JOLLY OLD ENGLAND

Armand Francis Lucier

HERITAGE BOOKS
2011

HERITAGE BOOKS
AN IMPRINT OF HERITAGE BOOKS, INC.

Books, CDs, and more—Worldwide

For our listing of thousands of titles see our website
at
www.HeritageBooks.com

Published 2011 by
HERITAGE BOOKS, INC.
Publishing Division
100 Railroad Ave. #104
Westminster, Maryland 21157

Copyright © 1996 Armand Francis Lucier

All rights reserved. No part of this book may be reproduced or transmitted in any form or by any means, electronic or mechanical, including photocopying, recording or by any information storage and retrieval system without written permission from the author, except for the inclusion of brief quotations in a review.

International Standard Book Numbers
Paperbound: 978-0-7884-0384-2
Clothbound: 978-0-7884-8886-3

CONTENTS

Foreword v

1720 1

1721 13

1722 35

1723 53

1724 77

1725 103

1726 135

1727 155

1728 175

1729 203

1730 237

Index 273

FOREWORD

I have but one purpose in mind in presenting this journal, and it is to share with the readers all the entertainment the 18th century public print gives me.

All articles in *Jolly Old England* were originally published in English newspapers. The following are some of the publications that were brought regularly from England to Colonial America: *St. James Evening Post, Daily Post, London Journal, Daily Journal, Post Boy, Mist's Weekly Journal, Monthly Mercury, British Journal, Country Journal, Daily Courant* and *Cork News Letter*. American publishers would set aside what articles they thought fit, inserting them into their own newspapers at will. Though they retained the dateline, they would seldom reveal the original source.

Every one of the 1333 items that appear verbatim in *Jolly Old England* has been printed in at least one of the following newspapers.

The American Weekly Mercury, printed by Andrew Bradford, Philadelphia. 1719-1732.

The Boston Gazette, printed by James Franklin, Boston. 1719-1720.

The Boston Gazette, printed by S. Kneeland for Philip Musgrave, (post-master) Boston. 1720-1725.

The Boston Gazette, printed by S. Kneeland for Thomas Lewis, (post-master) Boston. 1725-1726.

The Boston Gazette, printed for Thomas Lewis and Henry Marshall, (post-master) Boston. 1726-1727.

The Boston Gazette, printed for Henry Marshall, (post-master) Boston. 1727.

The Boston Gazette, printed by B. Green, Jun. for Henry Marshall, (post-master) Boston. 1727-1732.

The New-England Weekly Journal, printed by S. Kneeland and T. Green, Boston. 1727-1732.

The New-England Courant, printed by James Franklin, Boston. 1721-1723.

The New-England Courant, printed by Benjamin Franklin, Boston. 1723-1726. On February 4, 1723, Mr. James Franklin was banned by the Council from printing *The New-England Courant* (for articles he had printed). Because of this, he used his brother Benjamin's name as printer, from February 11, 1723, to June 27, 1726.

Armand Francis Lucier

1720

LONDON JAN. 2. By our letters from the West-Indies we have an account, That the pirates continue to be very numerous there, and to do incredible damage to trade, by taking, plundering, or destroying the ships of all nations, without distinction, that come their way.

The Port Mahon one of his majesty's ships, is come up the river from Copenhagen, and is going to refit, in order to go to sea again: His Majesty's ship Worcester is daily expected round from Scotland, where she was forced by stress of weather, and is to be laid up: Mr. Ely, the surgeon mate, who killed Mr. Bicknell, the first lieutenant of her, is brought in irons on board her, and will, on her arrival, be committed to the Marshalsea, in order to take his trial.

LONDON JAN. 8. About the hour of six yesterday morning a violent fire that was suppos'd to be all night kindling, broke out at the house of one Astall Esq; in Austing-Friers, where first discovering it self, by a strong smell the gentleman suspected fire, and went down to secure his books, having first desired his spouse to care of the plate; but being got down the fire soon got head enough to prevent his going up again, his poor wife, three children, a wet nurse, and a servant maid, were all in bed, the maid attempted to save her self by leaping from a window two story high, but, the violence of the fall was so great that she di'd in two or three hours time, the rest were all burnt; we hear of no more people being missing, but two more house adjoining were burnt down to the ground, 'Tis said that not one pennyworth of goods was saved out of Astall's house, the violence of the fire was so great; all this was an action of near about 3 hours duration.

LONDON FEB. 20. To day we were alarmed with an account of taking Brigadier Mackintosh, Commander and Chief of the Scotch rebels in the late rebellion, but it prov'd his brother Colonel John Mackintosh who broke out of Newgate at the same time. He was apprehended last night at the Four Swans Inn in Bishopsgate Street, by his Magesty's messengers.

Last week the Lord D____ was to have been married to the Lady Jane Douglass; the necessary apparatus being made for cellebrating the nuptuals; but a night or two before, the young lady, whether out of dislike to the Earl or any thing else is not certain privately withdrew herself from her friends, and has not since been heard of, to the no small disatisfaction of her consort; all the intelligence her friends have had of her is that she was carried by two chairmen to an India-shop in Leaden-Hall Street, from whence she escaped farther.

On Tuesday last was burnt by the common hangman before the Royal exchange, and in Palace Yard Westminster, a most scandalous and blasphemous book, entitled, A Sober Reply to Mr. Rigg's Merry Argument from the Light of Nature for the Tritheistick Doctrine of the Trinity with a postscript to the Reverend Dr. Waterland.

LONDON MARCH 3. The Revival Capt. Hughs, for Lisbon is lost upon a rock going into Plymouth.

This day warrants were given out for the impress of seamen to man the fleet for the Baltick; and accordingly a great many have already been impressed.

On Saturday last a ship bound to the West Indies was lost with all her cargo, near the buoy on the Nore; but the men got safe to shore in their boat.

BRISTOL MARCH 15. We have the following accounts given from the streight; That the Old Pompey galley, in her voyage to Leghorn, came up with a sail on the Coast of Portugal, which seemed by her colours to be Portuguese, on her deck appeared three men of that nation, who desired to be taken on board the Pompey, complaining they were in want of provisions and had lost their rudder: The captain sent his mate on board, finding them in distress, who searched in the hold found in the well a body of a man dead, with his head downward; and going into the cabbin, he found the liver and heart of a man, boiled, in a platter; but upon the deck lay a rudder unfinish'd which he believed had been designed by an Englishman. This gave the mate reason to suspect some piece of villainy had been acted; and therefore he was strict into examination of the portuguese, who gave him this account.

That being in the Port of Thesauruos, the captain, mate, and eight men being on shore the ship by stress of weather, was drove out of port; they had 28 days at sea, and in want of provisions; that they were necessitated to kill the man that was found pickled for their subsistance; that the man in the well went to see what water there was, and being faint and weak, was not able to get out, but died there.

The mate finding the rudder iron gone, and no hope of making the ship fit to sail took the men on board the Pompey, with several chests, as they desir'd, and left the ship adrift. In one of the chests was found a journal in English, which appeared to be the mate's and that he was living six days before; upon which the captain examined them again, and using some severities, they confess'd that one of them was the boatswain, that they had mutinied against the captain, and had thrown him, the carpenter, and several other men over-board, reserving the mate to bring the ship to port; who giving the daily encouragement, of coming to land, and being till their disappointment, they cast the mate over-board, then they remained five men one of which they fear'd would make a discovery, which was the person found in the well, they kill'd, on the first sight of a ship making towards them; the other was found in salt, and mentioned before, for their subsistance. The ship was Portugal built, loaded with salt, the captain, mate, and carpenter, were Englishmen, the rest of the crew Portuguese, the captain carried the three men into the streights, and deliver'd them up prisoners to Admiral Bing.

LONDON MARCH 22. On Sunday night about 12 a clock a fire broke out in the stabling of the late Sir John Parson's brew-house, near the Hermitage Stairs in St. Katharine's, occasion'd by a link which set fire to the hay. It consumed the stable and brew-house and several storehouses, wherin were butts of beer 18 foot deep, which it destroy'd and melted all the leaden cisterns, then taking hold of a warehouse near Burstreet, full of hemp, it increased its fury, and destroy'd that and about 17 or 18 warehouses and granaries on that side, in which stores of wine, brandy, &c. in their vaults, afterward the flames spreading themselves seiz'd the houses on the other side of the street, burnt 6 or 8, with part of Devall's Wharf, and damag'd several others; and all this in the space of 5 hours. It is observable of this fire, as of most others near the river, that it happen'd at low-water; and that among the unfortunate sufferers in this conflagration, is Mr. Astall, who was burnt out in Austing-Friers, his lost here being computed at 7000 £. Several other Russian merchants are considerable losers, but the dwelling houses belonging to the brew-house is untouch'd.

LONDON MARCH 26. We have an odd relation by letters, as the said in town from the Highlands of Scotland, which tell us, that the Highlanders having got possessions of some of the bodys of those which were killed on the side of the Government in the fight of Glenschell, would not suffer them to be buryed, but carrying them off, had exposed them to rot above ground, and that several of them having been lately found in that condition, had been buryed by order of the Government.

In the duelling Bill there are clauses making it death for any person to carry a challenge for a duel, and when ever a duel happens if one of them shall suffer death.

The Government having had information on Oath that in defyance of several statute particularly one in the Reign of King Henry 7th declaring it felony to hunt in the night or with disguise. That 14 men on horse back all armed with guns and some with pistols and two foot men with grey hound did in a violent and outragious manner on the 22 of February last at 4 in the afternoon, come into the forest of Windsor with their faces blacked and disguised some with straw hatts and others deformed habits and killed 4 deer 3 of which they carryed off whole and the haunches of the other. A proclamation is published offering 100 £. reward for aprehending any one of them.

LONDON MARCH 31. They write from Dublin of the 11th instant, that James Cotter, Esq; a gentleman of about 800 £. per annum was convicted of a rape committed on the body of Mary Squib, a Quaker, on the 12th of August 1718 near Farmoy in that county, and was sentenced to be hang'd as yesterday.

LONDON MARCH 31. On Sunday last in the evening the Duke of Douglas and the Earl of Dalkeith fought a duel behind Montague House, and were both wounded.

LONDON APRIL 9. We have account, That the Kingsale, Capt. England, homeward bound for Bristol, is taken by a Spanish Privateer, coming from Jamaica, the captain was set on shore at Bermuda, and lately arrived in England: He brings advice that the Milford man of war had lost all her masts, and was gone into Porto Bella, and that the Diamond man of war was going thither to tow her up to Jamaica.

LONDON APRIL 16. Last Sunday in the afternoon a new married gentlewoman richly dress'd, going to church in her coach, and two or three friends with her, were attacked at Brown's-hill between Enfield and Edmington, by a highwayman, who took from them jewels and gold watches to the value of 300 £. and then took leave, and rode off.

We have an account from Monmouth, that at the last Assizes there, an old woman was tried for the unnatural murder of her two grandchildren; it appeared that she sent one of them out in the morning, and in his absence most barbarously laid violent hands on the other; upon the return of the former she likewise seized him, took a knife, and cut his throat; the facts were fully proved against her, and she received sentence of death, which was accordingly executed upon her. And the Assizes at Herford, a woman was condemned for the murder of her Bastard.

LONDON MAY 3. On Sunday last at 11 at night a fire broke out at the lower end of Fleet Ditch next to the river Thames which burnt down two houses a large wood yard and did a great deal of damage.

LONDON MAY 5. This day a centinel was shot in Hyde Park for desertion, and three more whipt for the same crime.

LONDON MAY 7. We have an account from the west, That on Easter Tuesday 10 servants belonging to Shelton Calmady, Esq; member of Parliament for Saltash in Cornwall, took a boat at their master's seat called Wenbealy near Plymouth, in order to divert themselves on the water, but after having rowed about a mile from shore, the boat unhappily overset, and not one of them was saved.

LONDON MAY 8. Last Tuesday night, and Wednesday, the weavers assembled in great numbers, and did some small mischief to people whom they found wearing callicoes, and threaten'd many others. There were a great body of them down to the Parliament-House; and returning into the city, they threaten'd the East-India House, and several great shops where callicoes was sold; which occasion'd the guards to be drawn down, and an order for the militia to do duty, but this is all pacifi'd.

LONDON JUNE 4. One Mr. Etheridge, a tide surveyor, having seiz'd in the river some brass cannons, on board a ship from Venice, as being unlawfully imported, to the value of 2700 £. The legality of the seizure was disputed by the proprietor, who brought his action against the King; and last Saturday the matter was try'd in the Court of Exchequer, when the captain proving he had mounted the cannon and made use of 'em against the Spaniards, in his voyage from Venice: The Jury gave their Verdict for the Proprieter to the no small

Mortification of the custom house officer, who expected 100 £. to his own share.

LONDON JUNE 6. The weavers who had been apprehended for the late tumults, were discharged with a strict charge to avoid offending again in the like kind, least they should repent the abusing so much clemency.

Last Friday night a sessions ended at the Old Baley, when three persons received sentence of death, one which was John Hunt, for counterfeiting the 6d. stamp on parchment vellom, &c. about 9 or 10 are ordered for transportation.

On Thursday last Powell Hall, Collector of the turnpike near Hounslow, was try'd at the King's Bench Bar at Westminster, before the Lord Chief Justice Pratt, for a misdemeanor in stoping the post-boy, going with two expresses to Penzance in Cornwal, whom he detained two hours, and when he was told that he must expect to answer for stopping the King's express, he curst his Majesty, and said, he did not value him or his expresses neither, of which he was convicted, after a very trifling defence, and will receive sentence next term.

LONDON JULY 2. This day 200 warrants were issu'd out by Lord of the Admiralty, for the impressing about 2000 seamen for the equipping the squadron, to be commanded by Sir Charles Wager; who, as we hear, hoists his flag on board the Torbay.

A baker in Drury Lane, riding late to Finchley, to see his wife, was met on the Common by three highwaymen, who robb'd him of 30 s. and then commanded him off his horse, bound and threw him into a ditch with a neck of a mutton he brought with him tied about his neck.

LONDON JULY 8. On Thursday se'nnight the Right Honourable the Lord Carteret, one of his Majesty's principal Secretaries of State, passing thro' St. James's Square in a chair, was met by the Lady Harley in another; when a dispute arising between the footmen about giving way. They immediately came to blows; and the chairmen and footmen being engag'd with their poles and sticks, one struck his Lordship, as he was getting out of the chair; but whether accidentally or designedly we know not. In the meantime that person is committed to Newgate, and three of his brethren are bound over to the next session.

LONDON JULY 22. Thomas Gladwin, footman to the Lady Harley was convicted at the sessions at Hick's Hall for assaulting the

Right Honourable the Lord Carteret, and was sentenc'd to pay a fine of 5 pounds, and to be kept to hard labour at Bridewell for 3 months.

LONDON JULY 25. Letters from Dublin brings news of a very tragical and barbarous accident. That Major Johnson, a halfpay officer, coming into his parlour, where two of his sons were, one of them about ten, the other about twelve years of age; gave them each a pistol, loaded with powder and ball, and bid them to shoot at each other, which they refusing to do, the major drew his sword, and told them if they did not shoot, he would run them through; whereupon one shot the other dead. Upon the noise of the pistol, the major's wife coming down the stairs into the room, the major stab'd her, and afterwards himself, and both dy'd of the wounds.

LONDON AUG. 6. Our merchants have advice, that the pirates continue to infest the Coast of Africa, who some time ago, took no less than nine ships belonging to several nations in the River Gambia; but as the Swallow and Enterprize men of war are appointed at convoy to the 10 African ships that are going out, we are now getting ready at Portsmouth for that purpose, it is not doubted but that they will clear the coast of those robbers.

LONDON AUG. 13. Last week a woman was committed to Newgate for mortally wounding a man in Holbourn with a knife, which breaking a piece was left in his body. She is an old offender, having been at Newgate several times, and obliged the constable to treat her with a quartern of brandy, because she was first person he had brought to prison since his coming into the place.

LONDON AUG. 16. A gentleman going for the west country, was attacked by two highway men in a lane beyond Uxbridge, who robbed him, of 75 £. and afterwards making his dismouth, bound him, and tied his arms behind him, and being apprehensive that he knew them, they were for shooting him, but he protesting he never saw them before, they left him for a short time; but being still jelous that he knew them, they came again and told him they would kill for their own security, accordingly one of them fired a pistol but miss'd him; and he still denying he had the least knowledge of them, begging for his life, they spared him, and rode away with the booty.

LONDON AUG. 19. This day the Love of this place, John Thompson, master, arrived from Virginia. She met in her passage on the 11th of July, in the latitude 43 deg. 41 min. a Pyrate ship of 28 guns, and a sloop of 16, who after plundering her forced away 6 of her crew, viz. Miles Staterwait, carpenter, Michael Ashburn, Benjamin Woodburn, John Jamson, Thomas Waller and Roger Jackson, foremastmen.

LONDON AUG. 27. On Monday next the famous singer Beneditte, sings before their Royal Highnesses, the Prince and Princess, in Mr. Pecketman's Theatre at Richmond.

LONDON AUG. 31. On Wednesday night an upholsterer's apprentice in Houndsditch was kill'd by a banker's in Lumbord-street. They having fought together in Blowbladder street, the latter was worsted, upon which he ran after the other, and stabb'd him with a pen knife.

LONDON SEPT. 3. Last week the wife of one Price a bricklayer in the city of Gloucester, was safely delivered of four sons, who were all baptized; one of whom is since dead, the other three are' likely to live.

LONDON SEPT. 10. Sunday morning Charles Blunt, Esq.: cousin to Sir John Blunt, one of the directors of the South Sea Company, cut his own throat at his home in Broad Street; upon his falling down upon the floor, the servants ran up stairs and found their master weltring in his blood; a surgeon was immediately sent for, but came too late for the poor unhappy gentleman had done his business to effectually: The coroner's inquest sat on his corpse, and brought in the verdict Non Compos Mentis. He has left a wife and three or four children, and 'tis said, died worth 25,000 £.

LONDON SEPT. 10. A few days ago, five highwaymen came up with a gentleman coming from Windsor Hornslot-Heath, and very civily demanded his money, which he as readily delivering, they whished him a good journey and rode off. About the same time some sailors, were set on shore at Bristol, who belonged to the Tyger galley, of 250 tons, homeward bound from Jamaica, which having on board 35 men besides passengers, took fire upon the Coast of Ireland, by the negligence of a boy, who threw the snuff of a candle into the rum barrel; the ship was in a short time consumed. The captain and nine men saved themselves upon a raft, and were taken up by a fishing boat; the rest were either burnt or drowned.

LONDON SEPT. 17. On Monday last there appeared at Guild-Hall sixty five insolent debtors from Newgate, Twenty five from Ludgate, six from the fleet, seventy two from Wood-Street Compter, and sixty one from Poultry-Compter, and was all save six, found to be entitled to the benefit of the late act of grace, and were discharged accourdingly. 'Tis computed that this act will release throughout England and Wales, about 12,000 persons.

On Thursday one Mary Dampsey who is in the 103 year of her age, stood on the pillory at Charing Cross, for cheating Lord Cowler's Lady of a box of jewelry.

LONDON SEPT. 17. Last Wednesday a Board of Ordinance sat at the Tower, and appointed and nominated 50 gunners and bombardiers to go with all speed for Gibraltar; and the next morning they fell down the river for Woolwich, where they are to be shipped off with warlike materials and stores for Gibraltar.

LONDON SEPT. 20. They write from Strasburg, That a man has been tried there, found guilty, condemned to be beheaded and afterward burnt, and was executed accordingly, for transforming himself into a wolf, and carrying away and devouring a great number of sheep belonging to divers persons. They do not mention upon what evidence he was convicted, but it should seem, the Court of Justice which passed this sentence were transformed into another sort of animal.

Of the 61 felons transported from Newgate in May last, 16 men found means to make their escape in the following manner. The ship sprung a leak on the Coast of Spain, and the master caused them to assist him; which done, they bound him and carried the ship to Vogo, from whence 'tis supposed they are since all come over. Five of them being apprehended are in safe custody 3 or 4 of them for fresh facts; the rest of them are said to be on the Pad and shortly expected at Newgate.

LONDON SEPT. 24. Last week on Baron Downs near Canterbury, two highwaymen met two gentlemen travelling for France, from whom they took two hundred pounds in money, besides watches and rings; and afterwards, to prevent pursuits, cut the horses girts, and turn'd 'em loose.

LONDON SEPT. 24. We have an account from Holland, That a Scotch ship, with sixteen passengers on board, bound for Rotterdam, was lately cast away on that coast, and that all perished in her but a boy, who with great difficulty got to shore, where he found the poorest destitute of goodness enough to afford him the least supply towards preserving that life which the sea, had spar'd; a waggoner coming by, and finding him on the road destitute, was so kind as to put him into his waggon, and take care of him.

LONDON OCT. 15. A person lately proposed to rent the well in lamb's Conduit Fields of the Lord Powis, famous for many eminent cures of distempered people; but his Lordship generously rejected the proposal and declared it should be kept open and free for the benefit of the publick.

We hear that Mrs. Barbier, the famous singer at the New Playhouse, having gained above 5000 £. by South Sea stocks, has sung her last farewell to the stage.

LONDON OCT. 29. Yesterday Mr. Ambrose Page, one of the managers of the South Sea Company, was lamentidly beaten by an officer, who had sold his real and personal estate, and lost all in the South Sea stock, that if some people had not step'd between he would have killed him on the spot.

Tuesday morning at four on the clock 92 malefactors were carried from Newgate and put into a covered lighter at Black Friars Stairs, in order to go on board a ship waiting in Long Reich to transport them to his Majesty's plantations in America; among them is William Wrigglesden, the person that formerly robbed the King's Chapel at Whitehall, who had carried with him a great cargo of cutlets ware to traffick. At the same time several were sent also on board from Marshalsea.

OCT. 29. They write from Bristol, that a captain of a ship from the streights, who was ordered to perform quarentine, was shot at and wounded, as he was coming towards that city in a boat; upon which he returned back to his ship, and 'tis not known whether his wounds be mortal or not.

LONDON NOV. 1. The Lords Justices have published another proclamation, for requiring quarentine to be performed by ships coming from the Mediteranean, Bourdeaux, or any of the ports and places on the Coast of France in the bay of Biscay, or the isles of Guernsey, Jersey, Alderney, Sarke, or Man.

Poland is still distressed on every side by a most raging pestilence, by their civil dissentions, and by their apprehensions from the Muscovites, who with a powerful army still hover about their frontiers.

The affair between Muscovy and Sweden continues as they were, both fleets and armies are drawn off on either side, the one are laid up, the other gone into quarters of refreshment.

Twenty sail of Newcastle colliers are missing, which its feared, perished in the late tempest, on account of which the merchants are in pain for several ships laden with timber for Norway.

Extract of a letter from an eminent physician at Aix in Provence.

The contagious distemper which has become the reproach of our faculty here, for above a month past, is more violent than that at Marseille, it breaks out in carbunkles, baboes, livid blisters, and purple spots: the first symptoms are grievous pains in the head, costernations, wild looks, a trembling voice, a cadaverous face, a coldness in the extream parts, a low unequal pulse, great pain in the stomach, reachings to vomit; and these are so owed by sleepiness, delirium, colvulsion or fluxes of blood, the forerunners of sudden death.

In the bodies that are opened we find gangrenous inflimation in all the lower parts of the belly, breast and neck. About 50 persons have died every day for three weeks past in the town and hospitals. Most of them fell into dreadful frenzy, so that we were forced to tie them. We hear the distemper is so much abated at Marseilles that the inhabitants begin to return thither from their country houses.

A report has been spread here, that the plaque was at St. Molo, and also reported at Brussels, that it was discovered in Loyrain.

LONDON. A REPORT FROM MARSEILLES DEC. 28. The city is at present in so good a condition of health, that Messieurs de Chicoynecaw, Verni, and Soulier, celebrated physicians of Montpellier, are set out from thence to repair the ravages made by the contagion in the infirmaries of Aix, where for this month past 50 persons are said to have died in a day: It is observed that the violency of the distemper increases and abates according to the coarse of the moon. The Marquis of Cailous, Commander and Chief in Dauphine, writes words that a certain countryman has found a Specifick remedy against the plaque, by wearing a particular sort of girdle, which infallibly cures all who make use of it. As that account contains something very wonderful, it does not easily obtain upon belief of many people; how ever, if it proves true, its effects will soon get the better of the strongest incredulity.

# 1721

LONDON JAN. 21. The famous Newgate-Bird, known by the name of Filewood, having run through all the degree of art, from a little pick-pocket to a notorious house-breaker, has so much favour shown him as to be transported some months ago, and returned again, is taken and committed to Newgate for burglary, some have been so free with this extraordinary gentleman's character, as to say that he was born a pick-pocket, though they grant at the same time his father and mother were very honest people.

Advise from Edinburg says that Nicol Muschett of Bog-Hall, some time ago apprehended for the murder of his own wife, was executed there on the 6th instant, making full confession of that execrable fact, and on the persons that assisted him therein; for which two or three others, who have been seized, are likely to suffer.

LONDON JAN. 28. We hear that a corn-factor's servant in Water-Lane, Thames Street, falling violently in love with a maid servant of his master, she not fancying the man, and to avoid his importunity, left the service for a place in Woolwich; he soon hearing where she was gone, went after her, but still she continued insensible to him, and would give him no encouragement; this treatment throwing him into a violent distraction, he took a dose of poison, he had brought with him in his pocket, and swallowed it, and died in her presence.

LONDON JAN. 28. Last week a woman well dressed, came in a chair to the sign of the Green Man, a publick house, near Long Fields, and getting out complain'd she was ill, and desired to lie down, which she did, and was soon after brought to bed. She had two napkins, in one of which she had wrap'd the child, and tied the other about its head and face, and was going away; but the woman of the house, seeing her carry out a bundle, which she had not observed her to bring in, sent after her, and had her stop'd by which unlucky secret was revealed, and the poor woman delivered over the child to the secular arm of the honest church warden and overseers.

They write from Petersburg, That on the 20th past, a sentence, pronounced against a person for heresy and blasphemy, was executed there; in pursuance of which his right hand was cut off and his body burnt. His crime was, that being at the town of Moscow, and meeting the Archbishop, then engaged in a procession, he took the Cross out of his hand, and after having given him several blows with a club, uttered horrid imprecations.

Sir John Blunt, Bart., Sir John Lambert, Bart., Sir John Fellows, Bart., Sir Theodore Janssen, Kt. and Bart. and Jacob Sawbridge, Esq; Directors of the South Sea Company, are ordered into custody of the sergeant of Arms attending the Honourable House of Commons, and the two latter being members were first expelled the House.

Robert Sirmon, deputy cashier, and John Grigby accountant of the South Sea Company were also ordered into custody of the sergeant of Arms.

LONDON JAN. 28. Last Monday night there was a General Council at St. James's in which a proclamation was ordered forthwith to be printed and published, for apprehending Robert Knight cashier, or treasurer of the South Sea Company, who after his examination before the committee, thought it fit to fly from justice. A reward of two thousand pounds is offered by the Government for apprehending him.

It is reported, that Mr. Knight drove himself out of town on Sunday last in a calash, and that he was seen at Gravesend on Sunday morning going on board a small vessel, which was towed down the river, he being in too much haste to wait for the tide. But we hear orders are now sent to all the ports, to stop more of these gentlemen from going off.

LONDON JAN. 31. We hear, that yesterday the papers of Mr. Clerk, solicitor of the South Sea Company were seized by the master of the Black Rod attending the House of Lords.

LONDON FEB. 4. They are going to build four large fine streets near the New Church at the Horse-Ferry, Westminster, which are to consist of forescore houses each.

LONDON FEB. 4. It appears by a certain book, and by other sufficient testimonies, that above five hundred thousand pounds of

South Sea stock has been taken in, and a great part of it without any consideration at all; and that the same had been sold for one million two hundred thousand pounds. But the said book contains for the most part fictitious names to conceal those who shared the booty.

We hear that Mr. Knight cashier of the South Sea Company, sold out for himself 90,000 £. and Mr. Surmand his deputy 19,000 £. of the third subscription; to which sinister practices, and others of the like nature, our country owes much of its present ruin. It is said, that by the estimate which Mr. Knight drew of his estate before he fled, he appears to be worth sixteen hundred thousand pounds.

LONDON FEB. 9. It is said that the entire charge of the whole body of Directors of the South Sea Company, will occasion a thorough alteration in the inferior offices and great interest is making for places. 'Tis thought Mr. De Goltz, one of the cashiers of the bank will succeed Mr. Knight, as cashier of the said company.

LONDON FEB. 16. Yesterday the Lords in committee examined several of the Directors of the South Sea Company, namely Mr. Gibbon, Mr. Haws, Mr. Chester, Sir Theodore Janssen, Mr. Sawbridge and Mr. Holditch. The question put to all of them was, whether they knew, or heard of any stock to have been taken in, promised or given to any person in the administration, or of any member of either House of Parliament? To which Mr. Gibbon, and two or three others answered, that they had heard Mr. Knight say, that 5000 £. was taken from a certain Lord in high station, whose name we presume not to mention, and Holditch particularly said, he heard Mr. Knight further relate, that 20,000 £. was taken in for some Persons near the K—— ——; Likewise 10 or 12,000 £. for another deserving person, and 2,000 £. for a certain g——l.

Mr. Sawbridge was asked concerning 50,000 £. taken in by two gentlemen of the Sword-Blade Company, and answered, That the amount of the said stock was owed to them by the South Sea company; for that when there was a run on that of the Sword-Blade payment, it was demanded of Mr. Knight, who not having money by him, transferred, in lien there of, the said stock to them.

LONDON FEB. 18. A draught of 300 men is ordered to be made out of the regiment and four independent companies of invalids quartered at Portsmouth and Plymouth, to be sent over to General Nicholson, to South Carolina, to act in case of any necessity against the savage Indians, and each man is to receive 4 £. advance money.

This day the Commons on a motion of Mr. Walpole, came to the following resolution, viz. That the losses of the South Sea Company may sustain by money lent on stocks and subscriptions shall be made good out of the estate of the late directors, and the aiders and abettors: Also the losses by bying and selling stock for the said company.

'Tis said, that the fees of the directors of the South Sea Company, who have been discharged from custody, amount to above five hundred pounds.

LONDON FEB. 21. Yesterday morning between four and five a clock, a fire broke out at the corner of Cecil Street in the Strand, which consumed four of five houses.

LONDON MARCH 11. Several criminals have been lately brought up under a guard from St. Edmondsbury in Suffolk, and delivered to Mr. Forward a Virginia merchant, who pursuant to his contract with the Government, is to take care of their transportation.

On Sunday last the sessions ended at the Old Baily, when 17 persons received sentence of death for returning after transportation and several other convicts are ordered to be transported.

LONDON MARCH 25. Press warrants having delivered out, they are now executing them very vigorously for seamen to man the Baltick Squadron, which 'tis expected will be ready to sail the beginning of next month, under the command of Sir John Norris, who hoist his flag on board the Sandwich, Admiral Hosier on board the Prince Fredrick.

Letters from Jamaica advise, That the Oldfield, Capt. Mitchell, arrived here in eight weeks from Falmouth which brought thither between twenty and thirty miners from Cornwall, to work on the mines lately discovered in that island, in expectation of much richer ore that that at Cornwall.

Affairs on the side of Hungary are but in a doubtful unsettled posture, and the motion of the Turks seem to give no little alarm. They continue to march their troops towards the frontier, where their numbers daily increase, They fill their magazines, are strengthening their fortifications of the barrier towns, and are making many other such like signs of hostilities; though at the same time they talk very fair, and give the Imperial Court good words, and by their ministers there have assured the Emperor that they intend nothing against his Majesty's Dominions, or to do the disadvantage of the late Treaty of Passasowitz: But whether these infidels have not learn'd the method which has of late been much in use, of meaning the reverse of what they say, must be left to the event to make appear; and by the way, though they may intend otherwise than they act, and mean peace where they threaten war, yet it must be allowed to be very just to suspect those who by the whole tenour of their actions contradict all the bold assurance they give out.

LONDON APRIL 11. We are told some concealment of some of the late directors estates are discovered: if so there is like to be work for the hangman.

Last week several ships in the river received considerable damage by the high winds, which overset a boat a little below Greenwich, in which were two men and a woman, who were all drowned.

Last week a gentleman being in Newgate to take a view of a person he suspected had robbed him, had his pocket pick'd of six guineas, by one of the prisoners, but missing them in time, he with much ado got his money again.

LONDON APRIL 11. Some days since a gentleman coming to town from Cheshire was met on the road by three highwaymen, who took from him all his money; at which the gentleman was so enraged, that he offered to fight them all for it, one after another; but they thought fit to decline the combat, and rode off with the booty, telling him he was a madman.

We hear that Capt. Waller of the Robe galley, bound from Antigua, was stript by a press gang, belonging to the Baltick Squadron of Gravesend, of all his men, and had several women passengers most indecently abused by them, and also robb'd of a considerable value.

LONDON APRIL 12. Yesterday a foot-soldier in the park, carelessly leaning upon the muzzle of his piece, and playing with his feet, it went off accidently and killed him on the spot.

LONDON APRIL 20. An unknown gentleman did on Tuesday last feast all poor debtors in the Poultry-Compter, in this manner: to every four men he sent seven pounds of beef and each single person a quart of strong beer and four pence in money. The goodness of the victuals together with the clean and decent manner in which it was brought to prison, being all divided and covered, enhanced the value of the benefactor, and at the same time discovered the truly Christian temper of the benefactor, to whom we are desired to return to the greatful acknowledgement of those miserable people, who assure him they shall not cease to pray for his prosperity in this life, and his eternal happiness in the next.

LONDON APRIL 20. In the late engagement which the East India Company's ship had with the pyrates off of Joanna, the Cassandra lost 26 of her crew, and 30 soldiers which she had on board, and the Pyrates about 100. The engagement lasted 7 hours, and the pyrates were so enraged at the obstinacy of the captain of the Cassandra, that they offered 10000 crowns reward for the captain; but they soon chang'd their minds when they heard it was Capt. Maccra, which whom some of the pyrate's men had lately sail'd.

LONDON APRIL 22. There is advice from Rotterdam, That an Algerine ship of 22 guns, lately attacked not far from Bourdeaux; the engagement having lasted from four in the afternoon till seven at night: The rover was at last forced by a violent wind to stand to sea, and abandoned the Dutch ship, which had lost all her sails and masts, but none of the men were killed, and only one wounded.

APRIL 29. We have still most sad complaints of the proceedings of the smugglers and owlers in Kent, who are grown so intolerably outragious and impudent, that the custom-house officers are no manner of check upon them. They bring their goods a shore in open daylight, and tend the French sloops which come upon the coast with brandy, &c. by fourty and fifty in a gang; so that at present there's no power sufficient to oppose them. And they tell us, that one of the King's officers was shot by them a few days ago in the excise of his duty, and to render him a terror to the others, they stabb'd him in about 2 dozen places after he was dead.

They write further, That another officer, for whom those miscreants had a small regard, falling into their hands a few days after the commitment of the former fact, they did not think proper to treat him in such a barbarous manner, but obliged him to drink brandy as long as he was sensible; and after he was dead drunk, they poured it down his throat with a funnel, to the amount of about two quarts and a pint. This being done, they set him on horseback, tied him on, and turned his horse a drift, which carried him in that condition a mile or two; when, the cords breaking, he drop'd in the high-way, and there lay till the next day; when he was relieved by a passenger accidently coming by, and prevented his expiring upon that place.

LONDON MAY 6. Last week a person being apprehended for piracy, was carried before a justice in Rotherhith: As he was passing a publick-house; where a captain of a ship was drinking, the captain enquired what was the reason of the crowd, and being informed, it was occasioned by a person suspected to be a pyrate, he went to see him; who, to his great surprize, he immediately knew to be one that was on board a pyrate ship; and then before the mast, when he the said captain lost his first ship; and that he was lieutenant of a pyrate ship; and took him a second and third time; when, at the last taking his ship, he was for nailing the captain's ears to the main-mast. The said pyrate has impeached eight persons more, and the justice has issued out his warrants for their apprehending.

LONDON MAY 20. We hear that several of our merchants ships have declined carrying any more felons to the plantations, notwithstanding they have been very much pressed upon the score, and have had large offers to engage them in it; alledging in excuse, that though they may in the general be serviceable to the planters; yet they are so notoriously guilty in currupting the people there, that the country are heartily weary of them.

LONDON JUNE 3. One Mary Andrew, indicted for felony, being brought on her trial last sessions at the Old Bailey, refused to plead; and in the case by ancient law, was liable to be crush'd to death; but first having her thumbs drawn by the common executioner with a strong whipcord, she submitted to plead, and was acquitted for want of evidence.

On Sunday last one Mathew Clark, of the Parish of Wilsden, was committed to Newgate by Mr. Justice Dobins, for the murder of one Sarah Golderstone, living at a publick house at Neesden, by cutting her throat with a sharp knife, in such a barbarous manner, that he almost seperated her head from the body, and then rifled the said house; and we hear the villain hath since confessed, that he perpertrated the horrible fact, on the pretence of going to kiss her.

We hear that a gentleman at Hackney, has lately had his daughter trapan'd away in a manner not fit to be mentioned, and has since lost his own son. The young gentleman died last week, and 'tis said, he broke his heart with concern for the misfortunes of his family, through his sister's conduct.

LONDON JUNE 10. On Monday last, a hog went into Turnmill Street, and very much mangled a child, and is judg'd would have eaten it, the nurse being asleep, had not a neighbour who heard it cry, run in to its relief.

LONDON JUNE 10. Last Sunday a goldsmith did penance in Algate Church for calling an upholsterer's wife in the neighbourhood a whore.

On Monday the poor man bit by a viper in Hornsey Wood and since reported to be dead, was discharg'd from St. Bartholomew's Hospital perfectly well.

LONDON JUNE 13. The ingenious M. W——r has a design to give the world a new specimen of his ingenuity by establishing an account of a machine that will effectually preserve a ship in a storm; which if practicable, the world will certainly think, he deserves not only a statue of brass but of gold.

LONDON JUNE 17. Our merchants have advise that the Westbury, Capt. Bigloe, bound from Guinea to Jamaica having on board 176 Negroes was taken by pyrates.

We hear a young lady at Guilford upon discontent, took a lover's leap into the river, with a design to cure or drown her self; but her large hoop keeping her above water, and she finding that element too cooling and uncortly, screamed out for help, which was presently given her, and she was taken out alive.

LONDON JUNE 24. Last Monday the corpse of a young lady, which had been interred above a week in Covent-Garden Church, was taken up by her father and mother, also had been a long time in search of her. 'Tis said that the poor young lady had had the misfortune to be debauched by her own sister's husband, and died in child-bed. After her death, her parents, heard her, who suspecting she might have been murdered, had her body viewed by several surgeons, but we don't hear that any thing of the latter appeared. 'Tis impossible to express the misery this action has brought upon the family; the lady's brother, a hopeful young gentleman, and heir to a noble estate, broke his heart and died with grief; the parents are inconsolate, as well for the loss of their children, as the heavy scandal brought upon their family.

We hear that a large lead mine has been lately discovered in Cornwall, which produces the finest ore and will prove the richest mine of this kind in England.

LONDON JUNE 24. A considerable person, not far from St. James's being much addicted to gaming, by which he impoverished his family, finding he had no luck at it, made a rash wish; which was that if ever he play'd again, his right arm might rot off: in a little time he relapsed, and very shortly after, an inflammation fell upon his arm; and notwithstanding all proper means were used to heal it, it turned to a mortification, and killed him.

We hear Mr. Pierpoint the master of the Crown Coffee-House in the Jackie-Field, near Gray's Inn, who sold a jewel he lately found in the head of an old cane for 15000 £. has resolved to give 400 £. to be distributed among the poor of St. Andrews Parish in Fishborn.

Sir John Eyles, is said, received a letter last Saturday night from one of the Secretaries of State, signifying that the peace between England and Spain is actually signed.

LONDON JUNE 24. The plague spreads in a very dreadful manner in Province, most of the inhabitants of Toulon, men, women and children are dead; and they are in a most terrible constanation in France, for the apprehensions they are under of it spreading all the Kingdom over.

'Tis said that one Dibly, a journeyman blacksmith, having clandestinely married one Mrs. Tuberville, a fortune of sixteen thousand pounds, who was under the care of Mrs. Glandville and Mrs. Clarkson; they seized her a few hours after she was married (having first been bedded) and detaining her from her husband ever since, the said guardians were Tuesday last served with an order, to produce her before two judges. So that it will soon be decided, whether the man shall have his wife or not.

Last week one Christ. Clark of Hummerton, courted a young woman, and being in her company, upon some difference, he cut her throat, for which he is committed to Newgate.

The coachman of Sir George Brown, that was lately shot into the thigh by a footpad, as he was driving his master from Hamstead, is dead of the wound.

LONDON JULY 8. On Monday a High Court of Admiralty was holden at the Sessions House in the Old Bailey; where Walter Kennedy and James Bradshaw, mariners, were convicted: The former of two indictments, viz. for robbing, and afterwards burning the ship, Experiment, Capt. Cornet, on the high seas likewise for robbing the ship Loyal Merchant, Capt. Green, and barbarously treating the said commander. The latter was convicted of robbing the ship Loyal Merchant only, and one Fitwell, a carpenter, who appear'd as an evidence in his behalf, was by the Court committed to Newgate, 'till he should produce a certificate of his being acquitted of piracy, for which he himself had been try'd in Holland: And the Court pronounced sentence of death upon both the aforesaid criminals.

LONDON JULY 8. Came on at the King's-Bench-Bar Westminster, before the Lord Chief Justice Pratt, the tryal of Samuel Heathcore, of Queen's Square, Esq; and Ann Fletcher spinster, for betraying, seducing and corrupting a young lady, of the 15, from her parents at Clapton near Hackney. It appear'd by the evidence, that the defendent, Mr. Heathcore, being marry'd to the sister of the above mention'd lady, daughter of Justice Holworthy, had thereby an opportunity of frequent access to her at her father's house, till she was several months gone with child, when it was thought necessary to remove her thence; that accordingly about a fortnight before Easter, the young lady through a contrivance of Mr. Heathcore, and the assistance of Ann Fletcher her maid, was brought away in an abrubt manner from her friends to a tavern in Swithin's Alley near the Royal Exchange, where Mr. Heathcore receiv'd her, and carry'd her to lodging provided for her near Covent-Garden; where being brought to bed of a son, and falling ill, Sir David Hamilton visited her several times, and saw Mr. Heathcore in the room with her, who pass'd for her husband by the name of Stevens. Their cohabiting together as man and wife, was prov'd by several other witnesses. The lady soon after dying was bury'd in Covent-Garden Church; when the matter came to be discovered to her parents, who remov'd her corpse into Cambridgeshire, commenc'd this prosecution against the perpetrators of this horrid fact. The evidence being very full against the maid Ann Fletcher, as to her being aiding and abetting in the matter, the jury found them both guilty of the said indictment, and sentenced will be given them next term. The tryal lasted from 9 in the morning till four in the afternoon.

LONDON JULY 15. Last Monday night about 12 a clock, a foot soldier committed a robbery on the parade in St. James's Park: but was soon taken by one of the centinels upon duty; and we hear he hath discovered several of his gang, whereof one was taken on Tuesday morning.

LONDON JULY 17. On Monday last the Lord Castlemain gave a most splendid entertainment to his tenants, in the County of Essex at Wanstead. An ox was roasted whole for the populace, and ten anchors of brandy were made into punch. At midnight a great ball was provided for the gentry, and musick and other accomodations for the milk-maids, &c.

Last Saturday a young gentleman in Finch Lane, apprentice to an eminent attorney, unfortunately shot himself through the head with a pocket pistol.

The undertaker of the New Church in Great George Street, having receiv'd a sum of money, and going out of town with a friend, was set upon near Finchley, by two highwaymen dismounted, and drew from his pocket his silver watch, and with it about fifteen shillings; after which his friend persued them so close (though they struck him once on the head with a pistol, and fired upon him twice) that one quitted his horse: The owner of which lives at Highgate, and enquiry will be made to whom he lent the horse.

LONDON JULY 17. Sir Henry Prentice having reported to the King the proceedings of the Admiralty-Sessions on Monday the 2d instant, at Old Bailey; James Bradshaw was repriev'd, in order to be transported, and Walter Kennedy ordered for execution next Wednesday.

On the 26th past a young woman poisoned her self at Durton, within a mile of Northampton, upon some distress between her sweetheart and his master.

There happened lately a very sharp engagement on Enfield Chase, between a company of deer-stealers, and some people belonging to General Pepper. A relation of the general's had his horse shot under him, and several others were wounded, on both sides: But the aggressors being superior in number carry'd off their game, and we hear, that most of the gentlemens parks in Hertfordshire have been robbed likewise.

On Tuesday last, a gentleman coming from Hampton Court, was attacked by two highwaymen near Garden Wall, who, after robbing him of his gold watch, and about twenty guineas besides, used him very barbarously.

On Thursday morning, a drawer of the Horn and Horseshoe, in Chancery Lane, cut the cook maid his fellow servant's throat early in the morning, before anybody was stirring.

LONDON JULY 19. On Monday several physicians and surgeons belonging to the prince and Princess, attended by Mr. Lilly, their Royal Highness apothecary came to Newgate, to treat with the felons about undergoing the operation of inoculating into them the small pox, for an experiment, and agreed whith three of them viz. two men and one woman, who are to be removed into the airy part of the prison, in order to have their bodies prepared for the said operation.

LONDON JULY 22. Thomas Gladwin, footman to the Lady Harley, was convicted at the sessions at Hick's Hall for assaulting the Right Honourable the Lord Carteret, one of his Majesty's principal Secretaries of State, and was sentenc'd to pay a fine of 5 £. and to be kept to hard labour in Bridewell for 3 months.

On Tuesday sev-night a woman in years, unknown, and decently dress'd came to a grocer's in White-Cross-Street, and asked for half a pound of sugar, and the journeyman served her: Then she gave him a green purse of gold, which he at first refused; but she said it was his, and not hers, and persuaded him to take it, and then went away, and it has not been discover'd yet who she was. The man will not own the exact sum, but sath 'tis considerable.

Ann Gorbert alias Marchbank, was convicted of cheating Thomas Thorisby and Isaac Beach of several sums of money, with pretence of helping them to places under government.

Last Saturday the sessions ended at Old Bailey, when the following persons received sentence of death, viz. John Winchip for a robbery on the highway on the person of Christopher Lowther Esq; Mary Inman for the murder of a bastard child; Ann Meritt alias Walden, for stealing goods out of a dwelling house; Hannah Graham alias Grimes, for felony in a dwelling house, John Bickerton for robbery on the highway, Robert Hunter and George Post, for stealing plate, &c. to the value of 70 £. out of the dwelling house of John Thomas; Mary Goldstone for returning from transportation, pleaded guilty; William Gosling, for stealing out of the house of Mark Winn, Esq; his master, plate to the value of about 46 £. Anthony Cope and Mary Roberts, for picking of pockets.

LONDON JULY 22. A young lady living at Blackheart, having frequently appeared in hats, plentifuly set with bright stones; it was observed by some sharpers who thinking it to be loaded with more valuable ornaments, found means a few days ago to steal it. But discovering upon examination how they were deceived, they returned the hat with all its appurtenances a night or two after down the chimney.

LONDON JULY 29. A few days ago, a young gentleman of a good family, whose extravagancies had made him the aversion of his father, having got a considerable fortune, by a lucky run at the gaming table, waited upon the old gentleman, and with solemn promises of amendment and care of his circumstances, beg'd to be restored to his favour. His father pleas'd with his fortune, and his hopes of his reformation, embraced him in his arms; when the young gentleman desired, that he would accept a collation he should provide for him and some grave friends, at a tavern near Holbourn. The good old man agreed, and at the day appointed, appeared with some others at the place of entertainment. They were just upon point of seating themselves when our spark, seeing from the window one of his old companions passing by, he must need to speak to him, and downstairs he run, promising to return immediately. In about two hours he came back, but sadly altered: In a word, he made his father and friends acquainted that he was undone in that short time, and had lost again; the gentleman with whom he had been, having carried him to a gaming table in the neighbourhood, and there ruined him. The father, in the utmost anxiety, discharged the tavern reckoning, walk'd off, and declared he would never see him more.

LONDON AUG. 5. The town is at present amus'd with a very odd story, which however incredible it may seem, is justifi'd for truth: That on Tuesday last a little horse, for a wager of 150 £. went up the steps of the monument, to the top, and being there, the person that made the wager, rode him twice round the gallery, and then led him down again. 'Tis said he was brought up in the peek in Derbishire, where the rugged ways and craggy mountains, insures the horses to clamber very dextrously.

The malefactors that were on Thursday carry'd on board in order to be transported to Maryland, 15 from Newgate and a great number from the Marshalsea, that were sent up thither from several counties: about 130 more are to be sent away from Newgate this day or on Monday.

LONDON AUG. 12. The beginning of last week a young lady, upon the point of marriage, going to demand her fortune, which was a very ample one, of her guardian near Long Acre, he put her kindly off, till he had found means, in two or three days, to have her betrayed into a mad house, giving out that she was out of her senses; but the neighbourhood know the motive for the last: For the young lady before this misfortune had discretion enough, tho' the villany of this harpy, the disappointment of her conjucal happiness, together with the miseries of her confinement, have now bereaved her of her senses to all intent and purpose.

We have repeated accounts from Leeds in Yorkshire, of the happy increase of the woolen manufacture in those parts; their being at this time a greater demand for their cloth, and a greater number of hands employed in the manufacture than have been known there twenty years.

LONDON AUG. 17. That experiment of inoculating the small pox has been put in practice in London with apprehension.

CASSEL, AUG. 18. From the St. James's Evening Post. The Sieur S. Gravesande, Professor at Leyden, arrived here last week, to make tryal of the famous machine that is deposited in the Landgrave's Closet. That learned mathematician, as also an English gentleman in whose name is Fisher, are both of them persuaded, that this machine is the perpetual motion that has so long puzzled the searchers brains. The first of them is to write his opinion of it to Sir Isaac Newton, President of the Royal Society at London: Mr. Fisher has sent the exterior description of it to Dr. Desagullieres, demonstrator of the physical experiments of a wheel of 12 foot diamater, covered over with a wax cloth, to conceal its interior construction: It turns on an axel with such an extream velocity that it makes 26 rounds complete in the space of one minute: Each round it makes, a noise is made of 7 or 8 weights falling on the same side that the wheel turns: When a man lays his hand upon it to stop its motion and suffers it to turn only five or six times in the same minute, it regains its self by little and little its first swiftness. Its ordinary motion nicely examined into by a pendulum that shews the seconds, is always the same of 26 rounds in a minute. All the private experiments that have been made of it, have constantly shewn the same regularity, and the same strength of the machine in regaining its swiftness instead of losing it. If it be perpetual motion, as the Sieur S. Gravesande seems confident of it, the invention will be of great use in clockwork, and other arts. The Landgrave will not yet suffer any life to be made of this instrument, for fear the secret should be discovered, that Prince being desirous that the inventor should first receive from foreign countries the reward of so useful a discovery in case, upon the nicest enquiry, to which he submits himself, his machine should be thought justly to deserve the name of the perpetual motion.

LONDON AUG. 19. Last week a gentleman lately come from New-England going from town to Dolston, about nine at night, was robb'd near Whitmore House by three footpads, of four guineas, some silver and a diamond ring.

LONDON AUG. 19. Last week a person tolerably dress'd came to the Red Lion, a publick house at Hoxton, and desired that the shuffle-board room might be immediately clear'd, and got ready for some persons to come and play for a very considerable wager, the people willing to entertain such a guest as the fellow discrib'd, prepared the room, and brought a large silver tankard, and other suitable accomodations; but while the innocent landlord and his spouse were hurrying about the house, the villain found means to shuffle clear off with the tankard, and neither has been seen nor heard of since.

On Monday night last a journeyman to a toyman in Bowlane near Aldermary Church, thro' some discontent hang'd himself; as did the next morning another person in St. Thomas the Apostle; It is very remarkable that the latter being in bed with his wife call'd to her, and desired her to fetch a parson to pray for him, for that he design'd to hang himself; but she neglected to get up he rose himself, and going into the cellar, made it manifest that for once, he would be as good as his word. We hear, that thro' the instigation of the devil another person in wood's close by beat his wife's brains out, and that another hang'd himself in Aldersgate-Street.

When the convicts were lately carried on board a ship at Limehouse Hole, in order to be transported to Virginia, some few of them it seems were rich enough to lay in a little geneva and ginger bread for a viaticum; and a ginger bread cake belonging to one Taylor (who was once before transported, and whose father was hang'd) was accidently broke up, in which there was a file made up and bak'd with it, 'tis thought with a design to file off their hand-cuffs and rise upon the ship's crew: Upon this he was ty'd to the geers, and dealt with in a manner that is sometimes found necessary on board; but we do not find that he made any confession.

LONDON AUG. 19. They write from Norwich, That on Wednesday last the weavers of that city seal'd up their looms, according to their annual custom for the better facilitating the getting in their harvest, which could not be effected without a considerable number of that profession.

On Monday night last a little fellow that turns the wheel at a razor-grinders in Butcher-row, eat up at one time a leg of mutton, weighing about eight pounds, afterwards, to make up his meal, he eat about half a pound of candy.

Some days before, the same little Cormorant eat two dozen cucumbers, rine and all, for his breakfast, to the great mortification of the gentleman taylor in the neighbourhood.

We hear he hath likewise undertaken to eat a roasted cat or two, with a dozen of fry'd mice set round to garnish the dish, and other proper sauce.

The Mary man of war is arrived from Jamaica, having on board 40 pyrates, who were sent by the Governor of that place to be tried here, because several captains now in London, and were taken by them, are the only evidence sufficient to convict them.

LONDON AUG. 22. On Thursday night last, Mr. Cole, a custom house officer, seized in the house of Capt. Combes, near Manchester Court, Westminster, thirty large bags of tea, supposed to be part of the cargo of the two smuggling boats lately taken.

LONDON SEPT. 7. At the Assizes at Stafford three men received sentence of death, viz. One for murther, another for the highway, and the 3d for horse-stealing. This last being asked why judgement should not pass upon him, said, he thought it hard to be hanged for stealing of dogs meat, and begged for transportation. Being then asked, whither he would be transported answered, to any place where there is no dog meat.

We hear that several regiments of horse are appointed to patrole along the Coast of Suffex, to prevent the smugglers from sending away our wool, and the landing of French goods; which may prove of ill consequence, if it be true that the infection has reached Cherburg.

Our merchants have received account, that the Hope, Capt Wade; the Josiah, Capt. Stalks; and the Squire, Capt. Chamberlain, have been lost on the Coast of Ireland, Coningsby and Wales, in the violent storm about 10 days ago.

We hear, That the commissioners of the customs have now in their possession seized tea to the value of above twelve thousand pounds.

Last Saturday morning the Cirencester Flying Stage Coach, which set out between 12 and 1, was stop'd by two highwaymen at Knights Bridge: There happened at the time to be six passengers in it, and among the rest a sister of the Quakers, who told the highwaymen, she wonder'd how they could be so troublesome to travelling friends; but one of them clasp'd a pistol to her breast, and with an oath told her he was in hast; upon which she repli'd prithee friend, take away thy bauble, I have nothing but a few farthings about me. Another person in the coach had provided a green purse with 4s. 6d. in it, which she seem's very lost to part with, and which they with joy receiv'd. At the earnest request of a third, they return'd a key, and at last rode off, but very little heavier than the came.

LONDON SEPT. 9. We hear that a gentleman of a very good estate in Somersetshire, having married his only son to a gentlewoman of beauty, virtue and fortune in the same county, and living in the same house with them, the avarition genius of the old man took dire offence at the domestick expence of his children, which he often complained were excessive, and imputed to his daughter-in-law; that about three weeks ago, his son being abroad, and none but he and his daughter-in-law at home, he with an ax, in a fit of phensy, split her Skull. The son upon his return home, and the appearance of the bloody scene, finding his father yet in the house, charged him with the murder, and carried him before the Justice of the Peace in the neighbourhood, before whom he denied the crime. However he was committed to the custody of an officer, in order to be conveyed to the county goal; but the old man found means to get soon out of the hands of the officer, and has not been heard of since; but it is believed he is in or about London.

LONDON SEPT. 9. Last week the wife of a machanick, in the Parish of St. Andrew, died in a fit of scolding, being the first instant, we can give of this kind, but may be deem'd a dreadful warning and example to all women, who give their tongues to much liberty in this way, to beware lest they share the same lamentable fate.

LONDON SEPT. 14. Last Tuesday John Smith, who has already been tried, convicted, half-hang'd and then reprieved for his former crimes, has given a further instance of his destiny to be hanged. He has lived since this reprieve several years in and about the city, running on in the way of his fate, and committing divers little rogueries, was committed to Newgate again, got off, and is now the third time taken up, and it is reckoned that he will not now get clear. He seems to be one that sins by fate, and predestinated to be hanged for it; the cruel sifters seem to be now ready to cut the thread of live, which they have spun out for no better end. He will leave this world unlamented, and tread the path of death he has before set his feet in, and step'd back to life, a favour which very few have had.

LONDON SEPT. 15. By the last ship arrived, we hear, that upon the Eastern Coast of Africa 6 new pyrates have appeared, having about 3000 men on board, and carrying a black flag, and they have already taken several considerable prizes, as well from the English as the Dutch.

LONDON SEPT. 16. On Wednesday last a man, stark naked, was taken out of a pond at Maybone, having his hands and feet tyed. It is supposed he was first strangled and then thrown in.

LONDON SEPT. 16. Last week a certain baliff in York-Buildings, a bold fellow, had the courage to arrest a noted conjurer at Moorfield, who, by the rules of his art, could foretell the fate of others, but could not give a guess at his own.

LONDON SEPT. 19. They write from Devizes, That the small Pox rages there in a manner beyond whatever has been known in the memory of man, which has been fatal to a multitude of people. The trade of the town has been generally interupted, and the inhabitants are so universally fled from it, that the town is almost deserted, and the market place is covered with grass.

LONDON SEPT. 23. On Saturday night last the corpse of William Casey, one of the malefactors executed last Monday sev-night at Tyburn, was buried with great solemnity, his body having lain expos'd till then at his lodging in the Thieving-Lane in Westminster, till it became offensive. They came infinite crowds of people, of the lower class, to see him lye in state; the woman discover'd great marks of his innocence, as his bleeding at the nose, and other undeniable symptoms, but some nice observers took notice of the body's being very limber, and infalliable token some of the family will soon follow.

We hear a deplorable instance of the consequences of pride and extravagance in a young man lately dead. He had for some time, in spite of the remonstrances and admonitions of his friends, appeared in all the modern gayeties and excesses of life, till a narrow fortune he set out with in the world was quite vanished; with that went his credit, and soon after he disappeared himself, to the astonishment of all his acquaintance, who could get no news of him, till a few days ago that one of them accidently discovered he was languishing for very hunger, and for want of the common sustenance of life, in a mean lodging, at the obscurest part of town. He had no sooner got notice of the wretched abode and condition of the unhappy youth, but he went to the rest of his associates for their charities, and gathered a contribution of thirty guineas, which he carry'd to him with the utmost expedition in his power; but it proved too late, for he, wretched man, died from want of bread, a few minutes before his arrival.

LONDON SEPT. 27. Last Monday night one Mrs. Langworth, a gentlewoman of a very considerable estate, age about 50, threw herself out of a window, two story high in Love-Lane, & was kill'd by the fall. It being certain that she had lately been discover'd in her senses, the coroner's inquest brought in their verdict lunacy.

LONDON SEPT. 28. On Tuesday a woman was committed to Bridewell by Justice Ellis of Denmark Street, for tying her husband to a bedpost, and whipping him almost to death, being assisted therein by several of her gossips.

LONDON SEPT. 30. His Majesty's ship the Feversham, station'd at Barbadoes, has lately taken on the coast a pyrate ship carrying 16 guns; which ship was first called the Bumper, afterward the Gamboa Castle, and was commanded by Capt. Russel, in the service of the Royal African Company; but some time ago the said captain and his mate were set on shore in Guinea, and the rebellious crew, and 16 soldiers that were inlisted for one of the African settlements, ran away with the ship for the West Indies, and set up for pyrates. A few days since Capt. Russel by order of the African-Company, set out for Portsmouth, to embark on board the Crow, Capt. Wilkinson, for Barbadoes, as well to take possession of his ship, as also to give evidence against that crew of Pyrates.

LONDON SEPT. 30. A Court Marshal is ordered to be held at Portsmouth, on the pilot of the Royal Anne galley, for suffering the said ship to run upon the Brake near Deal, and afterwards to run afoul of a French ship in the Downs, whereby she received great damage.

We hear that a fever is so fatal in a village in Oxfordshire, that seventeen persons have died in a week there; which used to be accounted the mortality of the whole year.

Yesterday was sev'night a drunken man being very quarrelsome on board a ship at Fresh Wharfe, abused another man, and being engaged in fighting, they both tumbled overboard in the river. The aggressor was taken up alive, but the other could not be found; the former was immediately seized, and 'tis thought he'll have his tryal at the Old Bailey for the same.

We hear at Sturbitch Fair last, a poor country woman having brought her whole stock of cheese to sell, had her pocket pick'd of the money. The loss of which making her very uneasy, she sat upon a bank and cry'd very much: being lately delivered of a child, and her milk in her breast very painful for her, she desired a woman she saw with a child in her arms, to let the child suck her, which the other accordingly did. While the child was in her arms, a man come running by, and flung a large bag of money into her lap, and went off. Upon looking in the bag she found it to be the same she had lost, with a considerable larger quantity of money in it. It is supposed the woman who lent her the child was a comrade of the pick pocket, who seeing her with the child in her arms in the same place he saw his comrade, took the countrywoman for her.

LONDON OCT. 3. On Friday last an unfortunate accident happen'd at Barlow in the road to Cambridge: As one Mr. James Eaten, a young gentleman student in physick, was riding through the town on a gallop. His horse pitching on his head threw him forward, and then tumbling him so violently that he vomited great quantities of blood; and tho' several means very proper in that case were made use of, yet he expired in a few hours later.

Last Saturday was se'nnight, a goldsmith in Wapping having been robbed of a considerable quantity of plate, a letter was privately flung into his house the next day, acquainting him where he might find his goods. The goldsmith hereupon taking a constable, assisted by some neighbours, and going to the house, which the letter exactly described, found all the goods under ground, together with large quantities of other things, among which was abundance of plate.

LONDON OCT. 10. His Majesty having nothing more at heart than the preservation of his people from the direful calamity of the plague, which rages with such violence in the southern part of France, leave nothing undone that man contribute to so laudable and pius work, to which purpose frequent councils are held, and Sir. Hans Sloan, Dr. Mead and Dr. Athbothnot consulted, and the ministry apply themselves with great diligence to this business; in consequence whereof, we hear barracks are ordered to be built on Black Heath for the soldiers to be entertained, if it should please God to visit us with that dreadful judgement, in order to prevent the communication with this city and the counties of Sussex and Kent, where it is most likely to be received first, and that they began last Saturday to burn the goss or fuzzes of the said Heath; which kind seen at night in the town, gave ground to report, that several houses were on fire that way. On Sunday there was a council held at the Cockpit, where the aforesaid doctors attended, but came to no final resolution.

LONDON OCT. 12. Yesterday orders were sent to Whitehall, and the Admiralty-Office to the Governours of several seaports, concerning a Dutch frigate which lies in our channel, several on board having the plague; the said order are to force her away, and if she refuses, they have directions to fire upon her and sink her; There were 50 men in 4 days time thrown overboard which died of the plague.

LONDON OCT. 17. Sixteen men of war are in quest of the Dutch frigate having the plague. The first information relating to her was sent hither by Lord Whitworth, our minister at the Hague.

LONDON OCT. 14. Seven butchers in White Chappel were severally indicted for laying blood and excrements in the streets, and were brought by warrants, and pleaded guilty to their indictment. The Court fined them 40 s. a piece and discharged them when promising to take warning and amend for the future.

Sunday and Wednesday are appointed for a committee of Council to sit, in order to take into consideration proper methods to be used for preventing the spreading of the plague, in case it should be brought into these Kingdoms.

We hear the College of Physicians have had several meetings, according to the order of council, to appoint proper persons within the city and suburbs, viz. surgeons and apothecaries who shall be capable of regulating the bills of mortality, and of giving timely notice of any infection which may happen in order to prevent the same from spreading, and that none are to execute that office, but such as are examined by said college.

Orders are given to the board of his Majesty's works, to give an estimate of building barracks in 6 or 7 places near London; particularly on Black Heath, near Islington, near Hamstead, &c. in case of the plague should reach us, and the said estimate we hear will be laid before the Parliament, in order for a bill to pass for the building the same; but the report of burning the goss or fuzzes on Black Heath last Saturday, proves a mistake.

LONDON NOV. 2. At the last general quarter session held at Hick's Hall, the Court taking in consideration the great increase and progress of the plague abroad, and that all proper precautions ought to be used to preserve us from the infection, was the opinion, that the laws for preventing and removing publick nusances within the weekly bills of mortality in the county be put in execution.

LONDON NOV. 4. They write from Boston in New-England, Sept 5th, that the small pox is still so mortal in that city, that they are it is said, in great fear of depopulation. The chief of the inhabitants are gone into the country, to escape the distemper, which however has overtaken several of them. The Assembly sits at the George Tavern, the last house in the precinct of Boston, where they have a guard of soldiers to keep people out of the house that comes from Boston. "The truth was, in the months of May, June, July and August, there died in Boston, of the small pox only 46 persons. That several of the chief Boston people who had fled into the country were then overtaken with the small pox, is notoriosly false."

LONDON DEC. 2. We have received letters from very good hands in Boston in New-England, that during the height of the small pox in that town, near 300 persons had been inoculated for the same, every one recovered. The falsity of this is obvious to everyone. The date of the Boston letter must be sometime in the end of October, about which time not many more than 50 had been inoculated. On or about the 18th of November following, the number of 100 inoculations were completed. In the end of September dy'd the inoculated Mrs., D——l, and sometime before her dy'd two women, related to two of the inoculation promoters, under violent suspicion of inoculation.

LONDON DEC. 28. Word from Malaga, Spain is as follows. "They write from Tangier, that the Moors are fitting out eight frigates there, and some other vessels, on board which they intend to put 7 or 800 men, who are to make a descent upon some of the coasts of this Kingdom; but they are a great number of forces placed along the coasts of this Kingdom to prevent the communication of the plague, little noticed is taken of this intended expedition: however the Governour of this place has dispatched an express to Court to impart these advises. The same letter adds, that in most parts of Barbary the famine increases, and that several of the inhabitants of the country went to live in some of the Spanish towns in Africa, and other sold their own children, that they might raise a little money to help them from starving."

1722

LONDON JAN. 20. Petitions are come from several places against the Westminster-bridge-Bill, and the same is like to meet with great opposition.

It is computed, that when the new bridge is built from Westminster to Lambert, provisions will be sold at least 20 percent cheaper than they now are, in all the markets from Temple Bar to Hide Park Corner, as well in Westminster, there being more than the difference now in price between Southward, the City Market, by reason of the vast quantity of fish, fowl, beef, mutton, &c. which comes from Kent, Surry and Sussex, are (for want of another bridge) obliged to come over London Bridge, so that the out markets are saved at second hand.

LONDON JAN. 26. Yesterday there were very great crowds of people in the galleries of the House of Commons, to hear the arguement of the Council learned in the law against the Westminster-Bridge-Bill; Sir Constantine Phipps spoke a long time, setting forth the inconveniencies that would arise to the city of London and other places by this project; several witnesses were also examined to support Sir Constantine's allegations.

LONDON JAN. 27. Edward Crispe of Bury St. Edmond's in the county of Suffolk Esq; having been assaulted on Monday the last instant in the Church-Yard there, and knock'd down by persons unknown, and dragg'd to a dung hill, where he was cut and mangled in the following barbarous manner: His nose slit, one of his checks cut to pieces, his teeth and jaw-bones laid bare, one of his shoulders wounded to the bone, and his throat cut in two places, and there left for dead. His Majesty hath been pleased to promise his most gracious pardon to any of the persons concerned therein, who shall discover his accomplices, so as they, or any of them may be apprehended and convicted thereof. His Majesty is likewise pleased to promise reward of two hundred pounds, and he then said Crispe offers one hundred guineas more to such person as aforesaid, or any other person that shall make such discovery.

We hear two centinels in the foot guard are committed to the Savoy, in order to be tried by a Court Martial, for raising a nonsensical story of an apperation of several men without heads in St. James's Park.

LONDON JAN. 29. This day a book has been published here called, The Fortunes and Misfortunes of the Famous Moll Flanders, &c. who was born in Newgate, and, during a life of continued variety for three score years, besides her childhood, was twelve a whore, five times a wife, (where of once to her own brother) twelve years a thief; eight years a transported felon in Virginia, at last grew rich, lived honest and died penitent. Written from her own memorandums.

LONDON FEB. 3. On the 4th of January the British captives, being 26 masters & 26 seamen, redeemed by the late treaty with the Emperor of Morocco, came through the city to St. Paul's Cathedral, to give solemn thanks to Almighty God for their deliverance from slavery; A sermon being preached on that occasion by the Rev. Mr. Battyman, chaplain to the Right Rev. the Lord Bishop of London, and a collection made there for their relief, amounting to 138 £. 18s. 6d. They afterwards proceeded to St. James's to return the thanks to his Majesty, were admitted into his presence in the garden of the palace, and his Majesty was generously pleased to order the further bounty of 500 £. to be distributed among them. They went otherwise and presented themselves before the Royal Highnesses the Prince and Princess of Wales at Lancaster-House, and his Royal Highness was pleased to order two hundred and fifty pounds to be given them.

LONDON FEB. 17. The port letters for Falmouth of the 8th instant say, That a ship from Barbadoes for London, Capt. Witchel, was just come there, which bring advise, that his Majesty's ship the Weymouth of 50 guns, was taken on the coast of Guinea by two pyrate ships commanded by one Robert, whereof one carried 48 guns and the other 38.

LONDON FEB. 24. One Tuesday last a pick-pocket being taken in St. James's Park, was hunted by the mob a long time there, at length taking into Pall-Mall, they persued him with stones, and brickbats, and driving him into St. James's Square, used him there with such violence, that in a little time he fell to the ground and died.

LONDON FEB. 27. We hear the Royal African Company has agreed to furnish the South Sea Company with a sufficient number of Negroes, to make good their stipulation in the Assento contract.

LONDON MARCH 6. Last Friday Mr. Mills a victualler in Stock's Market, and a journeyman poulterer in Beadon-Hall Street, were try'd at Winchester Assizes, for robbing a lady in Buchinghamshire, and were found guilty.

WHITEHALL MARCH 10. Since the experiment made some time ago by Dr. Maitland of inoculating the small pox upon several criminals in Newgate, their Royal Highnesses the Prince and Princess of Wales being desirous for a confirmatian of the safety and ease of this practice that a further experiment should be made, six persons more had the small pox inoculated on them, the 23d and 24th of February last, which has succeeded very well the small pox being broke out in most of them; and the curious maybe further satisfied by a sight of those persons, at Mr. Foster's house in Marlborough Court at the upper end of Poland Street in Soho, where attendance is given every day from ten till twelve before noon, and from two till four in the afternoon.

On Saturday last the sessions ended at the Old Bailey, when 13 persons viz. 9 men and 4 boys receiv'd sentence of death for divers capital offences.

LONDON MARCH 12. We hear a relation from Jelingham near St. Edmondsbury in Suffolk of a plowman manuring a field there, accidently struck his plow-iron against something which gave so sudden a check as to recoil back; whereupon the man had the curiosity to look into the cause of it, and by digging found a large copper vessel which would contain about 16 gallons, and is near 3 inches thick; several other persons have found in the fields and waste grounds divers pieces of old coin, which has very much contributed to their maintenance.

Last Saturday in the afternoon the Assizes ended at Chelmsford, where seven persons received sentences of death one for highway, three men and a woman for felony and burglary and two boys for robbing their master to the value of 72 pounds, Charlesworth and Bird who were tryed for the highway on the evidence of one Everett, were acquited by the jury, to the wonder of some who heard the trial. A woman was also try'd and acquited for the murder of her bastard child, which was found smothered in a house of office. Two ordered to be whipt, and two to be transported.

LONDON MARCH 14. About 10 on Friday night a woman was thrown down in Witcomb-Street near Leicester-Fields, and had her pocket cut off with 10 shillings in it; one William Thomas, who was drinking at a publick house hard by, hearing her cry out, came to her assistance; she charged him with the fact, and swearing to it, he was committed to Newgate. 'Tis said the fellow has proof of being in the house all the time.

LONDON MARCH 17. Last Friday was sev'night a vitner near Golden Square, hanged himself in his vault, however not long enough to make his exit; for a gentleman coming in to ask for him they found him in a posture in that vault, and cut him down. It seems the cause was laid upon the wife, and he was weak enough to tell the company he did it to vex her.

LONDON MARCH 24. The following tragedy has been lately acted in the Venetian Territories: The Count de la Torre being married to a lady of good family, and unsuspected virtue, yet constantly kept lewd women in his house, and even committed the rudest indecencies before her face, insomuch that she found herself obliged to retire to one of her country seats. Among the ladies whom he entertained, one was of quality, of a family of Strafoldi, she proving with child by him, her brother pursued the Count, demanding a reparation of his sisters honour, by marrying of her. He consents; and in the presence of the two Counts, the pregnant lady, and her mother, 'twas agreed to dispatch the Countess. A woman is engaged in their service for this purpose; and as the vile instrument was delivering a letter to her, she shot her with a pistol; which not immediately killed her, the young Count Strafoldi, who followed the woman soft-up stairs, gave the expiring lady thirty three stabs with his poniard, and ended her miserable life. The murtherers are all seized, and likely to be made severe example of.

Our foreign letters bring the following tragical story from Modena, viz. A young lady was to be married against her consent to a rich cavalier, and accordingly went to church with him, where part of the marriage ceremony was read over, and when the question was put wether she would have that gentleman to be her husband? she answered no, but the person who stood behind him, meaning his rival; upon which the designed bridegroom drew his sword and killed the lady; the same instant her admirer stabbed the bridegroom, and the father of the young lady killed him. These three murthers happened in the church, where the priest who officiated was wounded in the hand. Let this be a memento to every parent, who is about to force his daughter into the arms of one she cannot love: If the consequences are not so fatal, let him not forget that he purges her into missery, by wedding her to her aversion.

LONDON APRIL 10. We have advice from Vienna, Viceroys of the Great Master of Malta has represented to the Viceroys of Naple and Sicily, that it looks as if the Turks designed to fall upon the island with all their power, and therefore he desires to be assisted with men and ammunition. The latter part of his request has been granted, but the first denied.

From Leghorn we hear, That the master of a Dutch vessel arrived there from Thessalonica, relates, that abundance of Turkish vessels are come into that port, laden with warlike stores, for supplying the places on the coast. He adds, That all the merchant ships in the ports on the Levant have orders to return to Constantinople, to be employed in the service of the Grand Seignoir. It is taken for granted, that the rupture with the Venitians will suddenly ensue.

LONDON APRIL 10. All Italy in general, and the Republic of Venice in particular are under dreadful apprehensions from the military preperations of the Turks.

LONDON APRIL 20. On Friday last died, at their house on Norfolk Street, Dorothy Clark, aged 81, and Grace Clark aged 75, two maiden sisters, who having liv'd lovingly together for many years, expired within two hours of one another, and were both buried last night at St. Duntan's Church in Fleetstreet, in one and the same grave.

LONDON APRIL 23. The youngest son of the Earl of Sunderland, and the only child living by his last Countess, having had the small pox inoculated upon him a few days ago, died on Saturday last of that distemper.

LONDON MAY 5. Last week a poor beggar woman having a child in her arms, was offered ten guineas by a practitioner in surgery near St. James's, to have it inoculated for the small pox; but she refused the offer with contempt saying, I'll leave my child in the hands of God Almighty and let thy money perish with thee.

LONDON MAY 8. Yesterday about noon, two gentlemen who were going through the Mint in order to take horse for the country, seeing a pig in a cook's shop which they liked, went in to eat some, were shown into a room where 2 other persons were at dinner: Soon after they had sat down, and their dinner was brought, a constable and 2 great company came in pursuit of the two others as highwaymen; upon which, they suspecting the two gentlemen to be come with design to see them, drew their swords, and without any word of provocation, as they were at dinner, stabb'd them in several parts of their bodies; and particularly gave one of them two dangerous wounds under the left pap several inches deep, and did a great deal of mischief to the other person; but being over power'd after desperate resistance, they were immediately carried before the Justice of the Peace, who hath committed them to Marshalsea.

LONDON MAY 12. His Majesty having receiv'd advise that several of his subjects having enter'd into a conspiracy to raise a rebellion in this Kingdom, in favor of the Pretender, the right Honourable the Lord Townshend, one of his Majesty's principal Secretaries of State, did on Tuesday last (by his Majesty's order) sent a letter to the Lord Mayor of this city, acquainting him with this traitorous design: And on Wednesday last the Lord Mayor and Aldermen met in Guild-Hall, and in the evening waited on his Majesty at St. James's with a loyal readiness at all time to defend his person and government.

LONDON MAY 17. Yesterday morning about one a clock, one Mr. Hancock, son of Justice Handcock, was killed in the camp in Hyde-Park by one Mr. Nichols, son of an apothecary in Westminster, lately a lieutenant of a company in the First Regiment of Guards. The deceased had 7 wounds 3 of which were mortal. Nichols was seized by Col. Murray, and being carried before Justice of the Peace, was committed to the Gate-House. Col. Murray is Major of the Regiment Scot Guard, who hearing a clashing of swords nearby his tent, he rose out of his bed, and seized Nichols. Handcock died in a quarter of an hour.

LONDON MAY 19. We hear from Ireland, that Nathanial Day, the Quaker, who escaped the county goal of Kerry, where he lay under sentence of death for high treason, was lately retaken at Bandon, a village whose inhabitants and a Mr. English, whitin 13 miles of Cork, and being carried to Cork was there hanged.

On Friday sev'night last Mr. John Moor, formerly an upholsterer in Pater-molter-Row, who by extravagancy was reduced to poverty, and by poverty brought to distraction and despair, hanged himself at the Bear Alehouse in Bow-street, Covent-Garden. Before he did it he wrote two letters, one to his mother, and another to a woman with whom it is said he kept company, charging the bearer not to deliver them till an hour after; which was acordingly observed. Wherein he told them, that death to him was more eligible than life; and that by the time they should read these lines he should be dead; which by the event they found true. The coroner's inquest having sat upon the body, brought in their verdict lunacy.

LONDON MAY 25. An under-butler, at Lord Buthurst's a strong and hale young man of about 19 or 20 years old, who was inoculated for the small pox, died on Saturday last, being the 12th day after.

LONDON MAY 30. They write from Youghall near Cork in Ireland, That a great number of persons are taken up in that Kingdom for treasonable practices, whereof some have made considerable discoveries, and impeach'd several of the confederates, some of distinction, particularly John King Lord Viscount Kingston, who is in custody of the high-sheriff; A son of the Lordship has left that Kingdom some time since, who is charg'd with being concern'd in enlisting men for the Pretender. A commission is sent to Cork to try several of them.

LONDON JUNE 9. The following pieces of news is an extract from a private letter, the contents of which are as surprizing as they are dreadful.

On Friday the 18th of May last, about 4 in the afternoon, at Eland in the West Riding of Yorkshire, they had a thunder shower which raised the waters so high, and so suddenly, that incredible damage was done. Rippodon waters carried away several mills, and large quantities of woolen manufactures; many persons were drowned, and several dead bodies were carried out of their graves by the turrent. I am told 200 £. will not repair the damage done by it to the chappel. Our river has also done much mischief, 14 or 15 persons having lost their lives. A mill was quite taken away with 3 men in it, the bodies of two of them, father and son, was taken up in our township. In another mill and house which were overwhelmed, of 10 persons only one escaped, by floating near two miles down the river upon a beam. To cut short, represent to yourself the following dismal scene: All manner of household goods, whole roofs of houses, trees, dead bodies, &c. floating on the water, and many who were in the morning in good circumstances, are now destitute of houses and goods, nay some of cloaths, having been forced to throw them off to save their lives by swimming.

LONDON JUNE 9. An English seaman, taken by the pyrates and detained in the service 18 months, came to town this week from Ostend, whither he escaped in one of the East India ships, and has given the Admiralty and the directors of our East India Company an account of the distruction of a French Pyrate ship of 500 men by an English pyrate. They it seems quarrelled about a point of honour, the former giving out that the he would reign master of the seas, and would neither give nor take quarters; the English pyrate hearing of it, was resolved to attack him, After a fight of 18 hours, and abundance of blood shed, sunk him down right with all his men. The aforementioned seaman relates, that he was in the engagement on board the English pyrate.

LONDON JUNE 12. Our merchants have advice, That the Alentejo, Capt. Berryman, was arrived at Maryland in 28 weeks from Lisbon; but by the tediousness of the voyage their provisions were spent, and all the men but three were starved to death.

LONDON JULY 14. On Saturday last a gentleman meeting a highwayman, near Hampstead, who had robbed him a few days before, immedeately drew his sword, and putting it to his breast, threatned to stab him if he offered to touch his pistol, which surprized the rogue so much that he surrendered without any oppositions, and was very peaceably convey'd to the College in Newgate-Street.

On Monday night last two hackney coaches coming from Belsize with nine passengers in them, viz. five men and four women, were robbed by two footpads; The men of their money, watches, rings, swords, hats, and wigs; and the ladies of what they had valuable about them. 'Tis remarkable that the highwaymen produced no pistol to scare the five pretty fellows; however they were so frightened that none of them lent any assistance to one of the coachmen who behaved himself like a man; nor were they moved when the fair ones in their company, were rifled by those ruffians; which the ladies have so resented, that some of these beaus have lost their mistresses as well as their money.

LONDON JULY 14. A few days ago two lads had some words at a boarding school in Hackney; The one being stronger than the other ty'd him by his hands to a beam in his room, and after having stript him and beat him, he drew his sword and 'stabbed him several places under the arm; which not content with, the cruel youth exercised his pen knife on him too. He then took him down, and finding he was not dispatch'd, hung him up again by the neck, and so left him; but some other lads coming into the room just afterwards took him down; and he is now in a fair way of recovery. Let this caution all parents how they arm their children with swords, before they have directions enough to rule their passions.

We hear from good hands, that Mr. Robert Knight was lately seen in Holland, not far from Hague, attended by his old and faithful servant the butler, who was allowed by his master to come in for about 8,000 £. hush money before their affair were over-set and detected.

LONDON JULY 18. By letters from Worcester we learn, That a young girl of about 13 years old, is to be tried at the approching Assizes there for the murder of her grandfather whom she dispatched with a pennyworth of arsenic, at the instigation of an old woman, who afterwards robbed his house. The case of the girl is much pitied, but the old woman is like to die unlamented, she having, as appears by her own confession since she was apprehended, been guilty in much the same manner about six months before.

LONDON JULY 18. We have an account from Hereford, That a lady who was the youngest daughter of a family there, and had been absent from her friends for forty years, is lately come down there to claim an estate of 600, per annum, which by the death of her brothers and sisters she is heir at law to; it seems there were so many of those when she left her father's house, that having no expextation of the estate, she never so much as enquired after it, and never heard of their death till twenty years after they happen'd.

Those in possession, however, are resolved to put her upon the proof of her being the person she says she is; and the cause was to come this month at the Assizes.

LONDON JULY 19. We hear that a French ship of St. Malo returning home from Cork with butter, cheese, hides, &c. took 4 Irish men on board as passengers, who murthered the master and his men, threw them into the sea, carried the ship to Ostend, sold all the cargo there, and that having disguised her so as she may not be known, they have brought her into some of our ports, where orders have been sent to seize her.

LONDON JULY 20. There being about 800 Palatines at Rotterdam, we are informed that the Duke of Montigue, hath sent an officer thither to ship off a great many of them to the Islands of St. Lucia, and St. Vincent, of which his Grace hath a grant.

LONDON JULY 22. The latter end of last week a servant of Mr. Hill, a brewer in Goodman's Fields, fell into a copper, & was scalded in such a manner that he died the next day.

LONDON AUG. 3. On Tuesday last one Elizabeth Jones was committed to the Gate-House by Nathaniel Blackerby Esq; being charg'd; on the oath of two other women with uttering treasonable and seditious words.

LONDON AUG. 4. Just before the Assizes at Cambridge, a Highwayman set on Mr. King a farmer, between Royston and Cambridge, and was robbing him, when a butcher coming up, encouraged the farmer to fight for his money, who collering the rogue and struggling with him, both fell from their horses, and by good fortune the farmer on the highwayman. The butcher immediately pull'd out a knife, and whetting it on his steel, persued the farmer to take it and cut the rogue's throat; which he did effectually that he died on the spot. The farmer was tried for the fact, and brought in guilty of manslaughter.

LONDON AUG. 11. The trade which the merchants of the opulent town of Leeds, in Yorkshire, pushed on with extraordinary vigour to Boston in New-England, and some other neighbouring ports, is dwindled away almost to nothing; those merchants having seldom or never found their accounts in the manufactures they have sent to that part of the world: Which they impute to the ill management of the people of New-England, rather than to the failure of any other essential in a branch of commerce. And this has been more particular a subject of complaint this year, than any other time.

LONDON AUG. 25. Yesterday afternoon the Right Reverend Father in God, James Lord of Rochester and Dean of Westminster, was seiz'd and examined at Whitehall by a committee of the Prevy-Council, and committed close prisoner to the Tower, upon an information. 'Tis said, of being concerned in dangerous design to overturn the present Administration of Government; and that several great persons of distinction are concerned likewise. His Lordship was at his deanry in Wesminster, when two officers of the guards, two messengers seized him. At the same time two other officers and as many messengers were dispatched to his palace at Bromley in Kent, who, with the assistance of a constable, search'd the house, and brought away what papers they thought proper. He is confined in the gentleman goaler's house, and none are suffered to converse with his Lordship in private. 'Tis said, that several letters of his own handwriting, though signed by fictitious names, have been intercepted, by which the Government have made some important discoveries.

LONDON AUG. 28. Our press begin to grow warm with the dispute about inoculation; as soon as the children of the Royal family, and some of our Ministers pass'd thro' this operation. The High Church began to open with clamorous and fierce wrath against it.

Mr. Massey, one of the party, and the van; and to make his sermon the more conspicuous preach'd it in Dr. Sacheveral's desk at St. Andrew Holborn. So it happens to be a party controversy among us.

LONDON AUG. 28. Our merchants have advice that the Hasting, Capt. Sergeant, bound from London to Petersburg, was lost near the latter, but it was hoped that both men and cargo would be saved.

On Monday morning last Justice Byer went to the Musick House at Richmond, and gave a strict charge that there should be no more gaming at cards and dice in that place.

LONDON AUG. 30. They write from Wiggam in Lancashire, the 22d instant, that a dismal accident happen'd there: A grocer's apprentice going for some soap up stairs with a light in his hand, unfortunately set fire to 3 or 4 barrels of gun-powder, he was blown into the air, and six persons overwhelmed below the stairs in the rubbish, four of whom were dead. Two boys at a 20 yards off, were much hurt by the concussion, many windows were broke thereby, and some adjacent houses shock'd. It happily fell out that the grocer, his wife and children, were all walked out.

On Tuesday night the constable came to Bartholomew Fair, demolished the gaming tables, and carried the gamesters to the comptor.

On Monday night a child of about four years old, was found stript of his cloaths at the Dead Wall behind Grey's Inn; He told the people that his friends lived in Soho; that a woman stript him who gave him a piece of cake. A barber's apprentice in Bedford-Row took the child to bed with him that night who died before the morning, the body being much swelled. The coroner's inquest was to sit yesterday on the body.

LONDON SEPT. 2. 'Tis said, that by some of the papers found upon the Lord Bishop of Rochester, it appears, that 70000 £. have lately been remitted by him to foreign parts; which he says was for the use of the Protestant Church abroad.

LONDON SEPT. 4. We hear, the Lord Bishop of Rochester desired leave that the Reverend Mr. Hawkins Chaplain to the Tower might be permitted to read prayers, and administer the Sacrament to him on Sunday last, but the same was refused by the commanding officer of the Tower.

They are very busy in repairing and strengthening the goal at Newgate, and particularly the miserable dungeon call'd the Condemn'd Hold, because this week 'tis expected the same will be tenanted.

LONDON SEPT. 8. On Tuesday morning the Dover stage-coach belonging to Mr. Smith at the Bell-Savage-Inn on Ludgate-Hill, was robb'd upon Black-Heath, by one single man on horseback, who afterwards meeting a young woman on foot, robb'd her likewise; she making to a gentleman's house alarm'd the people, who immedeately rode after him, upon which, seeing himself so closely pursu'd, he took his pistol and shot himself through the head.

Seven persons are convicted of capital crimes, viz. Matthias Brisden, for murder of his wife, Ann Morris, for the murder of her bastard child; Richard Oxey, alias Oxley, alias Thomas Hudson, for stealing a great quantity of plate out of a dwelling house, John Casey, Arthur Hughs, and Thomas Jennings, alias Milksop, for the highway, and the last for several indictments. Mr. Butler the smith who was to have been tryed for killing one Boyte, a bailiff, with a red hot poker, dy'd yesterday morning in Newgate.

LONDON SEPT. 11. A petition was presented lately in the name of Mrs. Morrice, daughter of the Lord Bishop of Rochester: praying, that she might visit her father and such restrictions as should be thought proper; and that application has also been made that Mr. Atterburry, only son of the said Bishop, might be permitted to visit his Lordship before he went to settle at Oxford; but the same could not be obtained.

LONDON SEPT. 14. Johnson, a bit-maker in St. Martin's Lane, and Kennedy a glover, falling out at an ales-house in Chandos Street about 3 weeks ago, fell to boxing of each other; soon after they came to the said house, paid for the window they had broken, and were reconciled to each other; since which the latter fell ill of a fever and died, and thereupon the former was charged with killing him, but the coroner's inquest having sat upon the body yesterday at the Plough in St. Martin's Lane, and the same being opened before them by an able surgeon, and no marks of violence appearing, they brought in their verdict, natural death.

LONDON SEPT. 15. On Monday last, in the morning, was found under the Gateway of Flower-de Luce Court in Southwark, a new born infant with its bones broken, and cram'd into an earthen pot; but the authors of this barbarity are not yet discovered.

The dispute between the King's troops and some of the Highland clans, is not looked upon as much importance, or as likely to cause any uneasiness to the Government of that side; the same being occasioned by the proper officers going to collect, or as they term it, to uplift the rents of the Earl of Seaforth's Forfeiting estate; upon which the Highlanders were mutinous as was expected.

The report said Earl of Seaforth's being there at the head of those clans, meet with no credit.

LONDON SEPT. 15. They write from Scotland, That Capt. Mack Neil march'd from Inverness with a detachment of his Majesty's forces to disperse a party of Highlanders belonging to the Earl of Seaforth who were lying ambushcade, in a wood; The said captain was order'd with a serjeant & party of 18 men out of the said detachment, to clear the woods of the said detachment, who let them pass without molestation; upon which Captain Mack Neil advanced at the head of his main body, The highlanders attack'd them, and in the fight the captain received 12 small shot, upon which he drop'd, & was carried off wounded, one of his Majesty's men was killed, and some wounded. Upon which the Highlanders left the said wood, with a design to draw his Majesty's forces to their parties, who were lurking on the hills; The King's troops pursuing them little imagining they had any more but themselves, a gentleman come to the King's troops, and told them, that if they advanced any further, they would be all cut to pieces: Upon which a Council of War was held, and it was resolved to retreat to Inverness.

LONDON SEPT. 15. Yesterday morning about day-light, Capt. Tempest & Mr. Grimes, who had been drinking together all the night at a tavern near Temple Bar, had the misfortune to quarrel, and went into the Temple, where they diverted themselves for some time at Tierce and catt, the latter was wounded in the arm, and then they parted.

Our merchants had advice, that the Bonetta, Capt. Margastroide, bound for Barbadoes to Philadelphia, was taken and burnt by the pyrates off Martinico, and all the men set on shore on the Island of St. Lucia.

LONDON SEPT. 16. On Sunday last the Rt. Reverend the Lord Bishop of Rochester was prayed for in most of the parish churches of this city, and those thereunto belonging, on account of his Lordships ill state of health.

On Thursday last a female infant, after driving some time with the tyde, was thrown into the Thames by the unnatural mother, or some of her agents, as soon as born.

LONDON SEPT. 18. Friday night last Mr. Bowen, engraver and print seller was taken into custody of his Majesty's messenger, for publishing a print of the Bishop of Rochester looking thro' a grate, &c. and the next morning one Edward Ward, who keeps a tavern in Moor-Fields, also taken into custody for being the author of the seditious verses under said effigies.

It is said that his Majesty and his Royal Highness will go for New Market, to take the diversion of the horse-race there in the beginning of October next.

LONDON SEPT. 22. A sad accident lately happened in Gloucester Court, in Whitecross-Street, where one Mr. Batchellor, a silver spinner, having some words with his wife, threw a tobacco pipe at her, which unfortunately hit a child she had in her arms, of a twelve months old, the small end of which entered its skull a considerable depth, of which wound it languish'd till Thursday last and then expired.

LONDON SEPT. 26. Matthias Brisden's daughter, convinced her father (who was one of the criminals condemn'd last session) of barbarously murthering her mother, being instructed by some wise woman of what importance it was to have her father's foregiveness, (tho' what she did was her unquestionable duty) did, with many tears, seeking that imaginary blessing while lay condemned in Newgate to no purpose; but in High Holborn, going up to the cart, where he was carry'd to execution, and kneeling down to him, she with much difficulty obtained it.

Yesterday one John Salt & Sarah his wife, commonly call'd Silver Sarah, stood in the pillory over against Chancery Lane in Fleet Street, pursuant to their sentence at the sessions at Guildhall, as notorious cheats; he having marry'd her by the name of Hayes by that she might try to get a maintenance, or at least, extort money from a certain gentleman of that name, with whom she pretended to have had an acquaintance; They were sufficiently pelted by the populace and the fellow in wrigling about at last fell down, pulling the pilorry along with him.

LONDON SEPT. 28. On Wednesday last in the evening, two of his Majesty's messengers went down to Brittel, to bring up the Earl of Orrery with his secretary; and yesterday morning Mr. De la Faye, with an officer and two messengers went to his Lordships house in Glass-House Street, and search'd the same for papers.

LONDON SEPT. 28. We hear that on Saturday last Mr. Shippen's house in Norfolk-Street (a noted member of Parliament) was searched by some of the King's messengers; and it was reported last night, that the said gentleman was taken into custody.

Col. Morron was order'd to bring up the Lord North and Grey from the Isle of Wight.

LONDON OCT. 6. The last mail from Lisbon brought a melancholy account of a English ship, freighted there for the islands, to lade corn for the Portuguese garrison of Mazagon upon the Coast of Africa. They took in at Lisbon a Portuguese captain and pilot, and being come towards the Azores, were met by a pyrate who took them, and cut the Portuguese pilot in pieces. The Portuguese captain they hung up at the yard arm by one leg till he was almost dead, and beat the English captain till he was in the same condition; then put them and their crew into a boat without provisions, and turned them adrift, though 12 leagues at least from any land. At last however they got safe to the island of St. Michael, after about 60 hours labour.

LONDON OCT. 9. Saturday last in the evening a man in Drury Lane stabbed his wife with a knife, and when he had done, stuffed a bit of rag into the wound to stop the blood, and led her to a surgeon: We do not hear the woman is yet dead.

LONDON OCT. 9. Last Thursday at the sessions held at Oxford, one Thomas Pocock a fruiterer was tried for sodomy; it appears he was 82 years, and had practiced that abominable vice near 20 years, which was proved by 5 witnesses; the most notorious was in June last, with the tapster at the Angel. The fact was clearly proved, and the jury found him guilty.

LONDON OCT. 20. Thursday morning early above seventy convicts, who lay in Newgate under sentence of transportation were ship'd to Virginia.

LONDON OCT. 27. In the last act of Parliament to impower his Majesty to secure and detain such persons as his Majesty shall suspect are conspiring against his person or government it is provided, that nothing therein shall extend to invalidate the ancient privileges of Parliament, or to the imprisonment of any member of either House of Parliament, during the sitting of such Parliament, until the matter be first communicated to the House and the consent of the said House obtained. According to which clause, a messenger was yesterday sent from his Majesty to the House of Lords, for their consent that the Duke of Norfolk might be secured, and, we hear, pursuant to the resolution taken thereupon, it was believed that his Grace would be sent to the Tower as last night or this day.

LONDON NOV. 3. Last week a gentleman bought in Exchange Alley of a person in a Clergy man's habit, 300 £. South Sea Bonds, They having a large interest due on them, he went immediately to receive it at South Sea-House, when, to his great surprize, the bonds were stop'd, having been picked out of the proprietors pocket long ago, who being well known, had got others of the company, upon giving security. The purchaser hurried to the alley, but to his mortification none could give him an account of his chapman.

At the close of last week, three men in lac'd cloaths took a boat from the Temple about 8 at night, and bid the waterman row to Whitehall; in his way thither they asked him, who he was for; he said for King George: On which they took him by the heels and threw him overboard, the poor man swimming well saved himself, otherwise he been lost, for they rowed away with his boat.

On Tuesday night the Alborough arrived at Spithead from Waterford in Ireland; from whence she has brought in chains, two of Rhoche's accomplices, who confessed they were concerned with him in the horrid murther of the company on board a French vessel.

There is orders to clean and fit the Alborough sloop, who was lately seized and carry'd into Limmington, a vessel of about 30 tons, laden with wine and brandy, belonging to the private traders at Christ-Church; which being made a prize of, will be first unloaded at Southampton and then brought here.

On Sunday last the Lord Mayor elect was sworn at Guild Hall as is required by the charter of the city of London. And on Monday he went with the usual solemnity to be sworn before the Baron of the exchequers, and then return'd as customary to make his procession thro' the city. It is remarkable that many of the Lord's of his Majesty's most Honourable Privy Council, six Knights of the Garter, the great officers at Court, Judges, &c. honoured his Lordship with their company at dinner at Godsmiths-Hall, where they were very suptuously entertained, several of the blue-Garters, afterward handed out the city ladies to dance at the ball.

This procession was attended with several unusual accidents, viz. A great fray between the Marcers and Plaisterers Companies at the corner of the Old-Baley, the latter endeavouring to break the march of the former brought the two bodies to blows, and after many wounds given on both sides by clubs lustily laid on, the latter prevail'd. Upon the whole the Mercers Company (as we are assur'd) will bring their action against the Plaisterers Company for the afore mentioned insult.

It was also observable that the mob stuck lawrels about the late Lord Mayor's coach, and huzz'd him in a prodigious sort, not without shewing some disposition of insulting the present Lord Mayor, so that the procession was obstructed. Upon which Capt. Bell of the Post Office was detatch'd back by the commanding officers of the city train'd bands, to disperse them, which he soon did accordingly.

The same day the stand belonging to the Coach Maker Company, which was erected in St. Paul's Church-Yard on the occasion of the Lord Mayor's Day, gave a sudden crack and fell forward into the street; but without any hurt to the life or limb to the persons, who were sufficiently bemused.

The tide of the Thames flow'd so high that the boats were row'd about the Palace yard at Westminster.

LONDON NOV. 27. Mr. Robert Knight late cashier of the South Sea Company has taken up his abode in Venice, from whence he has sent over, to a relation here, his picture in miniture done by an eminent Italian there.

We are assured by some persons very well skill'd in the coal trade that there is (one year with another) three hundred thousand chaldron of coal brought to the Port of London, which is an increase of ninety thousand chaldron yearly more than we had six years ago. The duty per chaldron is five shillings to the King, two shillings to St. Paul's Church, two shillings towards the new churches, six pence to the city orphan's, eight pence to the meeters, and half a penny to the Lord Mayor, which is called the Lady Mayoresses Pin Money.

LONDON DEC. 1. We are inform'd that the Viceroy of Mexico, on account of the continual depradations and barbarities committed by a sort of Indians, who had never been subdu'd by the Spaniards, sent towards the latter end of the last year a considerable body of forces to reduce them to the obedience of Spain; which force had the good fortune to take their King prisoner, and to make the entire conquest of their country. By this success, the Spaniards, 'tis said, have not only made themselves masters of several rich mines, but have had a foundation for the propagating Christianity, by Baptizing above 500 of their children.

On Wednesday morning last about three a clock a fire broke out at a confectioners shop in Bishops Gate Street near Cornhill, by which accident that house, the one next to it and the White Lyon Tavern behind them were burnt to the ground.

LONDON DEC. 15. On Thursday last a boy about ten years of age, who belonged to St. Clement's Danes Charity School, was unhappily bit by a mad dog; on which he instantly run mad, and died the next day.

We are under no small apprehensions of the villainous practice of willfully firing houses which is sure one of the most execrable crime that can be committed, when only for the probability of being able to steal something in the confusion and distraction people are put into upon those occasions, the villains secretly set fire to the house in the night, by throwing combustible matter in the cellar windows; and the two fires we have lately had, 'tis thought, were both of the begun this way. We hear that some gentlemen are determin'd to represent this affair to the Parliament, and to propose a punishment adaquate to the nature of the crime, to be inflicted on such wretches as shall be convicted of a fact so abominable.

LONDON DEC. 20. A misfortune happen'd lately at Capt. Lane's house at Bentley in Staffordshire: Mr. Lane and his daughter being drying gun-powder, the same took fire, blew up great parts of the house, and wounded the young gentlewoman in such a manner that her life is dispaired of; and Capt. Lane has receiv'd considerable hurt himself.

1723

LONDON JAN. 30. On Monday morning about 5 a clock the Bristol mail coming to London, in which were also the Gloucester and Hereford bags, was rifles by one highwayman, near Longford, who the post-boy says is the same fellow that robb'd it last time, just by the place where Hawkins and Simpson hang for the same fact.

Advice that the Sagmices, Capt. Scot, in her voyage from Barbadoes to the Cape of Verdes, was taken and burnt by the pyrates. Several of the seamen turned pyrates also, and the captain was wounded, and set ashore naked, and that five vessels had fallen unto the same hands of the pyrates about the same time.

LONDON FEB. 18. Some days since, at Chiswick, the wife of a supervisor in the excise, that had deem disordered in mind for some time past, took a dose of poison, of which she instantly died.

On Saturday night a disturbance happened at the New Play House in Lincoln's Inn-Fields, occasioned by a body of bailiffs and their followers investing the house, by order to carry of a gentleman who was upon duty in the play; but we hear, their design miscarried.

LONDON FEB. 23. We hear the Lord Bishop of Rochester still continue very much indisposed with a fever, and in great danger, being daily visited by his physician Dr. Friend.

We hear the Bishop of Rochester's coachman and footman, who used to go backward and forward, between his Lordship's house in Westminster, and the Tower, are taken into custody.

On Wednesday a poor man who used to work in the Bishop of Rochester's garden at Bromley, was taken into custody as was Thursday morning the Reverend Mr. Moore, Vicar of Aldesgate, his Lordship's secretary.

There is an new invention of a strange kind of machine for plowing of ground; the work is performed by one man and without horses: It is recon'd an extraordinary piece of ingenuity, and a great number of artists and persons of quality have been to see it now at the Golden Ball at Hyde-Park Corner.

LONDON FEB. 28. On Monday morning last, one Brittain a widow in Milford-Lane was marry'd to a brewer servant at St. Clement's Church in the Strand; who, being so advised by her learned counsel, or, as others say, some old woman in the neighbourhood, went to the Church-door without any other apparel on than her bare smock, to the great surprize and laughter of a numerous crown of spectators. By means of this cunning adventure, she thinks herself, it seems, not liable to pay any debts contracted by her former husband. At the Church-door her intended spouse took her in his arms, and carried her to an apothecary's house over against the Church, new cloath'd her from top to toe: after which whimsical transaction the nuptials were solemnized.

LONDON MARCH 1. On Wednesday the sessions began at Old Bailey when William Summerfield was convicted of a capital crime, for robbing on the King's highway.

On Monday a bill of indictment was found at Hick's Hall against Sally Salisbury for assault upon an honourable gentleman, with an attempt to murder him.

The same day a bill of indictment was found against Barton, a grave digger belonging to St. Giles's Church, for taking up and disposing of a dead body, as we hear, to practitioners in anatomy. The next day he pleaded to the indictment.

On Wednesday a bill of indictment was found at the same place against the four watermen of Islesworth, for the murder of Anne Aristow on Smallbury-Green.

We are informed, that soon after the ending of the present sessions, the old building of Hick's Hall will be pull'd down, and rebuilt at the charge of the County of Middlesex.

On Monday William Halewell master of the ale house on Smallbury Green, were the rape, robbery and murder was said committed upon Anne Aristow, died in Newgate; and the coroner's inquest having sat on the body, the same was delivered on Tuesday, to his friends, and was carried up the river to be interred at Islesworth.

The four watermen of Islesworth that are charged with ravishing robbing and murdering Anne Aristow of Oakingham on Smallbury-Green are now all taken; George Smith and Joseph Buckingham being taken at Gravesend on board a sloop bound for Holland, and committed to Maidstone goal; James Simpson taken at Pursleer in Erith, being carried before Sir John Fryer, Knt. and Alderman, was by him committed to Newgate; and on Sunday last Samuel Loyd, being taken at a house in Hart-street, Covent-Garden, and carried before Justice Vaugham, was likely committed to the said goal of Newgate; whither he was carried on Monday morning.

On Monday 36 felons, viz. 28 men and 8 women, were sent on board, to be transported to Maryland.

LONDON MARCH 2. Our merchants have advice, that the ship Baylor, Capt. Verney, having been slaving on the Coast of Guinea, and thence set sail for Virginia, turn'd pirate, the Negroes being thrown over-board. The said ship was afterwards taken by a Dutch cruzer, after a fight of four hours.

One elderly gentleman who was accustomed to shave at the barbers near the Royal Exchange, and who never found the way thither but on Sunday, had so tired the barber's boy with attending him on that day, that the youngster had contrived several ways to lose that customer, but to no purpose; however, about a month since, he fell on an expedient that did it effectually; and when the old gentleman came, and was under his hands (there being none in the room but those two) the boy on a sudden starting, seemed to be in a great surprize, and looking towards the corner of the room, cry'd out, I will not, which he repeated several times: The gentleman seeing him in such fright, asked him the cause; The artful youth repli'd, yonder stands the devil and tempts me to cut your throat for shaving this day. At which the old gentleman, who was something credulous, was so frighted that he run away with half his head on. This has had such an effect on him, that he can now find time to shave on a Saturday.

LONDON MARCH 2. On Sunday last, about three in the morning Mr. Jenny son in Law to Mr. Conningham, merchant in Ironmonger Lane, and Mr. Barnaby, a young gentleman who won the highest prize in the Dutch lottery, both intimate friends, being at a publick house at Holyhead, waiting for a wind to embarque for Ireland, were in a jesting manner, playing with their pistols, and having drank to a great pitch, at last Mr. Barnaby's pistol discharged, and shattered his friends head to pieces. Mr. Barnaby was immediately confined and an express dispatched to town, to acquaint Mr. Conningham with this misfortune.

The Duke of Douglas and the Lord Carmichael quarreling, on Thursday last fought in White's Chocolate-House Garden, but were parted before any mischief happened, and have since drank like friends.

At the sessions at Hick's Hall, Richard Roberts was indicted for assaulting Margaret Tomkinson, with intent to ravish her. He was found guilty of the said indictment, sentenc'd to pay a fine of 6 s. 8 d. and to undergo hard labour in Bridewell for six months.

The Bishop of Rochester, and everything that comes to him, is more strictly observed than hither to, for they say he had papers, pen and ink convey'd to him, on a barrel of butter from Bromley; and that he sent a breviate of instructions to his friends in a certain house, conceal'd in his foul linen.

LONDON MARCH 7. On Monday night last a Frenchman in Spittlefields, returning home in drink, was chid by his wife for staying out at a publick-house, upon which he took up a wooden bar of the door, and with it kill'd her, and he has since been committed to Newgate.

The next day a woman in Covent-Garden without any manner of provocation, stabb'd her husband, but we do not hear that he is dead.

LONDON MARCH 13. Wednesday last the stage-coach going to Exeter was overturned on the ridge of a hill, three miles beyond Salisbury, by which accident Mr. Pennick, steward to the Earl of Godolphin, was kill'd; Mr. Penrose so dangerously wounded, that his life is despair'd of, and two more gentlemen much hurt.

LONDON MARCH 23. We hear, that a blacksmith in Fetter-Lane, who has long been famous for his mechanical performances, has invented an instrument for engraving, which not only does the work much finer than it can be done by hand, but also performs more in one hour than could be effected in a month. It has for some time been the entertainment of the curious multitude of people going to see it.

They write from Yorkshire that a poor woman was about two weeks ago, delivered of five children at a birth, three girls and two boys, all living.

LONDON MARCH 30. Hampton Mason, who was brought up from King's Lynn, in Norfolk, to Newgate, being charged with burning his ship, &c. was lately carried to Doctor's Common and examined, according to the custom of the Court, in order to his tryal at the insuing Admiralty sessions. In his commitment mentioned is made that he took in goods at Rotterdam of Messiers Bower and Coffort, and insured 3000 guilders up on the ship there; 300 £. up on her at

London, afterwards run his cargo to Lynn, and then contrived to have her burnt to cheat both the insurers &c.

Yesterday Benjamin Ashe, son of Mr. Ashe a brewer in the city of Coventry, was shot to death in Hyde-Park, for deserting from Colonel Oughton's Company in the Second Regiment of Guard. It seems he was an old offender, and had been very riotous at the late election for the members of Parliament in that city.

Last Tuesday morning a captain of the 2d Regiment of Foot Guard shot himself in his lodging at Kensington.

Col. Chartres, who was charged with committing a rape about 14 months ago since in North Britain, for which he lately obtained his Majesty's most gracious pardon, travelling lately to his seat in East Lothian, was summuned to appear in Edinburgh, which he accordingly did, but not conforming himself in all respect to the ancient laws of that Kingdom with respect to offences of that nature, he was by the Lords of the session committed prisoner to the Talbooth.

LONDON APRIL 6. On Wednesday morning last between 6 and 7 of the clock, a duel was fought between two gentlemen of distinction in Marybone Fields, and before any could come up to part them, one of them was dangerously wounded, and afterwards carry'd to Mr. Coltheart, an eminent surgeon in Shandois Street near Covent-Garden, where he is now under care. We hear the other duelist is got off.

LONDON APRIL 6. Tuesday morning James Sandy, waterman to the Princess, was found in his house on Lambert-March, shot through the head, with his throat cut, and his apprentice boy dead in his bed, having his throat also cut; 'Tis said that he was a person of good circumstances, being owner of several houses in the neighbourhood. He return'd the night before from Crodon Assizes, where he went to prosecute another waterman, who some time since had by a blow kill'd a servant of his. Who was the instrument, of this tragical action, whether himself or another, we cannot pretend to determine.

LONDON APRIL 8. They write from Cloucester that one Pitts was tryed at the Assizes there for breaking of the arms of his Majesty's statue in that city, and attempting further to demolish it, and being convicted, was sentenced to pay a fine of 100 £. and to suffer three months imprisonment.

A melancholy accident happen'd last week at Carshalton near Epsom, where a man having singed a hog, some boys afterwards agreeing to try the experiment by way of frolic, one of them laid himself down to be singed; and a quantity of the straw being put about him, his playfellows setting fire to it, he was immediately suffocatted to death.

LONDON APRIL 10. We have received an account of a dreadful fire which happened last month at Wetherby in Yorkshire, the greatest part of which town belongs to his Grace the Duke of Devonshire. It began in a soap-boilers house, and burnt with that violence, that 36 houses were reduced to ashes, in less than two hours, besides barns and out-houses, the poor sufferers could hardly save their families and part of their goods, the loss in computed at upward of 13000 £.

LONDON APRIL 11. Last Monday a peruke maker's journeyman and apprentice, and a lapadary's apprentice in the city, were taken into custody, for desperate expressions an horrid intent to attempt the life of his Majesty.

LONDON APRIL 13. Last Saturday at the Assizes for Surrey, eight persons received sentence of death, five of which for robbing on the highway.

Yesterday William Burk was executed at Tyburn for robbery on the Highway.

LONDON APRIL 26. The Bill now happening in the House of Lords, for inflicting certain pains and penalties on the Bishop of Rochester, is to be read a second time on the 2d day of May next; when his Lordship will be heard by himself and Counsel against the said bill.

LONDON MAY 4. Last Thursday evening, a lady of Chelsea returning home, and having about her to a considerable value, was assaulted by several footpads, in the King's Road, who fired at the coachman because he neglected to stop; but the ball miss'd him. Upon the noise, one of the pensioners of Chelsea-Hospital, who was patrolling, came up and rescued the lady, by shooting one of the footpads dead; whereupon the others made their escape.

LONDON MAY 4. On Monday the Bishop of Rochester is to make his defence, by himself and Council, against the bill now pending for indicting on him certain pains and penalties, accordingly he is then to be brought to the bar of the House of Lords, where, for the more easy standing of his Lordship and Council, a convenient place is fitted up and covered with scarlet cloth.

LONDON MAY 7. Yesterday morning at about ten, the Bishop of Rochester, was guarded from the Tower, in the Deputy-Governour's chariot, who was also with him, to Westminster; and several witnesses having been examin'd by the House of Peers, his Lordship was remanded back to his prison in order to be carry'd up again this day.

LONDON MAY 10. Last Thursday night, several persons were committed for insulting the Bishop of Rochester, as he pass'd thro' King Street. This though his Lordship's tryal will not be over till next Monday.

LONDON MAY 10. As every thing relating to the fair sex will always be received in an agreeable manner by the polite part of mankind, surely the negotiation of a marriage, by way of correspondence in a merchantile way, must certainly be allowed a new way of falling in love. To proceed to the fact: An eminent merchant here, had receiv'd a letter from his French correspondent in one of the western plantations, who having acquired a considerable estate in those parts, acquaints him, that he cannot think himself happy, without the enjoyment of an English bride, and he disdains the hue of America's clime, thus marks out the female, which most suits his fancy. 1. He desires no portion with his intended spouse, but her person; and that she be descended of honest parentage. 2. Her age about 25 of a middle and well proportioned stature, a lasting face, and a sound constitution; able to bear the fatigue of the voyage, and the heat of the climate whither she is to be transmitted. 3. He assures his friend, that if he can find out an English girl, who is inclined thus to make her fortune by way of venture; that his having the above mentioned qualifications, and bringing a letter from him to prevent mistakes, he will marry her in 15 days, after her arrival. Our English merchant sent over a lass with all these endowments, and received by the last shipping a letter of thanks from the French gentleman, with an account of the joyful celebration of his nuptials.

LONDON MAY 15. Yesterday Alexander Day, the pretended Marmarduke Davenport, alias Fitch Esq; convicted the late sessions in the Old Baily, as a common cheat stood in the pillory, according to the sentence of the Court pronounc'd against him; The mobb, agreeable to their usual benevolence, bestow'd on the industrious cheat some hearty pelts of acknowledgement, and on his part, not having presently learned passive obedience, found means to discharge himself from the wooden ruff, and four or five times content alone against the multitude, and even returned some things thrown at him with great agility, upon the populace.

LONDON MAY 17. 'Tis said that the Lord Bishop of Rochester will make his first retreat to Brussels, and that proper dispositions are making for that purpose; and a certain gentleman, considerably interested in his Lordship's family, is about to dispose of a considerable station which he now holds, to attend his Lordship in his exile.

LONDON MAY 18. On Thursday last between eleven and twelve, Henry Roper, Lord Aeynham, an English Peer, one of the Lords of the Bed-Chamber to his Majesty, having been unfortunately disorder'd in his senses some days before, shot himself through the head with a pistol at his house in the Hay-Market, and died about an hour after: His Lordship was 47 years of age, hath left three children by his first Lady, none by his next, two by his last, daughter to the Earl of Suffex, who is now with child. His Lordship embraced the Protestant Religion about four years ago.

Yesterday Christhopher Layer, Esq; was executed at Tyburn, pursuant to his sentence at the Court of King's Bench for high-treason: The sheriff having demanded him of proper officers at the Tower, he was delivered up accordingly; and his fetters being knocked off was carried under a guard of wardens and soldiers through the little guard room, over the draw-bridge to the wharf, from whence he walked to the iron gate near St. Katherin's in the County of Middlesex, where he was received by the sheriffs officers, and carried upon a sledge to the place of execution, where he was attended by two Clergymen, viz. Mr. Hawkins and Mr. Beryman, who assisted him in his devotions. He made a speech at the gallows, and delivered a paper to the under-sheriff, and another to a friend of his: His head was afterwards sent to Newgate, to be set up, as we hear, at Temple-Bar, but his quarters were delivered to his friends, who put them into a hearse, and brought them round about Kensington to Mr. Purdy's an undertaker, in Stanhope-Street, Clare-Market, who had it sewed up in order to be interred in Cambridge-Shire.

LONDON JUNE 1. This day the Lord of Rochester is deprived of all his dignities and ecclesiasticle benefices whatsoever; and by the 25th of the instant he is to depart this Realm, and all other of his Majesty's Dominions, and to remain in perpetual exile.

LONDON JUNE 3. On Saturday night last about 11, one Thomas Taylor, an old master-hackney coachman, in driving down from Long-Acres into James Street, Covent-Garden, had the misfortune to run his coach wheel against a post at the corner of the street, and by the shock was thrown out of his box, and pitched upon his head died soon after. Yesterday in the evening the coroner's inquest sat upon the body, and brought in their verdict accidental death.

LONDON JUNE 4. Last Thursday several Quakers coming to town from the North England, and were robbed by a gang of footpads who treated them very unhumanely.

On Saturday last the sessions ended at the Old Baily, when four malefactors received sentence of death; viz. Joseph Chapman, John Tyrell alias Tenent, William Parsons, all three for horse stealing, and William Hawksworth a soldier in the Third Regiment of Foot-guards, for the murder of John Ranson a corn chandler.

LONDON JUNE 10. Yesterday about 3 in the afternoon a dreadful fire broke out in the warehouses in Hilleter-Lane, which burnt for three hours with amazing fury, consuming the whole range of warehouses, which were chiefly, filled-with Turkey goods of great value. Some houses were also destroyed, particularly the fine house of Col. Pertrain which was formerly Sir John Knipe's. Mr. Moier is said to have lost 60 bales of silk; and several rich Jews dwellings thereabout have suffer'd greatly. We hear this calamity was occasion'd by a fellow entering one of the warehouses, which was full of cotton, with a lighted pipe of tobacco. The whole damage is supposed to amount to near one hundred thousand pounds.

A baker's man in Bishopsgate-Street cut his own throat that morning, and died instantly.

Last night a fire broke out in St. Giles's near the Church, and today a baker's house in Mincing Lane also took fire, but with the assistance of the fire men was soon extinguished.

LONDON JUNE 13. By letter from Dublin we have advice, That one Daniel Carrol (who was concern'd in the robbing of Mr. Younge the first of July last, as he was coming in a chair through little Queen Street, for which his comrades, Cirrick and Mallons were executed) was apprehended there last week. The Lords Justices, soon after this fact was committed, believing he might return thither, issued a proclamation, with a reward of 40 £. for taking him, but he, it seems, was not discover'd till falling out with a mistress, she betray'd him to

Mr. Hawkins, goaler of Newgate, who seiz'd him in a house in Berwich Street, in Dublin; but Carrol being very desperate, he was first run through the body. He had 50 Molders, and other things of value about him.

LONDON JUNE 13. On Monday last, there happen'd a fire in West-Smithfield, occasion'd by a child playing with some paper by a fire side, which burnt one child & set fire to the cloths of another, who was much scourch'd thereby. It was extinguished time enough to prevent any considerable damage to the house.

LONDON JUNE 15. There was on Thursday a remarkable trial at Guild-Hall before the Lord Chief Justice Pratt, between a turner in Grace-Church-Street plaintiff, and a salesman's son in Hounds-ditch defendant; the former having su'd the latter in an action of 3,000 £. damage for criminal conversation with his wife, and the same being plainly proved, the jury gave him 500 £.

LONDON JUNE 18. Yesterday morning Capt. Lawrence, commander of his Majesty's ship the Alborough took water at Whitehall to go on board at Long-Reach in order to receive the deprived Bishop of Rochester, who went from the Tower in a barge this morning about eleven, to embark in the said man of war, for his transportation.

LONDON JUNE 22. On Saturday last, Capt. John Cross was committed to the guard-house Westminster, by Justice Gore, being charged on oath, by his confession, with assaulting and wounding with a sword in the cavity of the breast one Alexander Gwin of Spring-Garden, (a fortune-Teller) of which wounds he is in imminent danger of his life; Mr. Collaheart the surgeon in Chandos-Street hath him under cure.

LONDON JUNE 22. On Sunday last a gardner, a gentleman's footman, and a young lad, going to wash in the Thames over against the Swan at Chelsea, they both drowned.

LONDON JULY 6. The foreign seamen in the Czar's service grow weary of it, their pay being so small, and their victuals so poor, that many of them die through want, and were it not for the order given, not to let go any foreign seamen without the Czar's special pass, it is believed hardly one would be left in his whole fleet. The land officers are also full of complaint on account of their arrears, having received no pay this twelve months past, through the scarcity of money throughout Russia, which probably is owing to the large remittances the Czar has made to Constantinople, to bribe both the Grand Vizier and Musti to preserve the peace between him and the Grand Seignior. And this, no doubt, has occasion'd the project of laying a tax upon the nobility, gentry, &c. under the denomination of a free gift.

The Czar has sent assurances to the Danish Court, that he only manns his fleet, which now lies ready to sail from Cronslot, to discipline his seamen. The Lord Duffus of Scotland, is made a Rear Admiral therein.

It is now reported that an accommodation between the Grand Seignior and Czar of Muscovy is as good as concluded, and 'tis discoursed that a partition treaty is on foot between them and Meriweys, in order to divide amongst themselves the whole Kingdom of Persia, and new model its form of Goverment in matters ecclesiastical and civil.

LONDON JULY 15. The English seamen who formerly were so fond on entering into the Czar's service, we hear, are very sick of it, and endeavours all they can to leave it for their own, should the other foreign seamen in that service do the like, it is believed his fleet will not carry so much terror with it as it has heretofore done.

On Thursday a bill of indictment was found at the Old Baily against James Edmondson Esq; one of the late South Sea directors, for concealing part of his estate from the trustees, contrary to the Act of Parliament.

LONDON JULY 20. On Tuesday last Mr. Newsham in New-Street, Cloth Fair, London, play'd his new engine at the Royal Exchange, before several gentlemen present, which play'd several yards above the Dial, with a constant stream, above an hundred gallons each minute; which must be allow'd by all ingenious men that saw it, to exceed all sorts of engines whatsoever.

On Monday last, at Deptford, Capt. Dunning of Doven's new invented engine to force ships against wind and tide, was try'd upon a 30 gun ship in presence of the Lords of the Admiralty, the Commissioners of the Navy Board, and about ten thousand spectators. The engine answer'd the expectation of the beholders, and the success was proclaimed by the common voice of the people, and discharge of the cannon on the river. It is said, that by this invention, our merchants will not only avoid the dangers of Sallee and other rovers, gallies and pyrates, but our men of war will be capable of taking 'em in calms. Ships may at any time go out of harbours, and save their market, or come in to save themselves; so that the greater part of the dangers of the sea may be avoided. The engine is but a little change, and in no way incommodious.

LONDON AUG. 1. We hear by the last post from Naples, that great damage is done by the Vesuvius spewing out its volcanoes great quantities of cinders, and other combustibles and butuminus matter, and that some of the neighbouring villages have felt some shocks of earthquake.

LONDON AUG. 2. James Butler, and William Duce, who are to suffer on Monday next at Tyburn, have provided themselves with shrouds, which they design to appear in on Sunday next at the chappel of Newgate, as a token of their repentance, and to deter others from doing the like wise practice.

LONDON AUG. 3. On Thursday night, about 10 o'clock the wife of one Kefer, a German, living in Denmark Court near Exeter-Exchange, in the Strand, having left two small children at home, took her third, which was a girl of a year a half old, in her arms, to York-Stairs in York Building, and after stripping her stark naked, threw her, from the terrace wall into the Thames, it being at the time near high water, afterwards getting upon the wall she threw her self in. It happily fell out that a waterman was laying up his boat hard by and another person talking with him, who hearing them plunge, the waterman leap'd in at that instant, and having a pole in his hand, first reached the child just before the tyde had carry'd it under the Stone Arch; the poor infant crying mommy when it was thrown in, and as soon as taken out. They saved the unfortunate mother also, tho' against her will: She appears to be distracted, is now under means of cure, and is an object of compasion.

LONDON AUG. 10. On Thursday last a military officer was commited to Newgate for feloniously embezling a barrel of gunpowder belonging to his Majesty's stores.

LONDON AUG. 12. At the Assizes held at Norwich last week, two persons received sentence of death, viz. Hugh Robinson the father, and William Robinson his son, for willingly setting fire to several houses in Mortham near Yarmouth, in the County of Norfolk. William Robinson is to be hanged in chains on Northam Green, being the place where the facts were committed.

LONDON AUG. 17. A letter from an eminent physician at Salisbury brings advice that 1244 have been visited with the small pox in that city from Christmas last to the 29th ult. of which number 165 dyed. The same physician has sent a particular account to his Majesty's Sergeant Surgeon of 80 persons of all ages and conditions from the age of one & a half, to 50, who within these three months have been inoculated for the small pox in that city, and are recovered.

LONDON AUG. 22. On Saturday last one Flax, a cane chair-maker in little Turn-Style High Holburn, dash'd his wife's brains out with a pint-pot: Her body lay conceal'd till Tuesday last in the house where the fact was committed; the murderer having made his escape.

LONDON SEPT. 5. Yesterday morning Earnest Baker and Mr. Hare of East Acton Gate fought a duel on Old Oak Common, near Acton Wells: Mr. Hare was killed on the spot, and the other since made his escape; but the occasion on the quarrel is not yet known.

LONDON SEPT. 7. Last Saturday evening nine passengers were robbed by a gang of nine footpads, who lay concealed by a wood near Kingston, they gagg'd the passengers, took their money, and even stript'd some of them of their cloaths; and amongst the rest, one belonging to that town lost about the value of 100 £. The rogues were dress'd like sailors and the next day committed other robberies on the road.

A few days ago a gentleman giving alms to an old man that stood begging in an alley near Lincoln's Inn Square, with a long beard and very filthy tatter'd habit, another gentleman passed by at the very same time, looking wishfully in the beggar's face, knew him, and discovered him to be a person possessed of an estate of near 50 £. a year in Bucks, and 200 £. South Sea Stock.

The 30th past the sessions ended at the Old Baily when 5 persons received sentence of death, viz. Samuel Gibbons, Richard Wynne, Joseph Middleton, Richard Wallis and Humphry Angire; the four former for felony &c. and the latter 2 for robbery on the highway. Five were burnt in the hand, two ordered to be whipped, and 39 for transportation. One Benjamin Hurlock, that was tryed for ravishing a child about 4 years of age, was acquited; as was John Taylor, a soldier, of the murder of Thomas Lucas.

LONDON SEPT. 7. They write from Gloucester, that about eleven a clock one night last week a large mob assembled there, and in a riotous manner disturbed the camp near the city, bellowing out their usual nonsense; upon which the soldiers, who were at rest, were forced to turn out and fall upon them. Two of the mob were wounded, and some think mortally; and the rest were so well handed that it is best said it will be a memento to them for the Future.

LONDON SEPT. 10. Last Saturday Mr. Atwood of Grey's Inn riding to Oxford fell from his horse, broke his scull, and died immediately.

LONDON SEPT. 14. On Tuesday night a small party of the Blacks of Waltham visited Mr. Norton's seat at Southwick and carried of two deer besides wounding several others, which they were obliged to leave behind them; for no sooner were they discovered by the keepers, that an alarm bell was rung: Upon which the people of the town came to assist, but so have they been terrify'd by these smutty gentry, that, though they of Southwick were treble the number, they durst not attack them, but suffer'd them to go off with their landlord's venison; however, two fellows at Waltham are sent to Winchester, as being concerned, and two others from Southwick have been conveyed to the same prison under a strong guard of soldiers: They are both stout fellows and of a bad character; What makes them more suspected is that several deer skin have been found on them.

LONDON SEPT. 16. On Sunday the 1st of September, about 6 on the clock in the morning, one of the keepers was out in the Cole Forest, and saw some fellows disguis'd: He immediately returned back and called his fellow-keeper, and the rest of the men servants, and rais'd six men in all, whereof went with guns, and some with long sticks. After hearing two guns go off, they saw a fellow black'd and running from them, hollowing aloud; they left one of their company to look after him, and immediately espyed six more, who they very civilly offered to leave the ground and retire, which they refused, and parlying within 4 or 5 yards one of the villains presented his gun, and shot the keeper unexpectedly in the breast, and out of the back, who died immediately upon the spot; the rest stood a long battle, and the other servants did not fire till at last one seeing a hunter lift up his gun and present it at his fellow servant, who was a little before him, shot him in the thigh and broke the bone to pieces, so he fell. Three of them immediately ran away, and the other four were taken.

The letter adds, that out of the seven deer-stealers who lives above nine miles from Farmham and that the gang there, which has been much talked of is quite dispersed.

LONDON SEPT. 18. Mr. Heidigger, Director of the Opera House in the Hay-Market, has ordered 1000 £. for new paintings and ornamenting that house for entertaining of the quality this season, and some of the best masters are now at work on the same.

A few days since one George Wakins, a young lad belonging to a Holland's trader, lying off Crane Stairs at Greenwich, having loaded a pistol with a brace of balls, discharged it at a waiter that was on board the said vessel, but missing him, shot the mate, what induced him to commit such a villainous action we have not yet heard.

LONDON SEPT. 18. There is an account from Petherton near Chard in Sumersetshire, that one Darby, a barber-surgeon, having some words with his own brother, a cooper, took up a hanger and striking him on the belly, cut out his bowels, so that he died on the spot, and the murderer made his escape; the deceased is said to be the only one of five brothers who had any regard to and maintain'd his aged father.

They write from Hereford, Sept. 11, That great doings were made there the week before, at the annual Musick Club, singing, horse racing & for the view last, scaffolds were erected on Wigmore Marsh, on which several hundreds of ladies were seated to the best advantage, who had much better luck than vast numbers of the other sex, who had placed themselves there next morning when the buildings fell down by which unhappy accident, several persons had their arms and legs broken, and many very much wounded.

LONDON SEPT. 19. On Saturday last between nine and ten in the evening a couple of fellows came up to two warrenners of Wandsworth, and enquired of them if they did not belong to Mr. Brown of that place; upon there saying they did, these fellows bid them to hasten to his assistance, for they heard some persons, whom they had met just before, swear they would have his blood: Hereupon the warrenners made towards Mr. Brown's house, and the fellows following them a little way, and then knock'd them both down, and tying them very fast, joined some others who had fire arms, and went directly to Mr. Brown's; whose niece hearing some noise about the house, looked out of the window, and asked what they wanted: They cursed her, and said they wanted her blood and her uncle's, and immediately discharged a gun at her, and kept a constant firing for a considerable time. This alarm'd some persons in the neighbouring house; who calling out to know what was the matter, the villains bid them to keep within, and swore they wou'd shoot every person that show'd offer to come out. At length the people at the house farther off hearing this disturbance, but afraid of venturing out, rung a bell which they had at the top of the house; and this bringing the town folks out, the rogues made off. It is not yet known any of them were, nor what shou'd provoke them to such an assault, unless it might be Mr. Brown's prosecuting some fellows for robbing his warren. There happened to be no other mischief done that what the house received, which however was considerable.

LONDON SEPT. 21. They write from Wimple, the seat of Lord Harley in Cambridgeshire, that the painting of the chapel there is finished, the performance is Sir James Thornbills, for which, with the Altar piece, Sir James, we hear is to have two thousand five hundred pounds: The whole is look'd upon to be the compleatest and most beautiful of its kind in England.

A few days ago a gentlewoman was delivered, in this city a monster the upper part to the navel like a child, the remainder like a dog, it liv'd three days and then died. The mother was not allow'd to look upon it, nor does she yet know but what it was a perfect child, and born dead.

LONDON SEPT. 25. Yesterday evening one Bird, watchmaker, aged about 60, living in Bridewell Precent, first cut his own throat, but not doing it effectually, hanged himself afterwards at the Banisters of the stair case.

LONDON SEPT. 28. On Wednesday last at the Regiment of Footguards sitting by platoons, a recruit was ackward to his execise, upon which a serjeant, who is accounted one of the best in the Regiment, stept forward to reach him, but the wretch fired off at that instant, shot the serjeant in the face, by which he lost one eye, and his life is in great danger.

Last week a person of Darking in Kent, carried from that place to St. George's Church in Southwark (computed 23 miles) a bushel of wheat for a considerable wager, with which he rested but once all the way.

Last Saturday night four footpads set on two gentlemen, and robbed them of seven guineas as they were coming from Acton; they told them, that before they got to town they would meet with someone of their gang; but if they asked whether they met any body on the road, they were to reply no; but 'tis likely to be a fine day tomorrow, and they would be safe. Accordingly they met three more, and they acted as the rogues had ordered, by which means they got well home.

LONDON OCT. 5. The three foot pads, who robbed Mr. Huges's servant last week of 20d, near Bristow Causeway Hill and afterwards shot him, of which wound he died on Sunday last, were on Monday morning taken in their beds (one in Kent Street and the other two in the Mint) by means of a drover who saw them commit the fact, and traced them to their abode. They were carried before Mr. Justice Lade, who committed them to the Marshalsea prison, where they are closely confined and loaded with irons: One of them it seems, had been but a few days since discharged out of that very prison, and there is a fourth belonging to the same gang not yet taken.

LONDON OCT. 9. Last Sunday Mr. Winter an aged man of 80 years of age, hanged himself in Gardner's-Lane, Westminster. Some has it to be owing to his son's running out, and persuading the old man to give him leave to sell an estate, of which he soon after repented. Two or three accidents of this kind have happen'd since our last.

A ship lately arrived from Jamaica gives an account that in her voyage home, having taken a good quantity of dolphin, they put some in pickle to preserve it; of which the sailors eating, when no fresh was to be had, their bellies swelled as if they had been poison'd and some actually died by that means.

LONDON OCT. 10. Letter from Hapton in Warwickshire give account, that the drought this summer has been so great, that they cannot sow their wheat; and that the cattle have suffer'd very much by driving them so far for water as they have been obliged to do.

On Tuesday night two highwaymen were apprehended near Bristow Causeway, and committed to the Marshalsea. 'Tis said they have confess'd that the gang consist of 16, and all out that night, but those who murder'd Mr. Huge's servant do not belong to them.

LONDON OCT. 10. Letters from Brussels advise, that tho' the late Bishop of Rochester has taken a house, yet he sees but very little company; the Marquess de Frie having given him to understand, that the more retired he keeps himself, the more agreeable will be the Government, and also that not one Englishman of any character has been known to converse with him since his residence there.

LONDON OCT. 12. Robbery and murder seem to be as common among our rogues here as in France, and we now hardly hear of the first without the latter; Among other instances we have the following from Canterbury, from whence they write, that last week a gentleman's servant, having observed a poor drover receive a sum of money for some cattle he had sold in the market there, watched him out of town, and overtaking him on horseback, the drover being on foot, fell into discourse with, and offering to give him a lift, the drover got up behind him: They rode about two miles, when coming to a lane that led to a gentleman's house the footman told him, that being his master's he was obliged to turn off there; upon which the drover dismounted, in order to persue his journey. He was no sooner down but the footman followed, and clasping a pistol to his breast, swore he'd shoot him if he did not without the least noise, deliver his money; the poor fellow in the utmost fright, gave him all he had, and turning to go away the rogue shot him with two bullets into the hinder part of his head, and left him, as thought for dead, but before he expired, which was about an hour after, two gentlemen came up, when he was sensible enough to inform of his case, and which way the villain took; accordingly the gentlemen pursued him, and found him just come in to his master's where he confessed the fact, he was sent to Canterbury Goal.

LONDON OCT. 12. We have an account from Scarborough in Yorkshire, that a man being bit there by a mad fox died soon after notwithstanding their care, ranting, howling, & barking like a fox.

We are well assured from most parts of the Kingdom, that since the new distemper of vomiting and looseness, &c. vast demands have been made for that excellent purging medicine, so often advertised in the paper call'd The Great Cathartick, it being found to be the only remedy for curing the same, and if taken in time, for preventing it. Above 1150 bottles were sold in one week at the ware-house in Bow Church Yard.

A tempting fruiteress that plies about the Exchange, and who by her wanton leers, have captivated many a stock-jober, last week insnarl'd a stationer's servant in that neighbourhood: So complyable was the damsel, that she agreed to spend a night with him at a certain inn in Leaden-Hall-Street, but it seems the fly baggage had let her spouse into the secret, who so well observed his cue, that upon their ordering a pint of mull'd sack to be brought up to bed them, he obtain'd the favour of carrying it himself, which put the poor wharfer munger in such a confusion, that he was obliged to part with all his ready money to make up the matter, with which the husband was so contented, that he gave receipt in the following manner. Receiv'd of

Mr. _____ the sum of 4 £. 15 s. for use of my wife, and in full of all accounts.

LONDON OCT. 12. Mr. Hopkins a corn chandler in the Hay-Market who had been taken into custody of a messenger on suspicion of treasonable practices, is admitted to bail.

Robberies are very frequent not only here, but everywhere throughout Europe.

The River Thames is so shallow, on account of the dry season of the year, that people frequently ride over it on horse-back at Twickenham.

On Wednesday last Mr. Ward, son of a periwig-maker of that name in the strand, being on board a ship below bridge, and another vessel happening to strike against it, was by the shock thrown headlong into the hold, whereby his brains were dash'd out, and he died instantly.

Thursday evening, one Mrs. Ball who sold milk on Brook-Garden, as she was crossing the road at Hammersmith, was rid over by the eldest son of Mrs. Ayers, who kept the Goat Inn there, and died immediately. The occasion of this sad accident was by the said Ayers's riding full gallop, so that he could not stop his horse.

LONDON OCT. 14. On Tuesday last Mr. Allan of Dufwych was robbed in his chaise near Stockwell by two foot pads; and before they got out of sight, three gentlemen came by on horseback, who hearing what happened, pursued them immediately, which then obliging the rogues to betake themselves over hedges and land ditches into the fields; upon which two of the gentlemen alighted, and continued the pursuit on foot, while the third held their horses; and they took both, one at the Nine-Elms, and the other in a garden near Vauxhall; and being carried before the magistrate, they were committed to Marshalsea. About half an hour after, seven coaches were robbed in the same place by some highwaymen.

LONDON OCT. 15. About the middle of last week a horse fell down at Lambert, by which unfortunate accident two children were then killed, and a woman very much bruised.

We hear from Cambridge, That the small pox having lately been very rise and fatal in the town and University, has given occasion to begin the practice of inoculation there, which Mr. Warren an eminent surgeon of that place, had perform'd upon four of his children at the same time, with the desir'd success.

We hear from Cambridge, that part of the great publick building which is design'd for the Senate or Regent House, is, (by the generous contributions of several great personages, and the nobility of that university, and great care and inspection of the Rev. Dr. Snape the Vice Chancallor) so far advanced, that it will probebly be finish'd and open'd next midsummer commencement. And also that on a plain of Mr. Gibbs, a new college at King's will be begun early in the spring.

Last Saturday, a Court Marshal was held on board a man of war in the Medway; when a sailor, was try'd for the murder of a fellow sailor in the West-Indies; and being found guilty he was sentenced to be hang'd at the yard-arm. Also a lieutenant of a man of war was try'd for desertion; but proving that he had leave of captain to go ashore, he was acquitted.

LONDON OCT. 22. Last week the lyoness, commonly call'd King George's, brought forth two he lyons, to the great surprize of Mr. Martin, keeper of his Majesty's beasts within the Tower, the like having not happen'd before in this Kingdom: The dame is very tender of her young; and the keepers dare nor approach her without danger. We hear that soon as they can be conveniently mov'd, they will be carry'd to Court, to be shown to his Majesty.

LONDON NOV. 30. Some persons of distinction who lately arrived in town from Calais, have brought an account that a remarkable accident happened at a small village, called Beauleiu, situated on the road between Calais and Paris; where a captain and a private gentleman of the French King's guard, happen'd to set up at an inn in the evening of Nov. 5. Having taken their chamber, they supp'd and going to bed, one of the maid servants, informed them that there were seven dangerous Ruffians in the house, who would assuredly murder and rob them before they went out; In their dangerous circumstances the gentlemen consulted what was proper to be done, and finding no possibility of getting out of the house without meeting their fate, came to a resolution to force their way out, Vi & Armis, &c. Whereupon they loaded two pistols each came downstairs, and were going out, when the villains who were at supper, got up and opposed them, the captain discharged both his pistols, in an instant, as did likewise his companion, which kill'd four of them on the spot; the other three fell on their knees, and begged their lives, who, together with the master of the inn and his wife, were secured, and committed to prison.

LONDON NOV. 30. On Wednesday about four a clock three highwaymen stop'd a waggon near the Turnpike at Islington: A man being early up, and hearing a bustle, went out to see what was the matter; one of the highwaymen dismounted, and seized him; and scuffling together one of the rogues shot at the man that was seiz'd, but missed him, the bullet went through the lodge door at the Turnpike, and alarm'd them, two rode off, but the other was taken and is since committed to Newgate. 'Tis said their design was to rob the person who keeps the Turnpike.

Some days ago, a house-breaker got into the house of Mr. Warner, a wholesale apothecary in Cheapside, about nine at night, all the people being in the house; and opening a scrutore, we hear, took out 160 crown pieces: It seems there was in the same place notes to the value of 200 £. which he left; but not being content with his booty he searched further, and met with ten pounds belonging to one of the journeymen, which, with the others, he carried clear off without discovery.

LONDON DEC. 5. Yesterday the sessions began at Old Bailey, where David Bally was try'd for the murder of Thomas Anslo, Colonel Scot's coachman, and found guilty of manslaughter, and John Wilks, a drummer, was try'd for the murder of Francis Edwards, another drummer (who is reported to have before killed two men, and had been try'd at the Old Bailey) and found guilty also of manslaughter.

LONDON DEC. 5. On Monday night a gentleman's wife in Red-Lyon-Court Long Acre, being in some discontent, took a dose of poyson, and afterward acquainted her husband with what she had done. A physician was immediately sent for, who press'd her to discover what she had taken, that proper remedies might be apply'd in time; but she absolutely refused to discover that, or the occasion for her doing so: A short time after, the poyson began to operate, and she expired.

Letters from Froome in Sumersetshire, which came to town last week, mentions, that they have had in the neighbourhood very great convulsions of the earth, which they call there an earthquake; but they do not tell us any damage that has been sustained thereby.

Private letters from Hambourgh dated nine or ten days ago, bring advice, that about that time a considerable number of whales were brought in by a high tide at the mouth of the Ebbe of which 14 between 50 and 60 foot long, were left alive on the sands by the sudden reflux of the water; and when those letters came away, the people were very busy in converting them to proper uses, and they expected that the next tide would bring in more of those welcomed visitants, which may in some measure make amends for the bad voyage of the Hambourgers to Greenland and the last fishing season.

LONDON DEC. 6. There is advice that Captain Hamilton, commander of the ship King William, in the service to the South Sea Company was unfortunately drowned, with the boat's crew and that Mr. Nehemiah Winter, who went out chief mate, will come home captain.

LONDON DEC. 11. Last week we hear a linen-draper's wife on Tower Hill died in child bed through the inavertency of an apothecary's man, who, being in drink when the doctor's bill came to him, put mercury by mistake into the medicine, which kill'd her in two or three hours.

LONDON DEC. 12. Yesterday in the forenoon there arose a violent storm of wind W. N. W. which blew down many stacks of chimnies, and untiled several houses in and about the cities of London and Westminster: A great number of lighters and wherries were drove through bridge and staved to pieces, and the merchants were in the greatest consternation, as expecting to hear bad news from the downs, and other sea ports, the consequence of this dreadful hurricane which did not abate till about five in the evening.

The 24th died Mr. George Martin, a noted brewer in Westminster, in the 40th year of his age; he was judged to be the fattest man in England, and was got to such a bulk, that he thought he had dropsy; so that the day before he died he was cut several inches to be tap'd, but it was all through fat, which choked him. On Monday last his body was interred at the chappel in Stretton's Grounds Westminster. His coffin was 2 yards 5 inches long and ell and a half wide, and 3 foot 2 inches deep. It has been published by some, that there were 18 men to carry his body on a bier, which though it was made for that purpose, it was apprehended it would break before they got to the chappel. Those who reported this say, the corpse and coffin weighed 17 hundred weight, and was of so exorbitant bulk, that not being able to get it out of the door, they were forced to take the sashes down, and let it by tackle out of the window.

At the late race at Manchester, all the utensils of a taylor's shop board were run for by five of the stitching fraternity, each of whom were to have something, come in how they would; so that the last carried off a cabbage adorned with ribbons of verious colours.

We have an account from Bristol, That a gentleman near that city has lost his only son by the bite of a cat, which having seized one of his fingers they could not possibly remove her; and notwithstanding they cut off its head, yet its teeth continued fasten'd. The poor child was presently seized with distraction, and in two days died mewing like a cat.

One weaver, a soldier, hath been lately committed to Newgate for ravishing one Martha Wilson, a girl of about 11 years old.

In the Waste Ground near Thorn in Yorkshire, where they cut turfs for fireing, there has been lately discovered a great many trunks of trees buried far under ground, which lye all one way, and in the same position, and are so thick and close together, that no body can account for this being buried in such a manner, but by some extraordinary inundation. The timber is as sound and good, as if just cut.

1724

LONDON JAN. 21. Died of small pox within the bills of mortality, from Christmas 1721 to Christmas 1722, two thousand one hundred and sixty seven. Died the same distemper within the same bills of mortality, from Christmas 1722, to Christmas 1723, (the year of inoculation) three thousand two hundred and seventy one. Increase, one thousand one hundred and four.

LONDON JAN. 25. By the great storm that happened on Tuesday night, it is computed that about 100 boats, barges and lighters was staved to pieces, or sunk in several parts of the River of Thames.

On Monday night last one Margaret Cameron; an old woman of about 80 years of age, was burnt to death in her bed in Blue-Gate-Fields, near Ratcliff Highway. She took her fire pot upstairs with her as usual, to keep her self warm, having only some straw to be on and a mat to cover it, the miserable furniture took on fire, and so she perished, some of her limbs being burnt to a coal. Some people lay underneath, but was not appriz'd of it till next morning, when the fire had burnt its way through the floor.

On Tuesday morning between 4 and 5 of the clock 5 stage coaches coming to town from the western part of England, was attacked upon Salisbury Plain by three highwaymen, who robb'd and rifled the passengers.

About 70 convicts lying in Newgate under sentence of transportation and to be shipp'd off for the plantations the latter end of this week.

LONDON JAN. 27. On Friday last merchant Foward, transporter of felon convicts, came to Newgate to take an account of his effects there, and found near 100 heads of black cattle, lying ready for exportation to Virginia.

LONDON JAN. 29. The Neptune, Capt. Wadham, which came lately from the streights, and is now in the river, has lost one of his men by his running distracted. The fellow came to the captain one day, and told him he should die; and therefore desired that his wages might be paid to his father; nothing would satisfy him but such a promise, which at last he obtained of the captain. Some days after a storm arose, and the poor fellow fancied himself to be the Jonah who caused it, saying his comrades, better one man should die than all the company should perish. The commander hearing this again, reproved him, and bid him go down to sleep, which for the present he obeyed but the storm increasing, the main sail being blown away and the main yard down and the main mast in danger to be lost, he took his opportunity at two a clock in the morning, to run up the shrouds and get to the masthead, when taking hold of the vane spindle, he plunged himself from thence into the sea and was drowned.

LONDON FEB. 2. We hear that Justices of the Peace have given orders to constibles, &c. to take up all those people, who usually about this time of the year carry about and fling at cocks on Tower Hill, Moor Fields, Lincoln's Inn Fields and other such places; in order to prevent those mischiefs, mains and bruises, which to usually happen on such occasions.

As likewise all those loose, idle and disorderly persons, that go about with totums, whimsy-boards, barrows and dice, sweetners, ballard-singers, and the likes; to create a crowd to enable their comrades to pick pockets.

LONDON FEB. 8. Last week Mr. Rogier, whose wife belongs to Lincoln's Inn Playhouse, hang'd himself at his lodging in Wild-Street, while his wife was at play.

Last week the wife of a poor man in Fore-street, lying in the agonies of death, her husband ask'd a physician and apothecary that was present, whether there was any hope of her recovery? and being told there was not, and that she was then on the point of departing he seized immediately with distraction and died 12 hours after.

A miller on a sudden encompassed by an inundation, proposed to his wife to save themselves by swimming; accordingly he took her on her back, charged her to hold fast and not be faint-hearted; and the same time taking his child of about a quarter old, in his teeth by its blankets (notwithstanding which double weight and incumbrance) he had the good fortune to land his cargo very safe upon a rising ground. But his wife was so feared with the cold and fright, that as soon as she came to land she fainted; whereupon the miller swam back again to fetch a bottle of brandy, and returned just in time enough to revive her drooping spirit; but he had no sooner carried off the bottle, that both his house and mill were laid under water.

LONDON FEB. 13. Mr. John Woolanon, a Quaker and brewer in the city of Norwich was brought before the Court of King's Bench to receive judgement upon conviction for assaulting, wounding, and imprisoning a collector of the Assizes in the excecution of his office. The Crown fined him fifty pounds, and order'd him to stand committed till he pay the fine.

LONDON FEB. 15. On Wednesday last several young fellows, one apprentice to a barber, another to a wheelright, a third, a person who black'd shoes in the street, were apprehended for robbing the Chelsea coach when 4 gentlemen were in it, from whom they took watches and money to the value of 40 £. The shoe cleaner is become on evidence; and 'tis said, he discovered twenty one robberies committed within two months past, and that there were seventeen belonging to the gang, the eldest which is not eighteen years old.

We hear from Cambridge, That workmen, digging for a foundation of the new buildings designed for the King's College there found near a hundred broad pieces of gold, supposed to be coin of King Henry VI founder of the said college.

LONDON FEB. 18. On Saturday last Mr. Constantine MacCuinnis an Irish young gentleman, who studied at the law at Chambers in Essex Court in the Temple, murder'd in a most barbarous and unheard of manner on Frances Williams his landress, who was come at eight in the morning to light his fire, and to attend him. He being in bed, on a sudden leapt out, took his sword, stabb'd her in many places; and then dragg'd her down three pairs of stairs by the hair of her head, into Essex Court, where he publickly repeated the stabs. The poor creature died immediately; and there were found twenty five wounds about her body, mostly about her belly, but one quite through her head. She was then five months gone with child. He was laid hold of and carried before Justice Newton, where all he offer'd was, that the woman was a witch, had bewitched him. He was instantly committed to Newgate, where the next day he made an attempt upon the keeper, tearing his shirt, and striking him in the face, altho' he was in double irons; and discovering great tokens of lunacy, the officers of the prison have taken proper measures with him for their defence.

LONDON FEB. 22. Yesterday above sixty felon convicts were sent to Newgate to be transported to his Majesty's plantations in America.

LONDON FEB. 23. On Monday several of the directors of the bank of England went to Newgate, and after examining Baron Lodell, alias John Vhoick and John Smith, the two Germans charged with altering the notes of that company. They resolved to prosecute the latter, he being the chief contriver and promoter of the felony; and that the Baron should be admitted as evidence against him; who was thereupon allowed the liberty of seeing his friends, and permitted the use of a pen, ink, and paper.

LONDON FEB. 27. On Saturday night last between the hours of seven and eight, a person who execised the function of a shoemaker at Parson's Green in his return home from Fulham or Chelsea, was set upon by some foot-pads, who after knocking him down, struck him with a knife in at one ear, and out the other; then cut his throat in such a manner as made most people, who afterwards saw the body, believe it was perform'd by some butcher: They robb'd him of a silver watch, and some small quantity of silver money. On Sunday an idle sort of fellow, a butcher, was taken up at Falham, on suspicion of the murder &, robbery, and confined in the Cage or Round-house, all night; but being examined the next day before a magistrate, he was discharg'd. There is to be added to this relation something so remarkable in the case of the widow of the murder'd person, as it is not to be parallel'd in story, for which account we have very good authority, viz. She having had in all four husbands, everyone of which came by violent death, her first husband being executed for robbing on the highway; her second shot to death in Hyde-Park, about 11 years since, for desertion, he being a foot soldier; her third a waterman, drowned in the River Thames, and her fourth and last husband murder'd in the manner as above mentioned.

LONDON FEB. 29. Some days since a poor Quaker, who usually sold cakes about the streets for a livelihood hanged himself in the garret, where he lodged, at a victualling house in Cock-Lane near West-Smithfield; the coroner's inquest having taken disposition on the matter, he was buried at St. Sepulchres.

LONDON FEB. 29. On Wednesday night a gentleman in good circumstances, that lived in Red-Lyon-street in Clarkenwell, cut his own throat with a razor, but timely care being taken of the wound by a surgeon, he is not as yet dead.

LONDON MARCH 7. In Piccadilly, there happen'd a very merry adventure, a Welch footman belonging to an old Lord returning home potvaliant, and much inclined to show his courage for the honour of St. David, quarrel'd with almost every one he met; but at last caught a tartar engaging a rough-hewn sailor. A boxing match was agreed on; and taffy being told, it was the politest manner to enter the lists in buff, immediately stript, giving one his cloaths, and another his shirt to hold. The sailor gave out our ancient Briton a hearty mordern drubbing; but the honest fellow that held his fine Holland shirt (which he made to wear at the Welch feast) ran away with it; so the poor skip was forced to go home without one; and Hur is resolv'd for the future, to wear hur worst linnen on St. David's Day.

A few days ago there was brought to the Royal Highness, a calf that had eight legs, two mouths, six eyes, four ears, and other monstrous parts; but their Royal Highnesses not caring for such amusement, would not see it.

LONDON MARCH 14. At the last Assizes at Brentwood for the county of Essex, about twelve criminals received sentence of death, among which was an old woman, that is to be burnt, she cutting her husband's throat in November last, to whom she had been marry'd 45 years; she could not alledge any difference between them, nor give reason for the murder, only said, that she thought they had lived enough together. It seems they rented a farm about 40 £. per annum, and the old man having been with some goods at Chelmsford Market, and coming home in drink, she began according to custom, to scold at him, but he to get out of the noise, hasten'd to bed, and soon falling to sleep, she went up and cut his throat.

LONDON MARCH 14. Last week a man was brought from the Gatehouse Westminster, to Newgate, to be try'd for horse stealing, the prosecution being carried out by his own father.

Two boys, one of them about twelve years of age, are committed to New Prison from Highgate, for breaking open a gentleman's house in that place, when the family was at London, and taking thence plate and other things to a considerable value. One of them had bought a pair of boots and pistols, and was hiring a horse to go in quest of other adventures, when the warrant came which stopt his journey.

The watermen, who ply the River Thames, being drown very numerous of late, occasion'd (as it is thought) by a long peace, and their taking too many apprentices, have petitioned the Parliament for some regulation on their company, many of them being scarce able to subsist themselves, and their families. According to some accounts their numbers (including lighter men) amount to 9741 men.

LONDON MARCH 25. One of the malefactors order'd to be executed at Kingston, was a person who pretended to be blind and lame, and made his business to follow people about the country to beg money, and when he came to a convenient place, knocked them down and robbed them. The whole country cried out for justice against the offender.

Yesterday a dray cart, belonging to a very noted brewer, being standing at an ale house door in Newgate Street, while the servants were gone down with drink in the cellar, some persons unknown stole a large barrel of beer off, and carry'd it away without being discover'd.

Yesterday the Assizes for the County of Surrey ended at Kingston upon the Thames: Eighteen men received sentence of death for divers capital crimes, particularly Edward Arnold for shooting at and wounding the Lord Onslow, and three rogues for murdering and robbing a gentleman's servant sometime ago near Bristow Causeway; the principal whom, was last night brought back to the Marshalsea, he being order'd to be hang'd dead, and then in chains, on or near the said causeway.

LONDON MARCH 28. Yesterday two women were committed to Newgate for stealing a gold chain from off a child's neck in Bride-Lane.

On Monday a young man of about 21, was run over by a hackney coach at Whitehall, which broke both his legs, and thighs, he died the next day. The coachman got off, but a gentleman with great difficulty, got the number, so that the fellow will be brought to justice, and the coach and horses forfeited according to law.

The same day a carman in Thames Street, as he was driving his cart, fell down, and the cart ran over him, and killed him on the spot.

Last week several prisoners for debt in the goals of Middlesex, were discharged by the exemplary bounty and charity of the Grace the Dutchess of Kendal, who paid their debts and fees.

Wednesday se'nnight one Thomas Abdin, a man of 70 years of age, at Rickmansworth in Hertfordshire, fell into a little ditch of water, and was drowned, as he was coming home from the funeral of his nephew's child, one William Hutchings, who on Sunday before, had the same death by falling into a pond in his fathers yard.

Late Monday night the sessions ended at Kingston five were burnt in the hand, and 22 order'd for transportation.

LONDON APRIL 1. We are informed that the Bishop of Rochester will soon leave Brussels, in order to go and reside in Paris.

LONDON APRIL 4. On Monday night a watchman doing his rounds in Swan Alley by St. John Street, a mastiff dog belonging to a butcher there, broke out, flew upon the watchman, and left him in a miserable condition.

On Thursday night Serjeant Major Vandery was brought to town from Nottingham in irons, and committed to the Sevoy. He was Serjeant Major of the First Regiment about two years since, at which time he went off with 130 £. of the regiment's money. He was, when taken, enlisting in the dragoons quartered there; but known by one of the officers, and was sent under guard to town, and will be try'd by the next Court-Marshal for desertion.

LONDON APRIL 13. Yesterday was 7-night the following merry adventure happen'd within the rules of the fleet: Three women came in cloaks to a publick house and demanded a private chamber, and a minister being sent for, the eldest of the three women aforesaid undressed herself and put on mans apparel, and was presently married to one of the other women, and demanded a certificate of such their marriage. The people of the house seeing no man go into the room, and suspecting a trick, consulted with the parson, who refused his certificate till the suspected person was search'd, who appear'd to be the oldest of the three women. Its alledged the aforesaid woman was in debt, and made use of the stratagem to disappoint her creditors.

LONDON APRIL 16. Lewis Houstare, the French barber, who was tryed last sessions for the murder of his wife, and acquited, was now try'd for bigamy; both marriages were proved; but the first not being according to the rites of the cerimonies of the Church of England, the jury brought in their verdict special.

At the General Quarter-sessions of the Peace, held for the City and Liberty of Westminster, on Saturday last Mary Marchbane, alias Gaubert, formerly mentioned, was convicted, on her own confession, of defrauding one Joseph Bevan of 23 s. (part of a greater sum that was to be paid) under pretence of helping him to a place in the customs; and she was thereupon sentenced to be kept to hard labour in

Bridewell, Westminster for 6 months, she being an old offender that way.

LONDON APRIL 18. His Majesty hath granted license during his pleasure, to Mr. Morris and his wife, to visit the deprived Bishop of Rochester.

A project in on foot for employing not only the poor of this city, but all over the Kingdom, in working and spinning for the woolen manufacture by a certain engine newly invented. Shou'd it take place, there is no doubt but we shou'd soon see the number of beggars lessen among us.

A journeyman taylor, in the neighbourhood of St. Martins in the Fields, a few weeks ago, had a legacy of 500 £. left him: Giddy's with his good fortune, he soon set up a sumptuous equipage, and went on such a extravagant rate, that in a few days he saw the end of his legacy, and is now doing penance on his quondam shopbeard.

We hear his Majesty has been pleased to give orders against buying and selling places in the army for time to come; so that when an officer dies; the next to him in seniority in that company or troop will succeed, and the vacancy be filled up from such in pay.

LONDON APRIL 28. The following tragical story, how wide soever it may appear of truth, comes to us from a hand, that assures it to be a matter of fact. A gentleman named F_____, who he is said to be the natural son of a deceased nobleman, some weeks ago made his addresses to a young lady in the country, in which he was so successful, that the day was appointed for the wedding, and everything was got ready to celebrate the same. The night before, he was there so late, that he saw all the family to bed, and it proving rainy weather, he requested to stay there till morning, which was easily granted; but such ill use did he make of his time, that he obtained the last favor of his intended wife. He was no sooner up in the morning but he went home, under, pretence of going to prepare for the ceremony; but he never returned: The unhappy lady proved with child, and though she endeavour'd by all ways to let him know of it, he took no notice of her. When she was so far gone that she found it impossible to conceal her shame any longer, she imparted the secret to her mother, who, with grief, died in a very little time, and was soon followed by the distressed young lady. The father was seized with distraction, and we hear, is now under confinement. The brothers of the unhappy lady, 'Tis said, have in the most solemn manner, vowed revenge on the instrument of their great distress, and, fearful their resentment, the ravisher is reported to have taken his shelter in another country.

LONDON APRIL 28. Some days ago 3 men being in company in a publick house 2 of them wager'd with the 3d, who was a noted dram drinker, that he could not drink a pint of brandy off at once. He accepted the wager, and while he was drinking he fell off his seat the pot to his head, and died instantly.

LONDON MAY 2. We have account from Cirencester, that a few days ago 2 highwaymen robbed no less than 30 passengers in one day upon the North-East Road to that town. Since which one of them, being known by his horse, was apprehended and committed to goal, and they are in quest of the others.

LONDON MAY 2. We are assured from Birmingham, that a Volcan of that town courting a young woman there, and she (as many other has done before) found fault with the length of his nose, he went home and cut it off. Our intelligence is silent as the length of his ears, but we doubt not they bore some proportion to his snout.

We hear that warrants are issued out against many of the people belonging to the new Mint in Ratcliffe Highway, who, in riotous manner, attack'd a baliff in his own house, and took from him a prisoner which he had arrested a few hours before, and 'Tis said, that they will not only be proceeded against by law for the rescue, but also be prosecuted as rioters, for refusing to disperse after the proclamation had been read to them.

LONDON MAY 4. We hear several of the principal inhabitants about Hanover and Oxford Squares, have exebited a fresh complaint against their old neighbours the gallows, on account of divers inconveniences, which attend the frequent executions: Wherefore, its said, that eminent machine of justice will be forthwith moved to a convenient place near Hollowway, a small village between Islington and Highgate.

LONDON MAY 7. On Saturday last was try'd in Little Britain, a curious wind gun lately brought from Germany, which, being once charged, discharges thirty seven times either with ball or shot.

LONDON MAY 7. The Mission, Capt. Philips, and the Welcome, Capt. Mortimer, from Virginia, has been lately plunder'd by the pirates in their way home. From the former they took most part of her provisions, and not only strip'd the commander, but all his company of their cloaths, but what was far more unhumane, they killed the commander of the Welcome and afterwards cut his body in pieces, which they threw overboard. As these pirates were on board a small schooner some think her company to have consisted of transported felons, that had seized her purposely for mischief.

LONDON MAY 16. By our accounts from Cirencester, we learn that they are more infested with highwaymen, than ever was known there, for they write that in the space of two months past, above a hundred people have been robb'd within five miles of the town; but that they hope the gang is now in a way to be broke, two of them being apprehended, from whom they hope to come at the rest.

A few days ago a fire broke out at Market-Levington in Wiltshire, which consumed 32 houses, and burnt with such violence by reason of a strong eastern wind, that few of the sufferers had time to save so much as their wearing apparel. 'Tis said, the gentlemen of that town and neighbourhood have very graciously contributed to make up the losses of the unhappy sufferers.

On Tuesday last an unhappy accident happen'd on the river, below bridge, when a boat, with two men, four women, and as many children in it, was crush'd to pieces between a lighter and a ship, whereby two women and two of her children were lost.

LONDON MAY 23. Mr. Mist, who stood convicted of a libel against the Government, in his journal of June 8, 1723, was sentenced to pay a fine of 100 £. and to suffer one year's imprisoment, and to find sureties for his good behaviour during life.

Mr. Payne, who was convicted upon four several informations, of libelling the Government the Bench of Bishops, &c. in a late paper publish'd by him, called the True Britain, was sentenced to pay a fine of 400 £. viz. 100 £. each information, to suffer one year's imprisonment, and find sureties for his good behaviour during life.

As odd a robbery happen'd here last week, as perhaps was ever known in the streets of this city, viz. Two persons, well habited, came to a coach that was standing at Temple Bar, one of them getting into it, and the other mounting the box, drove away with it towards the Royal Exchange. 'Tis said neither coach nor horses have been since heard of, altho' 10 guineas reward have been offer'd for the discovering of either of the robbers.

On Monday last near 100 shoemakers met together at an ale-house in St. Giles's in order to decide a controversary depending about two prize shoes; on which occasion the dispute rose very high, and some baliffs entering with a writ, increased the fued, insomuch that it issued in a riot, and the proper officers were sent to keep the peace; but in the conclusion 7 journeymen of the gentle craft were apprehended and carry'd before Mr. Justice Ellis, who committed them to Newgate, for the said riot, and for the assaulting of the constable in the executing of his office.

A woman that kept a little shop on London Bridge, being compelled to leave it in a manner that did not please her; having cleared the house on Monday night last, the watch men found it on fire, which throws a suspicion on some body they have an eye on, and which, if it had not been timely discovered, would in all probability, have consumed the bridge.

WORCESTER JUNE 2. On Tuesday night last the felons in our goal, having made an agreement to break the dungeon and get out, had accordingly provided instruments for that purpose; and after having broke their hand-cuffs, neck collars, and sawed in two their bolts, & links, that, before morning they could not get through, and being prompted on by the 3 following notorious rogues (the ringleaders of the mischief) viz. Smith, Taveney and Cox, they agreed to the following bloody resolution: That as soon as the turnkey came to unlock them in the morning as usual, if he made any resistance they would kill him, if not they would only bind him and take the keys from him. The next who was to fall a sacrifice, was the Governour, whom they were to murder without mercy, and after having possess'd themselves of the keys, &c. they were to march off, but their bloody design miss'd off its intended effect; for as soon as the under turnkey came they seized and bound him; after that a fellow prisoner unaquainted with the resolution, met the same fate. They came to the turnkey who they seizes and bid him choose to submit to be bound, or to die; to which he courageously answer'd, that he would lose his life before the Governour should be wronged, upon which he called aloud for help, when one of them immediately knocked him down with an iron bar, after having given him several desperate wounds in the face and hands, struck off one finger, broke another and giving him many blows upon the back and shoulders, they were about to cut his throat, but were happily prevented by one Anderson hearing the noise, and running, with a spit, to his assistance; so that their bloody intent being discover'd and they overpowered, the Governour took care to secure them, and prevent their doing the like mischief, for the future.

LONDON JUNE 3. The account from Toulon are very melancholy, the plague increases there every day, and there are the utmost want for food and physick; all their hopes of the distemper abating are for the present at an end, and they seem to look for no deliverance but what may come from the malignancy of the contagion having wasted it itself, off from its own want of fresh objects to prey on.

Last Tuesday morning about three a clock, a quarrel happen'd at the lower-end of the Hay-Market between John Pierce and Richard Hoskins, one of the Knight Marshal's men, in which the former dangerously wounded the latter with a sword, and was therefore next day committed to the Gate-House.

LONDON JUNE 13. On Wednesday in the Whitson-Holy-Days, a race was run at Northampton for 5 guineas, between two bulls, four cows, and one calf; the first six were rid by men, and the last by a boy. The cows threw their riders, and the calf tumbled down with his, and was distanc'd; so that one of the bulls won the wager. Vast numbers of people gather'd together from that town and country to see such an out of the way diversion and were wonderfully pleased with it.

LONDON JUNE 13. They write from Bristol, That a certain Devonshire lady of great note, now residing in that city, stole out of the house when the family were abroad, and in a fit of lunincy threw herself into the river, but was happily observ'd by a waterman, who took her up and sav'd her life.

On Sunday last one Stampford was committed to Newgate for a robbery on the highway by taking from a woman her head-cloaths, and 9 s. in money.

Last Sunday seven night Mr. Coppard, comptroller of the customs at Hastings, observing a suspicious sail upon the coast, went out with some others in the custom house boat, and boarded it, and brought from thence into port upwards of 50 anchors of brandy.

LONDON JUNE 23. Latter end of last week, three persons were committed to Newgate by John Friar, for counterfeiting the stamp upon dice, which crime is a felon without benefit of clergy.

On Saturday last, a woman big with child was run over by a cart on London-Bridge and died on the spot. A surgeon open'd her soon after, and took the child out alive.

On Friday last about 5 in the evening, a dreadful fire broke out at Wooburne in Bedfordshire, at a house where they were brewing, it burnt with the utmost violence till about ten the next morning, consum'd about 100 houses, the George and Lion Inn escaped, and did also the church but with great difficulty. It is impossible to express the melancholy scene occasioned by this disaster.

LONDON JUNE 23. Yesterday a centinel was try'd by a Court Marshal at the Horse Guards at Whitehall, for drinking the pretender's health, by the name of King James the third, and for treasonable words, and found guilty.

Elijah Pitt, formerly convicted of defacing the King's statue at Gloucester having been try'd for the same at the Assizes there, and fin'd 100 £. and ordered to be kept in goal 'till 'tis paid.

Some days ago Mrs. Collins, a printer in Black and White Court in the Old Bailey, was robbed by a servant maid, of a considerable sum of money and other things, who was making off by water, for Rochester, when a gold striking watch, part of her booty, happening to strike in the boat, and her appearance ill agreeing with such furniture, she was seized on suspicion, and being carried before a magistrate, confessed the robbery, and was thereupon committed to Maidstone Jail. The said Mrs. Collins is since dead.

LONDON JUNE 24. Extract of a letter from Worcester dated June 14. On the 12th instant, about three in the afternoon, as I was sitting at a dining room window, with three others, a tea table only being between a lady and my self, there happen'd a terrible flash of lightning and a violent clap of thunder, which drove us men about the room, but the poor lady was struck thereby in such manner that she died within two minutes. We were all slightly hurt, but (thank be to God) are now recovered.

LONDON JUNE 25. Mr. Philip Hind, that kept the Bell and Castle in Winsor, was sometime since bit by a mad dog, and soon after was dipt in the sea &c. notwithstanding all the methods that could be used, he died mad on Sunday last.

LONDON JULY 7. They write from Dublin of the 18th past, that on the 18th of May last, in the night time, 11 persons, with their faces black'd, and arm'd with guns and pistols, did break open and entered several houses in the town of Dunnesee near Loughrea; in the County of Galway, in search for one William Degannon a weaver, who had lately inform'd against some persons in the town of Loughrea, for brewing privately, contrary to the act about excise, and so defrauding his Majesty of the duties; and having found the said Degannon, forcebly carry'd him to a wood, and there cut out his tongue, put out an eye, and cut off one of his ears, on account, as is suppos'd, of said information: Upon which the Lord Justices have published a proclamation for the discovering and apprehending the said offenders with a reward of 50 £. for each of the two first that shall be taken and convicted, and 20 £. for each of the others.

LONDON JULY 15. The commissioners for managing the new inland duties on coffee, tea and chocolate, has appointed twenty watchmen, with a salary of 40 £. per annum each, to watch every night from seven till six the next morning, at the 10 warehouses in London; hired for the reception of those drugs from the dealers therein, two at each warehouse & last night they went upon duty for the first time.

LONDON JULY 18. The letters from Petersbourg of June 22, import the following account, viz. That six days before there was found upon the dry land a sort of a whale 50 foot in length; and when it was opened, they found in its belly a lad of 12 years old, who had been missing from the 4th of June; his body was entire, only his feet began to rot; They are at a loss to account, whether the fish had swallowed the lad alive or dead, but his parents were of opinion that he had fallen into the water and then had drowned.

LIVERPOOL JULY 24. By a ship arrived yesterday from the Isle of Man, we have the following account, viz. That on the 9th instant, about 7 leagues from the Calf of Man, a ship of about 300 tuns, and mounted with 22 guns, called the Mary and Anne of London sprung a leak wich continued so violent, that they could not keep her free, so that she founder'd. A little before she went down, 18 men went into the hold, in order to get some valuable things out to put into the boats, but they all perished with the ship. The rest of the company were saved and got to the island. This ship had wine and other goods on board to discharge at Chester.

LONDON AUG. 1. They write from Norwich of the 20th past, that one John Jepson had been tried at the county-sessions and sentenced to stand three times in the pillory, for going about the country begging with a counterfeit brief for sufferers by fire: And that one Nathaniel England died there Thursday before raving mad, having been bit by a dog.

LONDON AUG. 1. Yesterday was se'nnight one Sheperd a notorious house-breaker, who lately made his escape from New Prison, and had impeaches his own brother, was committed to Newgate, having been retaken by Jonathan Wild: He is charged with several burglaries. &c.

At the Assizes at Chelmsford, one Lambert, a labourer, received the sentence of death for killing an old man near Colchester, robbing his house, and afterwards setting fire to it; so that, the next day, all that was found of him was a piece of his skull, part of his ribs, and one foot in his shoe.

LONDON AUG. 3. Last week Mr. Murray a Chichester gentleman, said to be a sufferer by the South-Sea scheme, threw himself out of a window at his lodging in the Old Exchange near Cheapside, and was so hurt that he instantly died.

On Wednesday, last week, the Assizes ended at Hertford, which proved to be a Maiden Assizes, as they call it, none having received sentence of death; in which case; according to an old custom, the sheriff presented the judges and officers of the Court, with white gloves.

Last Sunday a man and his wife, calling in at the publick house over against Mr. Faichild's Garden at Hoxton, known by the name of the Ivy-House, the woman taking a turn in the landlord's garden, plucked an orange from one of those trees that are planted there, whereupon a neighbouring Justice of the Peace, asserted his damage to the amount of twenty shillings. By the kind interposition of the Justice, the matter was made up for a crown. But the woman having received some bruises from the little struggle that happened upon her indiscretion, they are now obliging him to make reparation for assault and battery.

LONDON AUG. 15. Tuesday last King's officers made a seizure among the grocers and apothecaries at Salisbury of about a thousand pounds worth of tea, coffee, and cocoa nuts, which had not paid duty, and was not enter'd.

A fine young tyger was lately sent from Penama, one of the factories of the Royal Assiento South Sea Company, to Sir John Elves Bat. which that gentleman presented to his Majesty, who order's it to be sent to the Tower.

Last Saturday some rogues set fire to a farmer's barn on Muzzle Hill, in which were forty or fifty loads of hay, besides other goods, and while the farmer and his family were busy in extinguishing the fire, they took the opportunity of robbing the house of a considerable sum of money, and divers things of great value.

At the Assizes for Warwick two men received sentence of death; one for horse stealing, and the other for robbing a woman on the highway. He was stark naked when he committed the robbery and was taken before he had got all his cloath on.

LONDON AUG. 29. Their Highnesses the Princess Anne and Princess Caroline came on Monday last to St. Paul's Cathedral, and heard the famous Mr. Handel (their master) perform upon the organ, the Reverend Dr. Hare, Dean of Worcester attending upon their highnesses during their stay there.

LONDON AUG. 29. They write from Margam, in Glamorganshire, that a few days ago they had such a violent storm of rain and hail there, that caus'd such inundation as carried the cattle with it down from the hills to the lower ground; broke through a wall, and came into the houses there three or four foot, and that part of the Lord Mansell's house was in danger, several moveables and furniture being carried away.

Last week a bill was found by the Grand Jury of Middlesex against a sturdy beggar, for assaulting a gentleman near Tottenham Court, and putting him in danger of his life, for refusing to give him alms.

On Wednesday evening a taylor was set upon by three footpads in St. George's Fields; two of the rogues lay behind, while the other attack'd him; The taylor put his hand into his pocket, as if he was going to deliver his money, but pull'd out a knife, wherewith he cut the fellow cross the face. Upon this another of them came up, and the taylor, with his fork, stabbed him in the belly: The third, hereupon firing, the taylor ran away, and came into Suffolk Street in the Mint, where, soon after, he found the rogues dressing their wounds at an old woman's. They were immedeately secur'd and committed by Justice Machin to the new goal.

On Sunday evening a certain whipmaker, living near Fleetditch follow'd a lady home from Covent Garden Church to Dr. Chamberlain in King Street nearly adjoining; when she got out of the coach, went into the house with her; when being ask'd about his business, he said he was in love with her. But upon a narrow inspection, they found upon him two loaded pistols, one in his breast, and the other in his pocket. Upon which the lover was carried to the Round-House; and upon further examination before one of his Majesty's Justices of the Peace he was committed to Bridewell.

LONDON AUG. 29. Some deer-stealers having lately killed a brace of bucks in Richmond Park: And the beginning of last week, five of them made another attempt; but the keepers being prepar'd attack'd them. They stood each others fire several times; but at length the rogues were overcome, and two were taken and three made their escape by flight.

On Monday night last, between the hours of nine and ten, the corpse of a man quite naked, with his throat cut from ear to ear, was found in Shoulder-of-Mutton Fields, near Hackney, supposed to be robbed and murder'd.

The same morning one George Kerr, who formerly belonged to the foot-guards, but deserted, was seized by some soldiers in the Strand; with whom he fought, and after wounding three of them, made his escape.

LONDON SEPT. 3. Yesterday Mr. Fonseca was seiz'd and taken into custody at the Tennis Court Coffee House by Mr. Chandler one of his Majesty's messengers.

On Tuesday night the wife of Mr. Shepard was committed to the Counter for assisting her husband in making his escape, having been apprehended and taken that day by Mr. Jonathan Wilde.

LONDON SEPT. 3. On Tuesday morning, a gang of deer-stealers made another attempt in Richmond Park; but the keepers gave them a warm reception, and took two of them prisoners, one of whom, viz. John Briskford, alias Jack the Waler, was dangerously wounded, being shot thro' the body, and the ball lodg'd in the shoulder of one of his comrades: They were both committed to Kingston Jail.

LONDON SEPT 26. Yesterday Baker the grenadier, was shot to death in Hyde Park for desertion. About 9 in the morning he was convey'd from the Savoy, under a guard of musqueteers, to the parade ground in St. James's Park, and there received by a large detatchment of the guard, under arms, and conducted to the place of execution, the drums beating the Grenadier's March, and the prisoner marching in front between to clergymen, and another Devine following, with officers, who led the detatchment. The procession was slow and solemn, and very moving to the spectators. He gave signal for firing, and two balls only having been lodged in his body, he lifted up one of his hands, when the reserve fired at his head, which effectually put him out of his pain. His body after being exposed to the soldiers, was put into a coffin, and buried upon the spot. He behaved well, and died penitent.

CANTERBURY OCT. 3. The following account has been for some time the chief amusement of this city: A young spark, who is a mercer's apprentice here, was surprized in the middle of the day, by the apperation of his uncle, who has been dead some years: He appeared to him in the shop while two or three women customers were present. The lad knew him at the first sight, and was in the utmost consternation: The spirit, in an audible voice, bid him hasten to Yorkshire to save an estate he was heir to, upon death of a relation there, of which, if he did not take care of immediately, he would be cheated, and then instantly dissappeared. This you may depend on for the matter of fact, for the young gentleman is now in Yorkshire taking care of the affair, of which the apperation gave him notice.

LONDON OCT. 8. There happened lately a quarrel in the Fleet Prison, between two prisoners, about drinking a health, in which, we hear, Mr. Fitz Simonds, an Irish half-pay officer, happened to strike one Mr. Middleton upon the head with a chair, who died of his wounds last Tuesday morning. The deceased had been stewart to the Dutchess of Marlbrough, and was imprisoned there upon a suit with her Grace; but he was not the person with whom he had the dispute about the said health. And yesterday the coroner's inquest sat on the body of the deceased at it appearing that there was no malice in the case, that they were intimate friends, and that the fatal blow was directed at another person, they brought in their verdict manslaughter.

LONDON OCT. 9. On Wednesday last one John Sheppard, a malefactor, found means to release himself from the staples, fix'd in the floor of the apartment called the Castle of Newgate, where he was confined alone, by taking off great padlock from his legs; he attempted to pass up the chimney, but by reason of strong iron bars in his way, was prevented; in the midst of his endeavours, the keepers came up as usual with his necessaries when to their very great surprize, they found him at liberty in the room, they searched him from head to foot, and found no such as a pin, and when they chained him down again, the head keeper and others came and intreated him to discover, by what magick art he had that got himself from the staples, he reach'd forth his hand and took up a nail, and with that and no other instrument unlock'd himself again before their faces, nothing so astonishing ever known! he is now hand cuff'd and more effectually chain'd.

Tomorrow 97 felons are to be carried from Newgate, to be shipp'd for the plantations, among whom is the brother of the above mentioned Sheppard.

LONDON OCT. 10. On Tuesday came advice here from Capt. Gregory, commander of his Majesty's Yacht Catherine in the Haven on Ostend, that on the 24th of last month a passage-boat having on board the Lord James, and Charles Cavendish, sons of his Grace the Duke of Devonshire, was by a sudden gust of wind overset under the counter of Capt. Gregory's Yacht, and were all taken up by Capt. Gregory's people except Lord Charles, who by the force of the tide was drove under the bottom of two ships, and after that fortunately rose up under the bow of the Catherine, and catching hold of the head fast was taken up tho' almost dead, proper means being used, he as well as his brother are recovered, their baggage being lost.

LONDON OCT. 10. On Wednesday last one hundred and three persons went to Mr. Hughes's Garden at Swan at Haggerstone & saw his large cucumber of 33 inches long. Three guineas was then bid for the same, but refused, upon which a fellow attempted to steal it that night, but was prevented by a great dog, who almost tore him in pieces; since which the landlord keeps the cucumber in a chest under lock and key.

LONDON OCT. 10. The following unhappy accident in what you may depend on. A village upon the Worlds, call'd North Delton, having been infested with rogues, who attempted to break into houses of some of the richest farmers there; one of which, living at the farthest end of town, hearing a noise in the back yard one night, got up and call'd out a window twice or thrice to know who was there; but nobody answering, he let fly with a fowling piece he had ready charg'd and unfortunately shot his own son, who was just married and lived in the same town, and who was come out of carefulness to see whether his father's house was safe or not. This fatal accident has thrown the old man in a melancholy distraction; which, 'tis thought, he will never get over; and the tragedy has clear'd the village of the rogues, who found by it what they are to expect from the inhabitants.

LONDON OCT. 12. Twenty one felons from Lincolnshire and Nottinghamshire, that were on board the ship Robert and Mary to be transported to Maryland, mutiny'd against the captain and seamen the 26th past, and having seized the boat, made their escape on shore near Harwich.

LONDON OCT. 14. Last week at Assizes holden for the Isle of Ely, before the Worshipful John Ruby, Esq; Deputy-Recorder of the city, two parish officers were indicted for carrying a poor sick woman and two children in a cart to an open field, a mile distant from any town, and there leaving them expos'd to cold and hunger to ease their parish of the charge; and being found guilty, they were sentenc'd to a fine and imprisonment.

LONDON OCT. 14. We have the following account from Bristol of the murders of Mr. Stoaks, a butcher who constantly used that market, viz. That the said Mr. Stoaks being drinking with some company in a house at Palton Revel, near Dunderry, there came in upon them in a riotous manner eight sturdy fellows, and being ask'd what they wanted, they all swore, they wanted blood, and blood they would have before they went away: Whereupon Mr, Stoaks, being a constable commanded peace; upon which he was knock'd down, & maim'd in a most dreadful manner, his skull being beat to pieces and dy'd soon after; several others were so wounded, that their lives was dispair'd of: Upon which, two of them, Samuel Tyler and Solomon Gune, both of High Littleton were secur'd but the other six made their escape, whose names and places of abode are as follows, viz. James Green of Clutton, John Cook of Chedder, William Tyler and Isaac Cune of High Little, Benjamin and Jacob Quarman of Temple; and warrant are out for apprehending them. The two that were secured are committed to Ivelchester Goal. The deceased lived in Stowy.

Last Wednesday sevennight Hurford and Sarah Steel were executed in Ivelchester, just at the setting of the sun; the former for robbing the Bath and Bristol coaches, and the latter for stealing 26 s. in money, 8 yards of dowlas, 6 yards of woolen cloath, out of the house of Robert Davey of Chiselworth, near South-Petherton: She was 91 years of age and went with crutches. Four more were condemn'd at the same time, but are repriev'd.

LONDON OCT. 14. On Wednesday last five malefactors were executed at St. Michael's Hill Gallow, viz. John Philips, of the parish of Penrose, near Monmouth, age 30, and Richard Roberts of the parish of Penalt, near Monmouth age 28, for a robbery by them jointly committed; James Williams, of Bradford in Dorchestershire, age 23, for counterfeiting the current coin of these Kingdoms; Constant Smith, of the city of Dublin, age 31, for a street robbery; Daniel Cross, of St. Olive's Southwark age 18 for shoplifting.

LONDON OCT. 15. Some nights ago an attempt was made by the felons on the common side of Newgate to escape, they had cut several iron bars asunder, and some of them saw'd off their fetters; and if they had not been timely discovery made of their design, about sixty desperate villains had been set loose into the world. Most of them have since been put on ship board for transportation.

Yesterday Jonathan Wilde, the famous thief-taker, attending the sessions at Old Bailey in order to give evidence against one Joseph Blake alias Blewskin, indicted for breaking and entering the house of William Kneebone, a woolen-draper in the Strand, along with John Sheppard and William Field, Mr. Wilde went into the place under the Sessions-House here he said Blewskin with other prisoners, was kept to wait tryal, and had some friendly discourse together, when Blewskin on a sudden took Wilde round the neck, and with a small clasp knife cut his throat even to the windpipe in a very dangerous manner and afterwards rejoiced, saying, he should be hang'd with pleasure if Wilde did but die before him; Mr. Dobbining and another surgeon were sent for who sew'd up the wound; and they have hopes that Wilde will recover.

Blewskin being examined what motive induced him to commit so base an action, after Mr. Wilde had supported him at his own expence since he had been in Newgate declar'd, that he had fully determin'd to murder him; and that his intentions was to have cut off his head, and thrown it into Sessions-House Yard among the rubble, and curs'd both his hands and the knife for not doing it effectually.

Yesterday the sessions began at the Old-Bailey; when two men were convicted of capital crimes, viz. William Grove for robbing his master, a barber, in Little Knight-Rider Street, of 25 guineas; and Moses Oafenan a Jew, for privately stealing a large sum of money.

They write from Edinburgh, that a woman was hanged there for muthering her bastard child, and after hanging two hours was cut down and brought to life again by her friends, and carried to Musselbrick, 4 miles from Edinburgh, and re-married to her husband, the proper officer has been to demand her for re-execution, but those of Musselbrick refused to deliver her up, she being in another district.

LONDON OCT. 15. Last week died one Mr. Trig, a tallow-chandler. He left his brothers sole executors, ordering them in his will to deposit his body in the roof of a barn, at Stevenage, and his body to lie there 30 years; otherwise his estate consisting of 2 or 3000 pounds to go to the parish. His will was accourdingly comply'd with; and on Monday night that copse was to be deposited as aforesaid, but to be laid in a leaded-coffin, to prevent its being an offence to the neighbourhood.

LONDON OCT. 17. We hear that near one hundred gentlemen and merchants of this city, have lately form'd themselves into a musical society, the one part performers, the other auditors, who meet weekly at the King's Arms Tavern in St. Paul's Church Yard. They open'd concert last week with a very good performance, to the entire satisfaction, and pleasure of all the members. Mr. Young of St. Paul's Church Yard, a noted master of the science, and one of his Majesty's Chapel, is President of the same.

On Thursday night John Sheppard found means to unchain himself from the staples fix'd in a strong room call'd the Castle in Newgate, by twisting and breaking the irons, and unlocking a great horse padlock, having got off his hand irons, with only the help of a flat iron bar, which he took out of the chimney, with that he broke through a thich wall into another strong room, the locks were of had not been open'd for seven years past; he wrench'd them off and forc'd his way through five other strong doors, breaking all the locks and bolts in his way, and got to the top of the goal on the leads, and decended by a blanket, which he fastn'd to the wall, on the house of Mr. Bird, a turner, adjoining to the prison, enter'd the same at a trap door, and got down the house into the entry, making his way out the street door without the least disturbance to the family, and made an entire escape.

LONDON OCT. 19. On Monday night last a foot soldier quarter'd at Reading shot himself there, upon his being foresaken by his sweetheart: He Discharg'd his pistol into his mouth, and the ball tore his head almost in twain, so that he was, when dead the most specticle that ever was seen.

LONDON NOV. 3. On Saturday night last, the famous John Sheppard was apprenended and taken in the manner following viz. between 11 and 12 o'clock, he came to the shop of one Nicks, a butcher, in Drury Lane; and having agreed for three ribs of beef, he desir'd Nicks to go with him to Mrs. Campbell's a chandler's shop a door or two further, intending to treat him with a dram of brandy, and to pay him for the same: Nicks went accordingly, and whilst they were drinking, an ale-house boy, belonging to Mr. Bradford, who keeps the Rose and Crown against the house, came in and ask for pots, and seeing Sheppard went and acquainted his master, who being a head borough, took to his assistance the watch, and seiz'd Sheppard in the brandy-shop, who was dress'd in a handsome suit of black clouths, a diamond and cornelian ring on his finger, and a light type periwig of about seven pounds value, three other plain gold rings in his pocket, two tortoise shell snuff-boxes a tortoise shell watch, and five guineas, and two loaded pistols in his pockets: Mr. Eyles a constable was sent for, who together with the head borough aforesaid, the watch &c. put him in a hackney coach and convey'd him to Newgate, several thousands of people being assembled in Holborn, as he was in the coach he call'd out murder, help for God's sake, rogues, I am murder'd and am in the hands of blood-hounds, help for Christ's sakes, &c. Being brought to Newgate, he owed, that last Friday morning he broke open the shop of Mr. Rawlings, a pawn broker, at the Four Balls in Drury Lane, and took from thence a suit of black-cloth cloaths, a light type perywig, and a gold watch and a tortoise shell watch, two tortouse shell snuff-boxes, a silver-hilted sword, a night gown, and other goods to the value of about 60 £. He is now put into an apartment, call'd the Middle Store Room, adjoining to the Castle, and is loaded with 300 pounds weights of irons. When he was brought in, he was pretty much in liquor, and had the impudence to tell the keepers, their utmost strength and art should not confine him long. But it's generally believ'd (if they observe that due caution, when cheated a first and a second time beware of the third) we shall hear in a little time, whether Sheppard's next tour will be in a coach or a cart; and whether he will steer from Drury-Lane or Tyburn.

LONDON NOV. 14. On Tuesday last the notorious thief and house breaker John Sheppard, who was some time since convicted of a burglary at the Old Bailey, and thereupon received sentence of death, was carried to the bar of the King's Bench, Westminster, pursuant to a motion made by Mr. Attorney General in that court of Saturday last. The record of his conviction was removed by a certiorari, as was his person by a habeas corpus; and the proper evidence attending, he was proved to be the very same malefactor that had been so convicted and sentenced, and afterwards escaped; whereupon a Rule of Court was made for his execution on Monday next since which he has been remov'd to the condemn'd hold, where he is chain'd down to the floor, and is watched by two men day and night.

Among the crowds who went to Newgate to see this noted criminal, there was a famous painter, who thought it worth his while to pencil out his face. What use he may make of it, we cannot say; but after he had done it, he shewed it to Sheppard, asking him if it was not like him? who replied, that he thought it too old; where upon some amendments were made to it.

The woman lately committed to Newgate as the accomplice of John Sheppard (and whom some will have to be Molly Frisky) was taken in the following manner. She came with a man and a boy to the Dolphin Ale-House in Long-Alley near Moorfields, and pretending herself a stranger just come up from Gravesend, got the people of the house to look out for a lodging for her; and leaving several bundles in the ale-house while she went with them, the man of the house gathering from some circumstances, that she was no stranger to John Sheppard, opened the bundles and finding many materials to confirm suspicion of her confederacy with him, then got an officer ready and apprehended her on her return: upon which the man and boy that attended her took their heels, and got off. The broker Sheppard last robbed being sent for, came and owned the goods that were found on her.

We hear that frequent robberies are committed at this time on the northern roads by the felons that lately escaped from on board the transport ship near Harwich, who has dispersed themselves in gangs up and down the northern counties.

LONDON DEC. 1. On Monday last the notorious house breaker, John Sheppard, was executed at Tyburn, pursuant to the rule of Court of Assizes King's bench, Westminster: As he was an enterprizing fellow, his hand-cuffs were continued on him even to the very gallow. Never was there a greater crowd assembled on any occasion, than to see this criminal; and however undaunted he might appear before, he was greatly shocked at the fatal three; and probably the more, in that to the instant had meditated an escape; for on his entrance into the cart, a naked knife was found on him, with which 'tis thought he designed to have cut the cords that tied him, or the fatal noose, and so have thrown himself out, and taken refuge amongst the mob. At Tyburn he declared he would confess no new robberies except one, which he committed in Monmouth Street since his last escape. So amazing have been the actions of this desperado, that we hear, they have got the escapes of John Sheppard, or Harlequin in Newgate, now in rehearsal, at the New Play-House; Mr. Lun not doubting but to make as much of him as he has done of Dr. Faustus. The person who plays Sheppard it seems, went to see the original in Newgate, and told him, he should be glad to have it in his power to play his own part.

LONDON DEC. 5. The Paris letters say that there is now depending in the Parliament there a very curious case concerning a gentleman, who desired his descent may be fixed to get the inheritance of one of his two reputed fathers. The case is this, two gentlemen traveling together with their wives, both with child, it happen'd that they lay in both at the same time, and in the same room. The midwife laid the two children before the fire, without any mark to distinguish them: One of them died soon after, and the two fathers not knowing whose son the living child was, they agreed to have him brought up as their son in common, &c.

LONDON DEC. 10. Last week died at Newgate John Chambers a Scotch man, who had been a prisoner about 29 years in that goal for the assassination plot against King William.

An unhappy accident happen'd on Monday morning last in Fleet Street, where, as some young men were playing at football, a coach came amongst them, the pole of which struck an unhappy youth on the head, knocked him down and broke three of his ribs, and so fractured his scull, that he died that evening.

Letters from Weymouth, which came on Wednesday, advise, That the Scinner, of Chichester, is come in there, having on board Capt. Hunt, and 11 men belonging to the Thomasia, from Hamburg, who were stranded on the 27th past, whom they took up in a boat: They left on board three men, who shifted in the ship till the last instant, when they were saved by a fishing boat, who put them ashore.

LONDON DEC. 19. Yesterday 48 convicts under sentence of transportation, in Newgate, were carry'd from the said goal on board a ship, to be transported to the American plantations, in pursuant to their said sentence. But one Sykey, in going to the water side, took his opportunity to run away, and got clear off, having not been heard of since.

They write from Edinburg, Dec. 5. That a young woman there who lodged in a private room by her self, told some of her neighbours that she was going next morning into the country, and went to bed in perfect health. She fell into a deep sleep, which continued 14 full days and nights. On her waking and appearing abroad, her neighbours welcom'd her well but told her, she had certainly been thinkidly out in the country, for she looked like a spectre: But she told them she had been sleeping in bed all the time.

1725

LONDON JAN. 1. Letters from Newcastle upon the Tyne, say, that on Wednesday last, about eight a clock in the evening, a fire broke out in a merchant's house near the great church in that town; whilst endeavours were using to extinguish it, a great quantities of gun powder, which was in the house unknown to the crowd, took fire and tore the house to pieces, driving the stones and timber among the multitude, so that thirteen people died upon the spot, and about fifty were sorely wounded, many of which are since dead. During the burning of the fire, the Mayor and member of Parliament, Mr. Carr, was very active in encouraging the people and giving directions for the extinguishing of it, sometimes he was in great danger when the gunpowder took fire, several having fallen dead about him. He has since order'd all surgeons thereabouts carefully to attend the wounded poor people, and has given fifty pounds as a reward to the people that were diligent in putting out the fire.

LONDON JAN. 2. The widow of a famous horse jockey of Smithfield, left worth above 10,000 £. having remov'd lately with her only daughter to Hanover-Square, that they might live and converse like themselves, an Irishman found means, under the title of a Lord, to get into the house with them as a lodger, and to marry the daughter with 5,000 £. down for her dowry. Quickly after marriage he was so successful as to get 1,000 £. more from the old woman to help him in pretended purchase; and immediately after the money was paid, he was discovered to be an imposter, which has brought such shame and confusion upon the widow and her daughter, as may be better imagined than express'd.

On Saturday night last two watchmen in Castle-Yard in Holbourn, being contending together about lighting a gentleman home, they fell to blows, and in the fray one killed the other, and was thereupon apprehended and secured in Bridewell till the coroner's inquest sat, which they did on Tuesday last, and their verdict being wilful murder, he has since been removed to Newgate.

About twelve a clock yesterday a young man, supposed to be in drink, wandering out of his way among the new buildings near Old Street Square, happen'd to fall into a well there, which by negligence, having been left both uncovered and unclosed: He was rather staved than drowned; for the water did not reach above his breast. It seems that a woman in the neighbourhood of the well, heard him cry out; but the noise was so dismal, that she had not courage to go out. 'Tis said, that the coroner's inquest, who sat upon the body, have brought in their verdict accidental death.

LONDON JAN. 9. On Monday last Charles (commonly called captain) Towers, formerly mentioned, was executed in the New Mint, near Wappings Wall. He was convicted the last sessions at Old Bayley upon the Waltham Act, for going with arms disguised, to the great terror of the peaceable part of his Majesty's subjects &c. At the place of execution he declared, on the faith of a dying man, that both the facts, and the disguise sworn against him at his tryal, were absolutely false. He ow'd that the dread of prison had caused him to retire, with other unfortunate persons, to the place called the New Mint. In a word, he died bitterly inveighing against the balliffs.

LONDON JAN. 9. Last Monday one of the daughters of an eminent merchant in this city, a favorite of the family, and the admiration of all that knew her, standing to have her maid lace on her stays, cried out, without any previous indisposition, that she was stricken with death, and dy'd about two hours after.

LONDON JAN. 16. They write from Colchester, that several hundreds of workmen having gather'd together in a riotous manner there, on account of their masters lowering their wages. A detachment of horse marched into that town on Saturday last, to prevent the ill consequences that might have attended such tumults; which had the desired effect.

On Tuesday night a young man of about 22 years of age was taken up between Pancrass and London, very dangerously wounded, having received several stabs in his body. The account he gave of himself was this: That he courted a young woman who receiv'd his addresses, but he not being look'd upon as a sufficient match by his mistresses mother, she had provided another lover for her daughter, but the girl's affection was so settled upon the former that he was look'd upon as an obstacle in the way of her good fortune; the consequence if this was, that he received a letter in the young lady's name, to meet her that night at a house at Pancrass, whither he was then going; but was waylaid by two men, who gave him the wounds above mentioned.

They write from the Hot Wells at Scarborough in Yorkshire, that a certain nobleman having out of a frolic, caused a sack of meal to be immediatly made into an hasty-pudding, and offering a reward of two guineas to the person as should eat most of it, a certain number of country fellows enter'd lists; two whereupon eat to that excess, that the one died on the spot, and the other two days after.

LONDON JAN. 19. At Chigwell in Essex, a man was lately kill'd by his wife, who struck him under the ear with a poker. He was bury'd on Wednesday last, and she is committed to the county goal.

LONDON JAN. 23. We have the following very true relation of a combat, which happened last Sunday in the afternoon, in Sermon Time, in St. George's Fields, betwixt a game bull and an informing constable as follows.

The bull it seems, is used to graze about the fields on Sunday without molestation, altho' baited there twice a week; but last Sunday some unlucky boys got together and hunted him, till at length, the bull very wisely runs up to the magistrate's house (which it seems, is in the fields) for shelter, he looking thro, his window & seeing him, as well to shew his power and his valor, immediately takes the sign of his magistracy, and goes forth, thinking thereby to deter this fierce creature, but it proved quite the reverse, for Taurus, not dismay'd, immediately makes at him, catches him in his horns, and flings him over the pales into the next neighbour's-yard, which it seems, is a notorious bawdy-house, shewing thereby, that he ought rather to have been going about to search those houses, than at home drawing drink in Sermon time. Upon the whole, he was immediately blooded, and put to bed, his wounds being dress'd made by the horns of his combatant is in better way of his recovery than desired by his neighbours for they say, the bull ought to be shot for not thro'ly doing his work as well as the fellow was wished hanged for half cutting Jonathan Weld's throat.

Last Wednesday pursuant to several considerable wagers laid between some Italians and English gentlemen, at Slaughter's Coffee House in St. Martin's Lane, there came one notable boxing-match, at Fiff's celebrated amphitheatre in Oxford Road, between Stopa l'Aqua, a Venetian gondalier, or waterman, and John Wetacre, an English drover. The battle was fought with equal spirit and resolution on both sides, but not with equal stature, strength or skill, the Italian being the tallest by several inches, but the Englishman being the most sturdy; for he received all the attack of the Italian, without much hurt or concern, gave him several terrible falls, without having one himself, and beat him so sorely, that he was forc'd at last, to cry out Busta, which signify'd that he was basted enough. There was a numerous and uncommon appearance of the spectators, Seasemberg, and other foreign ministers being present, together with several of the English nobility, and members of Parliament, to see which nation carry'd the day.

LONDON JAN 23. By the letters from Dublin, there is advice, that the Lord Mayor had himself lately visited most of the baker's shops in that city, and had committed to goal some of that profession, for selling bread under weight, in order to be prosecuted for the said offence.

LONDON JAN. 30. We hear that not withstanding several surgeons, for the space of sixteen months, had attempted to cure a certain noble lady's breast, in vain; she is now return'd to her house in London, perfectly cured by one Mr. Scotsmir, surgeon, at Saxmundham in the County of Suffolk; and that the Earl her husband presented him with a purse of two hundred guineas for the cure.

LONDON FEB. 2. On Monday last above twenty persons, supposed to be sodomites, in regard some of the gang have been convicted of, and stood in the pillory for that filthy crime, were apprehended in a house in Hart Street, near Covent-Garden, in masquerade habits, and secured in several prisons, in order to examination.

LONDON FEB. 9. On Saturday last one Kite was apprehended at the Fountain Tavern in the Burrough of Southwark, on suspicion of robbing the Chester mail, and other felonious practices; who being carried before three of his Majesty's Justices of the Peace was by them committed to the New County Jail in the said Burrough. We hear, he is charged with erasing and altering bank notes for 20 £. to 70 £. and passing it for the latter sum; and with altering one other note of the like value in the same manner; which last he sent by a drawer of the tavern aforesaid, to be changed for specie; but the master of the house observing some suspicious circumstances, order'd the man to call at the post office, and to give an account of it there on his way to the bank; by which means he was seized and committed as above.

LONDON FEB. 9. At the close of last week a duel was fought between Mr. Cooke, a captain of dragoons in the service of France, who came over with the French embassy, and Mr. Stapleton; in which the former was wounded in the body and the sword arm.

LONDON FEB. 13. On the 4th instant one Carter, who was gentleman to the Earl of Suffolk, now in the Tower, was committed to Newgate, by virtue of an order from the House of Lords; he having been found guilty of procuring and selling written protection to divers persons, to the great oppression of their lawful creditors, and in breach of the standing orders of the house of Peers: And also found guilty of other offences. He is sentenced to pay a fine of twenty nobles, to suffer three months imprisonment and to stand twice in the pillory. On Thursday he stood for the first time, before Westminster Hill Gate, and on Thursday next he is to stand before the Royal Exchange.

On Monday last a woman servant in Stone-Cutters Street, near Fleet-Ditch, being perceived to be ill, was bid to lie down on the bed, when being by her self some time she was delivered of two children, whose backs she broke, and then thrust them into a picture, which she hid under the bed, with design to convey it away, but was discover'd, she died a few hours later.

LONDON FEB. 18. This day two baliffs, with an attorney of Furnival's Inn, going together to execute a writ against a gentleman from Africa; they mistook the house, and their man, and enter'd the lodging of Acton Baldwyn, Esq; member of parliament for Ludlow, and put him under arrest, as he was dressing in his chamber, to the great surprize of himself and family, and for all that Mr. Baldwyn and his servants could do to persuade them that they were wrong the wretches persisted, and were inexorable, and began to use him after the mode of their profession; the one crying confound us why do we wait? While the others meekly replied, Jack be patient, 'tis a civil gentleman, and I know will consider us: But soon being made sensible of the gross error they had committed, and of the penalties their rank zeal had made them liable to, they fell on their knees, and with prayers and tears besought a remission of the trespass, assault, false imprisonment, and breach of the privilege of Parliament. We hear they will be prosecuted by law.

LONDON FEB. 22. Robert Tranter, the baliff, who was formerly try'd at the King's Bench Bar, for being concerned in the death of Captain Luttrell, having most grossly abused the Duke of Leeds, his Grace brought an action against him, which was try'd the 13th instant; and, we hear, the jury gave his Grace 200 £. damage.

LONDON FEB. 25. Yesterday about 11 a clock a fire broke out at the Earl of Cardigan's house in Lincoln's Inn Fields, which ranged near 2 hours with great fury, and burnt down the said house to the ground, but did little more damage by reason of the timely assistance of the fire engines, except burning down a cupola of the New Playhouse, adjoining it, which was a very great damage of being totally consumed.

We hear William Morgan of Tredegar Esquire, designs to appear in one of the most splendid equipages that has been seen in England, on the 1st of March next, being the anniversary of the birthday of her Royal Highness the Princess of Wales, and the feast of St. David the Welch Tutelar Saint.

LONDON FEB. 27. Last Wednesday, as they were digging the foundation of a portico to the new church at St. Martin's in the fields, they took up a stone coffin, in which was a human skull, with a glass bell by the side of it, and a thigh bone; all the rest being moulder'd to dust.

The Skettle-grounds in and about the City and Liberty of Westminster and county of Middlesex are, by order of the Justices, suppress'd, tending to induce apprentices and servants to idle away their masters time, and embezzle their money.

They write from Gloucester, That a gentleman who lives at Slymbridge, in that county, has a goose now living, which is above fifty years old; and that the very last season she hatched two broods of young ones.

LONDON MARCH 6. Monday being the birthday of her Royal Highness the Princess of Wales, who (being born in 1683) then entered into her fifty third year of her age, the morning began with ringing of bells, and guns of the Tower, &c. were fired at noon, and flags were display'd all day, and at night there were bonfires and illuminations in the high streets of the cities of London and Westminster. Her Royal Highness received the complements of the nobility and gentry of both sexes at Leicester-Fields; and afterwards went with the Prince to St. James's, where his Majesty was also pleased to complement her: and at night there was a ball.

LONDON MARCH 6. On Wednesday night a gentleman, going home through Long Lane, was knock'd down, and robbed of 300 guineas and his pocket-book, in which were bills and bank notes to the value of 300 more.

Francis Kite, convicted of misdemeanor, for altering a banknote eras'd and alter'd, received sentence to stand once, in the pillory on Tower-Hill, to suffer six months imprisonment, to pay a fine of 20 £. and find security for his good behaviour for twelve months.

LONDON MARCH 12. His Majesty has granted letter of patent to Thomas Smith Esq; who for the improvement of navigation, hath invented an engine to row ships ahead with oars against wind and tide, or swimming in current, carrying ships out of war in or out of harbours, or line or battle, useful for fire ships, or bomb vessels, also to get up with, or leave any ship at sea, when wind is waiting; and more particularly useful to those ships that use the Lisbon Straight, Gibraltar, Vere Messina and the East and West Indies.

LONDON MARCH 13. We hear from Edinbergh, by letters of the 1st of March, that the pyrate vessel called the Revenge, commanded by Gow, alias Smith, who hath lately committed several pyracies and murthers, is taken at an island in the north of Scotland. The ship is seized, and said captain and his crew made prisoners.

A vessel is ordered for Scotland, to bring to London, the pyrates taken there, belonging to the Revenge. They being about thirty five in number, cammanded by one Captain Smith, a Scotchman.

Last week a waggon, coming to London, from Canterbury, loaded with bales of silk, and other rich commodities, belonging to some mercers in this city, to the value as said, of near a 1,000 £. The waggoners, smoking his pipe, set fire to the straw, which consumed or damaged the greatest part of the goods, as the waggon likewise. The loss is computed at 600 £.

LONDON APRIL 3. His Majesty's ship the Greyhound, Capt. Peter Solgard commander, arrived at the Nore the 24th past, with 30 of the prisoners on board, that we have mentioned to be taken in the pyrate ship called the Revenge, in the north of Scotland, seven of whom were condemned in murdering the captain, mate, surgeon and super-cargo, at their first seeing the ship: They have also brought a prize with them, which proved to be a ship of about 200 tuns, and has

18 guns mounted. As the Greyhound is since come up the river, these prisoners are all secured in the Marshalsea against the next Admiralty Sessions.

LONDON APRIL 13. Last Wednesday night Cladius Angeau a German watchmaker, was taken up at Sadlers Wells for robbing Baron Hattorf's House at St. James's; and several rings, jewels, &c. being found upon him, and sworn by Justice of the Peace, he was committed first to New Prison, and then to Newgate and a bill of indictment is found against him for the said robbery.

Jackson the quack-doctor, condemned at Hertford, for robbing the Chester mail, was, we hear the single person who robb'd the Bristol mail, sometime since. He is to be hang'd in chains, with his companion Rowe, near the place where the robbery was committed. Jackson is said to have taken some poison a little before his trial.

Last week a farmer, going from Havant, was stopp'd by one footpad, who demanded his money, but the farmer being unwilling to part with it on such easy terms, the fellow thought to oblige him to it with a pistol, so that he very narrowly escaped, for he was shot thro' the hat, but finding himself not hurt he briskly took to his heels and got safe away.

LONDON APRIL 17. They tell us from Greenwich, that a boy of that town having soon gone clandestinely, along with some other boys, on board a bomboat in the river, and breaking open a cask, drank about two quarts of the spirit, and died instantly.

LONDON APRIL 27. They write from Portsmouth, April 20, That some days before Mr. Oglander, attorney at Newport in the Isle of Wight, hang'd himself; 'tis said he was driven to that fatal action by his nexessitous circumstances.

Some days after, Mr. Short, a considerable upholder at Chichester, hang'd himself likewise; 'tis thought his losses by South Sea Stocks occasioned the sad catastrophe; before which he wrote a remarkable letter of good advice to his children, which was found in his pocket, and it is as follows.

My dear children,
Notwithstanding the unhappy circumstances of my death, let it not so effect you as to decline the ways of virtue and religion; and whatever station God cast you in, behave yourselves with humility and industry, and let not pride once take place, which it has done to my ruin. You may expect from the worst sort of people some reflection; but bear it with a Christian patience, being conscious to yourself you had no

share in my guilt. Never fail of doing your duty by praying to God morning and evening; with out which you cannot expect but blessing. Love God, love your fellow creatures, and be sure to assist one another all that's in your power: And may God of Love and Peace dwell within you to the end of your lives, and you with him to eternity Amen, Amen.

LONDON APRIL 29. On Tuesday last, the mate of the Triumph, Capt. Hammerton, now in the river, bound for Lisbon, being disorder'd in his senses, shot himself with a pistol through the head, and instantly dy'd.

One night last week the Dutchess Dowager of Rutland being to go from her house at Chelsea to Kensington, to pay a visit, and one of her Grace's footmen being on horseback, and slinging his blunderbuss to attend her, the same unfortunately discharg'd and shot a young lad, and helper in the stable, into the body, who died in two days after. The coroner's inquest sat last Saturday on the body, and brought in their verdict, accidental death.

LONDON APRIL 29. On Tuesday night a gentleman very much in liquor going home about 12 a clock thro' Causton-Street, had the misfortune to fall down, and was so little in his senses, that instead of attempting to get up, he fell fast asleep, and lay there till a coach run over him and broke his leg.

LONDON MAY 8. On Thursday last, about 11 in the forenoon, commenced the tryal of the Earl of Macclesfield, late Lord Chancellor of Great Britain, at the bar of the House of Lords. 'Tis thought the same will hold some days.

Madam Johnson, the wife of the famous Roger Johnson, a Burger of Rotterdam, who is said to have stolen to the value of about 2,000 £. at the late installment at Windsor, has been committed prisoner to Clerkenwell Bridewell; where she lives in splendid manner, being, as we hear, attended by several servants among whom is a French cook.

LONDON MAY 18. Yesterday there was a tryal at the Common pleas Bar, Westminster, between Mr. Barker a master taylor, plaintiff, and Mr. Huntingford a baker, defendant; for assault and battery and main, committed by the latter in throwing down the plaintiff, and dislocating his thigh bone in such a manner, that the same is become incurable, and he renders now incapable of providing for himself and his family, being in the 76th years of his age; but it appearing that there had been a friendship between them, and that the misfortune was merely accidental and without the least malice, The Jury gave the plaintiff 20 £. damages.

There was also a cause tryed at the same Court between Mr. Barnes a painter, plaintiff, and Mr. Jobson an officer of the excise, defendant, for a criminal conversation with the plaintiff's wife. The jury gave 200 £. damages.

LONDON MAY 18. An order is gone down to the Mayor of Bristol to send up from thence in safe custody the captain of a Virginia ship, in order to his tryal at the Admiralty Sessions the 26th instant, at the Old Bailey for the murther of his cabbin boy, in the voyage home from Virginia; he being now a prisoner in Newgate in that city for the same.

LONDON MAY 22. It appears by several informations upon oath against Jonathan Wild, condemn'd last Saturday at the Old Bailey, That he hath, for many years past, been confederate with great numbers of pick-pockets house breakers, shop-lifters, and other thieves. That he hath form'd a kind of corporation of thieves, of which he is the head, and director; and that notwithstanding his pretended services in detecting and prosecuting offenders, he procured such only, to be hang'd and conceal'd their booty, or refus'd to share it with him. That he had divided the town and country into districts, and appointed distinct gangs for each, who regularly accounted with him for their robberies. He had also a particular set to steal at churches in time of Divine Service, and also other moving detatchments to attend at Court and Birthdays, balls, &c. and upon both Houses of Parliament, Circuits, and county fairs. That the persons employed by him were, for the most part, felon convicts, who returned from transportation before the time for which they were transported was expired; and that he made choice of them to be his agents; because he had it in his power to take from them what part of the stolen goods he thought fit, and otherwise used them ill, or hang them as he pleased. That he hath, from time to time, supplyed such convicted felons with money and cloaths, and lodged them in his own house, the better to conceal them, particularly some, against whom there are now informations for diminishing and counterfeiting broad pieces and guineas. That he both not only been a receiver of stolen goods, as well as writings of all kinds, for near fifteen years last past, but frequently been a confederate, and robbed along with the above mentioned convicted felons. That, in, order to carry on these vile practices to gain some credit with the ignorant multitude, he usually carry'd about him a short silver staff, as a badge of his authority from the Government, which he us'd to produce when he himself was concern'd in robbing. That he had under his care and direction, several warehouses for receiving and concealing stolen goods, and also a ship for carrying off jewels, watches, and other valuable goods to Holland, where he hath a superannuated thief for his factor. That he kept in pay several artists to make alterations, and to transform watches, opals, snuff-boxes, rings, and other things, that they might not be known; several of which he us'd to present to such persons as he thought might be of service to him. That he seldom or never helped the owners to their notes or papers they had lost, unless he found them able exactly to specify and discribe them, and then after insisting on more than half the value. Lastly, it appears, that he hath frequently procured false evidence to swear persons into facts they were not guilty of, sometimes to prevent them from being evidence against himself, and others for the sake of the great reward given by the Government.

LONDON MAY 22. We hear a reprieve is come down to Newgate for Mr. Jonathan Wilde, upon his promising to discover the persons that robbed his Majesty's Exchange; and to make several important discoveries which greatly concern the publick.

A servant of Col. Pelham shot himself on Tuesday night, in Conduit-Street, with one of his master's pistols, thro' the breast and died immediately.

We hear that one of the masters of a noted school in Essex, is charge with committing, the abominable crime of sodomy with some of the scholars, and that a warrant being issued for apprehending him, he hath absconded.

This morning between one and two, a pastry cook's wife from Swithin's Lane stabb'd her husband, so that he died, immediately. She was seized and secured in the Compter.

The children of the Charity-School, in London and Westminster, to the number of several thousands, all new cloathed, conducted by their respective trustees, teachers, &c. proceeded, according to annual custom, on Thursday last, to St. Sepulchre's Church, the Rev. Dr. Barryman preached a suitable sermon to them on the occasion.

LONDON MAY 22. Early Tuesday morning a person well dress'd was found dead in a ditch in St. George's Fields, supposed to be robbed and murder'd. He is said to be one Mr. Smith, a clerk to an attorney.

His Majesty's ship the Argyle, Capt. Bowler, is expected suddenly from Lisbon, having on board James Williams, lieutenant of the new pyrate ship called the Revenge, formerly mentioned, with whom the pirational crew quarrelled, clapt him in irons, and put him on board the Triumvirate, Capt. Davies, (taken by them 10 leagues off of Vogo) who carried him to Lisbon, and delivered him to the man of war, in order to his being brought to justice.

DORCHESTER JUNE 1. One Mr. John Felton an officer of the excise here, lately seized two and twenty anchors of brandy between East and West Lulloth, a notable place for running goods, the rendezvous of smugglers. The wife of Richard Card, one of the smugglers, willing to save a large canister of tea, about twelve pounds in weight, claspp'd it betwixt her thighs. The officer observing, when she walk'd her legs were very stiff, and seemingly deprived of muscular motion, presently divin'd the good woman to be grown pregnant with some prohibited goods, and that the hour growing night, a speedy delivery would be necessary: He then lifting up the hem of her garment, brings forth into the world an innocent canister of tea, to the great diversion of himself and the spectators.

LONDON JUNE 12. There are melancholy accounts from several places in the country, great damage done by the floods; in the vale of Evesoam, the River Avon overflowing its banks, tracts of land under water. The like hath happened in some parts of Leicestershire, and Bedfordshire, and the post-boys from Wellingborough and Derby were in great danger, being oblig'd to swim their horses in passing the river.

LONDON JUNE 14. Yesterday betwixt 1 & 2 in the morning a deplorable accident happened at the house of Mother Valentia, a gentlewoman of the street in Little Suffolk-Street in the Hay-Market, where a person of quality & a lady being communicating their love together, the bed-chamber (by their careless placing the candle) took fire, and immediately raised a flame lot greater than their zealous passion. The lady governess, together with her doxies and their companions, had but just time enough to escape in their shifts, and the house was, with all its furniture, destroyed immediately.

LONDON JULY 3. Notwithstanding the terrible apprehension people are under, the mischief done by the late bad weather is not so great as was first imagined in the vales which are flooded and round the towns where things are forwardest 'tis thought the farmers will suffer greatly; but in the hill counties they have a very fair prospect of fine harvest.

Last Monday a young boy, an apprentice to a farrier in Hay-Market, hang'd himself in his master's garret.

A large vault has been lately discover'd in the Meuse, curiously tiled and motto'd, it appears to be the bathing-place of Queen Elizabeth.

LONDON JULY 3. At the last sessions on Thursday Anne Mitchel, a girl of about 14 years of age, was try'd upon an indictment for stealing some wearing apparel from one Mrs. Sylvester of Bond Street; it appear'd by the evidence, that the said Sylvester kept a disorderly house; that there was a contract between them in relation to this affair, and that she furnish'd the girl with the cloaths to keep company; which it seems she did till she got the foul disease, and then went off, carrying the cloaths with her. The jury considering the matter acquitted her of the indictment; and the Court order'd that she should have a copy of the same, that madam may be prosecuted for so vile an infamous practices.

LONDON JULY 8. Private letters that came on Tuesday from Hamburg gave further account of the success of the South Sea Company's ships employ'd in the Greenland fishery, viz. that they have taken in all forty five whales, worth several hundred pounds each.

One day last week Mr. Guerin, an agent crossing the Thames in the ferryboat at Putney, his horse startled by the sail of a boat passing by, fell with him into the river, and threw him off; but having the good luck to catch his mane, the horse dragg'd him safe to shore.

LONDON JULY 10. Letters from Newcastle mention, that on Wednesday night, June 23, a coal-pit belonging to an alderman of that town, suddenly fir'd, and by the blast 15 men were killed, and 4 very much wounded. 'Tis said likewise, that 19 horses were destroy'd by it, but in what manner the letters do not mention.

LONDON JULY 10. Mr. John Morris who kept the Ball Inn in Ladenhall-Street, having receiv'd advice from the country on Tuesday night of the death of his wife, shot himself last Wednesday morning, and dy'd immediately.

LONDON JULY 17. We have a just account of the tumult at Glasgow, which had been falsely represented in several of the papers; since then the story is confirmed with divers particulars as follows;

Edinburg, June 29. The Malt Tax in North Britain commencing on the 23d instant, the Commissioners of Excise have received information a day or two before by letter from several of the officer at Glasgow, that they were threatened to be stoned if they should attempt to take an account of the stock of malt in the hands of any person there; and that some of the town's people had laid at the door of every malt house great heaps of stone to convince the officers they were in earnest. Hereupon the Commissioners made application for some troops to Major General Wade, Commander and Chief of his Majesty's forces in this part of the Kingdom; who in compliance with this request, sent from hence Captain Bushel, with two companies of Dolorain's Regiment of Foot, to aid the magistrates of that town, in case they should demand his assistance against any that should make a riot, and charging him strictly not to resent any abuse language, or proceed to any manner of violence, unless he should be driven to extremity. The two companies marched from this city the 23d instant, and notwithstanding, very great rains, and the distance of 40 miles, they arrived in Glasgow about six in the evening of the 24th, when they found a mob got together, consisting chiefly of women and boys, who gave them the worst of language, and threw stones at them. But the officers desired them to be quiet for that he was not come to do harm to any body. When he came into the midst of the town, he applied to the provost that he might lodge his men in the guard-room; the provost answered, that the mob had secured the key of the guard-room, and he could only give him billets for his men; whereupon the officer contended himself with hiring a publick house for his men. Not long after a drum being beat about the town by one of the rioters, a vast number of them drew together, and about 11 at night they began to break into the houses of Mr. Daniel Campbell of Shawfield Representitive in Parliament for the town of Glasgow, and destroyed or took away the furniture, and whatever they found in it. Then they broke open his cellars, drank themselves drunk, and staved the rest of his wines. Captain Bushel had timely intellegence given him, that the mob were going to plunder the said house; and therefore kept himself ready with his men in expectation of being called by the provost to his assistance; but not hearing any thing from him, he dispatched an officer to the provost to let him know he was on purpose to assist the civil magistrate on this occasion; but the provost returned answer, That he did not think he had a sufficient number of men, and therefore he did not think it fit to make use of them. Thus the mob gutted the house, and not one magistrate to discountenance their violence; for some had withdrawn from the town some time before, and the rest were (or pretended to be) intimidated. The officers of the excise had hid themselves, before and during the riot; but some of them were found out by the rabble, and were unmercifully beaten and abused.

It was thought the rioters were satisfied with the mischief they had done that night: But about three in the afternoon of the 27th, the drum began to beat again by a man in woman's cloaths. Captain Bushel was then at dinner, and finding there was some mischief in hand, he began to suspect there was a design against the troops, in which he was not at all mistaken, for in a very little time the mob were got together to the number of 2 or 3,000. The fellow in woman's cloaths advanced to the captain and endeavoured by kissing his hand, and other submissions to amuse him till the mob should draw nearer. The captain telling him he was not to be imposed upon, and bidding him to dismiss his people, of whom he seemed to be the head, the pretended woman ran away, which was a signal to fall on; for then came a shower of great stones and clubs at the soldiers heads, with a continual cry of drive dogs out of town; They wounded several of them, broke the locks of some of their arms, and told the officer they knew he durst not fire at them. The captain with some difficulty, prevailed with a constable (for want of a superior magistrate) to read the proclamation against rioters, before any harm was done by the soldiers; but the poor man seeing himself in danger; when he bagan to read it, threw the proclamation down and ran away. Upon this the captain called some of his men to fire over their heads, in hopes to terrify them without hurting them; but instead of his finding the effect from this tenderness towards them, they, fell upon the troops with redoubled violence; so that the captain was at last obliged to order his men to fire in their own defence, by which three or four rioters were killed. Then the mob retired a little, and the provost, sent a messenger to the captain, desiring him to retire with his men out of town. The officer complied, but this retreat gave new spirit to the rabble, and they pressed upon him, he retiring in good order; and which about 10 of the rioters were killed, and several wounded.

The mob persued him about six miles, there being 3 or 400 of them armed with flintlocks, but durst not come near enough to him when he was in the open country, to kill any of his men. And preserving he was making his retreat towards Dumbarton Castle, they sent some horsemen full speed to threaten the people at Dumbarton, that if they gave any shelter to the soldiers they would come and burn their town. Two of the soldiers fell into their hands in Glasgow, one of whom they thought they had killed, but some time after a woman dragged him into a house and in about two hours time recovered him a little from the miserable condition he was in by the wounds he received. They came to a resolution to hang the other; but a man, who was desirous to save him told the mob to amuse them, that the best way was to carry him to Shawfield's house and hang him there. When they dragged him thither, the fellow told the mob again, that it was almost dark, and that it would be better to hang him the next morning by daylight, for an example to others. After which, in the night, he got the soldier out of their way. Four others were missing by the way in their retreat, being fallen with the fatugue of the long marches and their wounds but two of them are since arrived at Dunbarton Castle; The other two cannot yet be heard of. These are the chief particulars, which we have received by divers letters, and by persons come from Glasgow on this occasion.

MAIDSTONE JULY 17. Last night Mr. Underdown, the distributor of the stamps, for the county, was robb'd on Floxly-Hill of his money and cloaths, by some footpads. After they had taken his money (which did not exceed thirty shillings) they led him according to their custom, into the wood, and bound him; so setting a watch, they looked out for another adventure: But having no luck, they came and released him, without further abuse; than striping him of his coat and waistcoat, shirt and perriwig. The person who watch'd him, told him, their business was come to nothing, and that he had a great mind to leave off trade.

NORWICH JULY 17. About 7 a clock last night some gentry were robbed in a coach, at the Gravel-Pits near Brook, by two men on bay horses, a gold watch, 2 gold rings, besides money, one of 'em was a little man, pockfretten, in a light fustian frock; the other lusty, ruddy complexion, in a dark cloath suit.

LONDON JULY 17. On Monday last one Thomas Dean a grenadier in the Second Regiment of Foot Guard, was whipp'd in Hyde-Park, the second time for desertion: His wife there upon hang'd herself in her own room, in Exeter Court in the Strand, in which dismal posture she was found last Tuesday morning.

LONDON JULY 17. On Monday last three deer-stealers shot and carried off a buck at Enfield Chace and next day were so insolent as to shoot another in sight of General Pepper's house, who is ranger of the said chace, upon which the keepers and some other servants came out upon them, and tho' they were 11 in number the deer-stealers fired at them, and would have carried off the buck, but as one of the three stooped down to load his piece a keeper that was behind him shot him at the fundament, and the bullet came out of his breast; the other two mounted their horses and escaped, and the wounded person who was a wheelright on Tower-Hill, died on Tuesday night.

LONDON JULY 20. Last week Henry Norris a player at the New-House, son of the celebrated comedian of that name, had a encounter with Mr. Goddard, belonging to the Old Play-House, in which the latter was so wounded that he died in two days after: and Mr. Norris who is much wounded, is gone, as we hear, for Ireland.

On Friday evening three milk women were committed to Newgate, by Mr. Justice Brown of Islington for robbing a young fellow of 25 £. which he had been entrusted with by his father to pay away in town; but in his way meeting with these women, he went into a publick house with them, where they robbed him.

LONDON JULY 24. They write from Lincoln, that Mr. Bishop a malster, who is a prisoner in the Castle there for the murder of his mother, a widow, in a village near Spilsby, and ripping up a gentleman's belly that lodged in her house, who is since recovered, has twice attempted to poison himself: That the coroner's inquest, after several consultations, had found the fact wilful murder: and that great endeavours are using to prove him lunatick at the Assizes.

LONDON JULY 24. The lady Child is given over by the physicians at her house in St. Anne's Parish. This Lady is great grand mother to the Dukes of Grafton, Bedford, and Beaufort; and mother to the Lord Middleton, the Dutchess of Chandos and Lord Castlemain.

Yesterday morning an unfortunate accident happened in Piccadilly, where a baliff and his two assistance attempting to execute a writ against Capt. Dellegal an officer in Col. Philip's Regiment in Placentia, burst open his chamber door, and put his wife, (who was that instant in labour) into a terrible fright, with the rest of the family. The captain shot one of the fellowers into the body, and also ran him through with his sword. The fellow ran into the street, and drop'd down dead in the highway; But the other two carried off the captain in a hackney coach; and he was committed to Newgate. And in about half an hour after his wife was delivered of a dead child.

Last week a merchant in this city was arrested with his shopkeeper and footman. One Jubeenville a banker at the corner of Cocq, who has been arrested for a bankruptcy, of above 500,000 livres, was carried last week to his house, to be presented at the taking of the seal put on his house, but nothing was found therein, and 'tis believed he'll be put into the pillory.

LONDON JULY 24. They write from Norwich, That a great number of men, women, and children were assembled together in a riotous manner at Stokesley, and had pull'd down a mill and several gates and fences belonging there to, on repentence, that they had a right of common there, which a certain gentleman had encroach'd upon, by hedging in the ground: persisting in those practices two or three days, the sheriff thought fit to go with an armed company to quiet them, but they made no opposition: whereupon 10 of them being taken up, were carry'd to the city, and examined before the justices there, who used them with great clemency, and admitted them to bail till next Assizes, upon promise not to offend again.

A certain young lady of good fortune, whose parents neglected to provide for her sprightly constitution required, has within a few days gone away with an inferior officer of the troops.

Relating to a friend of mine an account from Newcastle, upon the Tyne, which I had seen inserted in one of your late journals of a melancholy accident which happen'd there in some coal-mines, whereby 15 persons were kill'd; He sigh'd at hearing of it, and told me, that some time ago himself was concern'd in an unhappy blast of that nature, whereby 72 persons were torn to pieces, the colliery set on fire and destroy'd, and in which his own loss amounted to upwards of 300 £. per annum. He added, that they are called sulphurous blasts, or fire; That they will take fire at the smallest flame of a candle, or any thing else, but are no way effected by red hot coal or iron; That the blast blows up all before it like gunpowder, makes a report like a cannon, and like that tears everything to pieces that comes within the extent of the power: But daily risques do coal-miners run for a slavish livelyhood. If you please to insert this you'll oblidge.

Your frequent reader A. B.

LONDON JULY 24. Yesterday about noon a baliff and his follower arresting a gentleman a little without Temple-Bar, the gentleman drew a pistol and swore he'd be the death of one, or both of them if they detain'd him; accordingly, the officers persisting to secure him, he fir'd, and kill'd the follower upon the spot: for which rash and bloody action, being carry'd before a justice he was committed to Newgate.

At the Assizes at Chelmford for the County of Essex, a woman was try'd for attempting to murder her child, by leaving it exposed near the road on Epping Forrest. It appear'd that she had an husband, who left her just before her reckoning was out, and that she was deliver'd at an inn in Gracechurch-Street on Saturday the 4th instant; but being turn'd out on Tuesday following, she travell'd with the infant, and left it the next day in the forrest, where accordingly to her own confession in Court and other circumstantial evidences, the infant had lain till Saturday, when it was discover'd, without any sustenance, and which is very surprizing was still alive. Her design of murdering it did not appear, but the barbarity and unnaturalness of the action was so notorious, that the judge thought fit to sentence her to the House of Correction for three months, and to be whipp'd three times a week for the last two months.

LONDON JULY 24. At the Assizes at Hertford a gentleman, of that town try'd his coachman and footman, for taking wine out of his cellar for their own drinking; the fact appearing very plain, they were both order'd for transportation.

On the 16th instant at the Assizes of Chelmford, for the County of Essex, a notable practitioner of the game of thimble and ball, was convicted of cheating several persons of their money, and received sentence to stand in the pillory, and suffer a year's imprisonment.

LONDON AUG. 7. On Tuesday morning the body of a man, supposed to have been murder'd was found upon a brike kilne near Stoke Newington. He appeared to be a labouring person.

They write from Doncaster in Yorkshire, that on Monday was 7-night they had a terrible storm of thunder and lightning, one Simon Lee a flax dresser was killed by it, and his shop set on fire, a shoemakers prentice of the same town had also one side of his face taken off.

At the Assizes held for the County of Buckingham, Martha Shephard age 71 years was try'd and convicted of felony and manslaughter, in feloniously killing one Margaret Beale widow, age 70 years, and burnt in the hand; the quarrel was occasion'd by jealously.

LONDON AUG. 11. Last Saturday morning between 9 and 10 of the clock, two houses fell down in Soho Square, whereof one was lately inhabited by Capt. Carey, but then empty, the other was Mr. Brigham's house (son of Sir Orlando Brigham) who marry'd the Lady

Anne eldest daughter of the late Earl of Bradford who is near her time of lying in: The Lady who was in bed, was carry'd backwards by a servant that perceived the house to crack on the fore part; but her housekeeper was unfortunately kill'd. The sad accident is said to be occasion'd by the workmen (then at breakfast) not having sufficiently shor'd up the house, as they were enlarging the vault under the front.

LONDON AUG. 11. Some days ago a fellow that was reputed half a fool, having gain'd the good-will of a maid servant, who had saved a pretty handsome sum, privately married her, and afterwards pretending he had a letter that gave him an account of an estate left him in the country, enticed her to go down with him to settle there; she consented and carry'd all her cargo with her. The villain waited his opportunity when the coast was clear, and riding into a by-place, knock'd the poor woman off her horse, and stabb'd her so barbarously that one of her eyes dropt out; not satisfied with that, he gave her several other wounds, and then taking her money, left her in that miserable condition but providentially a person happen to come into that very place in a little time after the villain had left it, and seeing such a deplorable object, administer'd such assistance as brought the poor creature to her senses. Upon her discovering the barbarous author of her wounds, he was pursu'd and taken, and is now in custody in Lancaster. 'Tis hop'd the woman may recover: but however, the barbarity of the action, together with the villain's having another wife, as it appear since he has, make it very probable, that if ever he goes to heaven it will be in a string.

LONDON AUG. 11. We hear that on Wednesday next there is to be a terrible and furious encounter at Mr. Figg's Amphitheatre, adjoining to his house, in Oxford Road, between the famous Mr. Sutton, champion of Kent, and a couragious female heroine of that county on the one side; and the celebrated Mr. Stokes, and his much admir'd consort, the invincible city-championess on the other. Forty pounds are to reward the valour of either hero or heroine that gives the most cuts at swords, and the most blows at quarter-staff, will have a title to twenty; so that the triumphant conquerors will be gainers of threescore pounds, besides the sole command of all the immense treasure which shall be taken the day in the box.

This week Hanna the wife of James Gibby was committed to the Gatehouse, Westminster, by Justice Railton, for cursing his Majesty, in words not fit to be named but in a Court of Justice.

LONDON AUG. 14. The Lords Justices having promised a reward of 40 £. for apprehending either Thomas James, Aaron Maddox, William Gatts, and John Caster, four notorious deer-stealers, who assaulted and grievously wounded Henry Best, one of the keepers of Endfield Chace, on Friday the 30th of July last, in that part of the said chace which is call'd Ridgeway.

On Saturday last, several mobbish fellows that were taken up the night before, for rifling a hearse, plucking off the escutcheons, tearing the velvet, and raising a mobb and tumult in the Parish of Shoreditch, were carried before Colonel Mitchel, a Justice of the Peace, and bound over for the same; which 'tis to be hoped will go a good way towards breaking a practice so savage and barbarous.

LONDON AUG. 14. Last week 4 tradesmen were drinking at an alehouse about 4 miles beyond Craydon and staying till after the day was shut in, two of them one of which was a butcher bound for London, resolv'd to go that night, and tho' it was extraordinary dark, laid a wager of a guinea, that he'd get first to Craydon turnpike and notwithstanding the other two dissuaded them from it, they mounted their horses and went away full speed, the one coming to the turnpike found the butcher's horse there before him, but no rider on him, and telling the people of the turnpike what had pass'd, they went back with him with a light to see for the butcher, whom they found in the road within a mile of the house they started from, with his scull broke in a dismal manner, and his head and body all over blood, without life; it was suppos'd that falling down, his horse kick'd him, and perhaps the other rode over him, whereupon he was carry'd to the house they set out from, where the other two remain'd, the utmost endeavours were us'd to bring him to life but to no purpose.

Yesterday morning Robert Carr, a journeyman perriwig-maker, was found hang'd and dead at the bellfrey door belonging to Lincoln Inn Chappel. He was related to, and had been from three years old bred and employ'd by Mr. Carr, a noted perrywig-maker by Lincoln's Inn, who is very much concern'd at his unhappy end. 'Tis universally agreed, that he was author of his own death, but the cause assign'd for this unnatural action are different; some attributing to too much love, a young woman, for whom he had a very passionate respect, having the day before been married to another person in that very chappel; whilst others will have the cause to be too little money; occasion'd by his own ill conduct, he having left behind him the character of a great deal of honesty but little prudence; we shall not pretend to say which was the certain cause; but if any of his acquaintance shall have reason to believe the latter, it may not be amiss for them, and all persons who shall hear of it, to reflect how literally the wages of his sin and death.

LONDON AUG. 14. On Sunday last an attorney of Lincoln-Inn was married to a gentlewoman aged 80 two years; who was, withal, so infirm, that it was the work of two or three people to support her while the ceremony was performed.

At the Assizes at Durham were try'd J. Brown and Gr. Richardson, the one a butler, and the other a gardner, for attempting to poison their master William Cartwood, Esq; by putting arsenick into his chocolate, and they were both found guilty, and sentenc'd to close imprisonment, one for five years, and the other for three; to stand four times in the pillory, and to be whipt ten times round the market place.

They write from Lincoln, that on Friday the 30th past, one Bishop was hang'd there for the horrid murder of his own mother on the 10th of June last. It appear'd by the evidence that he rose out of bed where he lay with his wife, and went into the room where his mother was in bed, and cut her throat most inhumanly, and afterwards stabb'd her three times, under the left pap, and once under the right: The cause of it was her refusing to yield up to him an estate of about 100 £. a year that she enjoy'd, which was to decend to him after her death; tho' otherwise she was a most indulgent mother: He also cut a man across the belly so dangerously, that part of the omentum or crawl came out, which being expos'd to the air some time before it was dress'd, the surgeon was forced to cut off as much as weigh'd four ounces; notwithstanding which, in five weeks time he was perfectly cured, and the man appear'd at the Assizes as an evidence against the murtherer.

We hear that complaints has been lately made of a poor woman who perished merely for want in Wesminster Gatehouse, where she was detained only for her fees, as was reported by the coroner's Warrant.

On the 5th instant a gentlewoman of Ham near Stratford in Essex, who has long been disorder'd in her mind, though in good circumstances, murder'd her own child, a girl about nine years old, by strangling her; after which she told her neighbours of it with little fear of punishment, as if she had done no harm. For this unnatural crime she was committed next day to Chelmsford Goal, where we hear she has some intervals of sober reflection, in which she discovers such a remorse of her barbarity, in shedding the innocent blood of her dear little angel, as she calls her, that she abhors the sight of her guilty hands, wishing they were cut off; and that she has since attempted to murder her self, by running a fork into her throat. The coroner's inquest has sat on the body of the child, and brought it in an act of lunacy.

CANTERBURY AUG. 21. The magistrate in this city, as also those of Faversham, have forbid the county people both from bringing to town or selling in the market all sorts of plumbs, several people having di'd in those places by eating that sort of fruit, which, it seems thro' the excessive rains proves very unholsome this season.

SARUM AUG. 21. At Barford, four miles from hence, a notable encounter lately happened about a Maypole; A neighbouring gentleman suspecting it was stole out of his woods, came in the night with a large posse to carry it off; but the inhabitants being alarmed, rose upon them, and tho' they rallied twice, at last gave them an entire defeat, and sent them back with many broken heads.

LONDON AUG. 24. We hear that the government is going to erect at Port Royal in South Carolina, in order to be a security to our trade in its return thro' the Gulf of Florida.

LONDON AUG. 30. About the middle of last week, a very odd accident happened at the Lady Killagrew's, relict of the late Admiral of that name, within two miles of St. Alban's. An ass that had gone in the wheel to draw water fourteen years, now grown old and peevish had no mind to work; and being forced into the wheel by a man whose business it had been to put him in for that space of time, he got out in a fury, fastened his teeth in the calf of the man's leg and tore it to pieces. The man cry'd out, but no body heard him; and the ass came again, sucked his blood, and he died on Saturday morning. The ass was shot immediately.

LONDON SEPT. 1. On Sunday night last some robbers made an attempt upon a house at the corner of Gutter Lane in Cheapside, who having made therein a breach, to their great mortification, found it to be an empty one, and so went off as wisely considering an old philosophical maxim, viz. That out of nothing can come nothing.

LONDON SEPT. 2. There is advice from the ship Martha of London, Capt. Bull, who went commander, died in the voyage to Guinea, that in their passage from that coast to Jamaica on the slave trade, the Negroes had form'd a design to surprise the crew in the night time, but being timely discover'd were prevented after 20 of them being kill'd by the ship's company.

LONDON SEPT. 4. On Tuesday about three or four a clock in the evening, during the hurry of the sessions, twelve convicts that lay for transportation, and two others that lay for fines, found the opportunity to cut the chains that fastened the main door on Common side of Newgate, and to make their escape, the lock and keys being sent to be mended above ten days before; and if the lower door had not been immediately secured, many more would have escaped, and had goal delivery their own way.

LONDON SEPT. 9. Last night between 11 and 12 a clock a most dreadful fire broke out upon London Bridge, near the corner of Tooley-Street, and rag'd with inexpressible violence for five hours, till it had consumed all the houses on both sides of that part of the bridge, which is without the gate towards Borough of Southwark, The gate it self is a stone building, and it happily prove an impregnatable rampart to restrain the progress of the flames, which in all probability, would otherwise have destroyed the whole pile of buildings upon the famous structure, the houses all built of wood. 'Tis said to have begun in a haberdasher's house, by means of some shavings left by the workmen, who had been new sashing the front; the master of the family at some time being out of town. The bridge by the fall of the timber and rubbish render's impassible, for coach and carts. At the beginning of the fire, the tyde being low, and they wanted water to supply the engines, what they got out was full of mud that chocked them; the damage was very great.

LONDON SEPT. 11. Col. Turner about 18 years ago receiv'd some hurt on his forehead, a bunch grew thereon which was suppos'd to have occasioned the distemper of the falling sickness; he had been for late years importun'd to have it open'd, but would not consent to it, till a few days ago, when an eminent surgeon made an operation with that success, that he found the point of a sword in his skull of an inch long, which he took out, and since that the colonel is very easy, and in a fair way of recovery.

On Wednesday morning a butcher in Long-Lane, near Moorfields, hanged himself out of discontent, (as some say,) for having found another in bed with his wife.

LONDON SEPT. 11. We hear from Edinburgh, That the brewers of that city have at last consented to brew; for that the people will no longer be under an in'ispensible necessity of living sober.

LONDON SEPT. 16. Yesterday two baliffs, who had a writ against a worsted thrower in Fetherstone-Street Bunhilfields, went and knocked at the door his wife, not knowing what they were, open'd it, but upon rushing in hastily, she mistrusted their designs and endeavour'd to oppose their going farther, whereupon they threw her down the entry, and kick'd her in a most barbarous manner, till she was all over bloody, then arrested her husband, but a crowd gathering about the house, they were secur'd and carried by the constable to a Justice of Peace.

Mathias Cater, an under steward of the Right Honourable the Earl of Suffolk, having been convicted at the Assizes at Maidstone of robbing his said master, and thereupon order'd for Transportation, attempted some days since to make his escape by breaking the goal, but was prevented by the keepers; however, he was resolv'd either to effect it, or to perish in the enterprize, and the latter happen'd, for last week as he renew'd the attempt he was shot dead by one of those, whose business was to keep him in safe custody.

A Valet de chambre to one of the Lords of the treasury has been dismiss'd his place, and is ordered to be prosecuted with the utmost severity, for permitting a tallow-chandler to conceal a great quantity of candles in the houses of his master, to defraud the King of his duty, where there were seized by the officers of the excise.

LONDON SEPT. 18. On Friday se-nnight one Rowler, a bricklayer, being at work on a house in St. Martin's Court, his wife with a young child in her arms, came to ask him for money for subsistence for his family. Whereupon he threw her down a shilling from the top of the house, with this answer: God damn her, he would knock out her brains if ever she came to ask him for anymore. Which words were no sooner spoken, but he fell down, and dash's out his brains against the pavement.

We hear the famous ostrich died a few days ago in Strourbridge-Fair, and that his body was afterwards dissected at Cambridge by Mr. Warren the surgeon. He cut about 6 inches deep in fat. Many stones and nails, and a half pence, and some pieces of silver, all turned black, were taken out of the crop and gizzard. The silver, especially about the edge.

Yesterday a centinel of the 30th Regiment of Foot Guard received 600 lashes in Hyde-Park for desertion. He had been whipt four times before for the same crime, and had writen a letter to his colonel, saying, if the Court martial would find stripes, he would find back, which impudent letter was yesterday read to the soldiers in Hyde-Park.

Mr. Cockrell, a gentleman of Gloucester City, worth 140 £. per annum, having lately marry'd one Mrs. Abigail Cole who was set up for a West India fortune, possess'd a plantation in Barbados worth 1000 £. per annum, and other fine things, being dress'd in deck'd in a manner answerable thereof; but proving to be only a servant maid without any fortune at all, indicted for a conspiracy in persuading and inducing him, & to marry her; the same was try'd at the Old Bailey, both sides, the jury without going out of Court acquited them both.

LONDON SEPT. 18. We have an account from Grantham in Lincolnshire, that the wife of Mr. Wheeler, of that town, having been in labour 3 days, was taken in a deep swoon insomuch, that her husband thinking her dead, caus'd her to be buried; and one Hanks coming over the church-yard about 2 o'clock next morning perceiving a rumble under ground, ran and called the sexton to open the grave, where they found her deliver'd of two children dead; but perceiving life in the mother, sent immediately to her husband to come and bring necessities & assistance to get her home, where they put her in a warm bed, whereby bleeding, and other means, she came to her senses in about 24 hours.

LONDON SEPT. 29. On Monday six women and three men, commonly called Gypsies, who go pilfering about the countries, under pretence of telling people's fortunes, were by Sir Francis Forbes, committed to Fleet-Street Bridwell; there to be kept at hard labour.

On Tuesday last a remarkable accident happened at a house in Curley-Street near Lincoln's Inn Fields; where a poor woman, being at washing, was taken with a fit, and her head falling into the tub of water, she suffocated and died immediately.

Two persons having collecting a quantity of corn under pretence of leasing, the man that kept the Crown-Alehouse on Turbam-Green, in a jocular manner examin'd them how they came by it, upon which they presently fell upon him, and beat him in such a violent manner, that he died the next day. His wife thereupon Miscarried, and died; and both husband and wife were interr'd last Sunday at Chiswick, and a suitable sermon preached upon the occasion.

FALMOUTH SEPT. 30. On Tuesday last we had a violent storm of wind at S. W. but no danger was done to the shipping in the port. I am sorry to acquaint you that there are six ships lost at Mount's Bay, and most of the men drown'd viz. Capt. Newels, Capt. Lobbs, and

Capt. Brewers, three colliers, and a Norway ship laden with timber and deal.

LONDON OCT. 2. The storm last Tuesday was se'nnight has done a great deal more mischief than was at first reported; it was so very strong, that in places which were exposed, the longest trees have been rooted up. They begin already to tell us from Holland, that a great many ships have been cast away upon the coast, but they could not yet give any particular account of them, but supposed most of them were Dutchmen.

LONDON OCT. 9. We have an account of sixteen ships and vessels being lost on the northern and western coast of this Kingdom, with near 300 men, in the late stormy weather, besides several damag'd; some having lost their masts, and others their anchors and cables, particularly between Nore and the Downs.

Two Englishmen having robbed their grandfather, a watch-maker, of several watches in London, fled to France, and was there secured and put into prison, by the application of the English ambassador to the Duke of Bourbon.

LONDON OCT. 9. The distress of the poor hay makers, who came from different distant parts, to get their bread by the sweat of their brows, has been so great, occasion'd by the late extraordinary wet weather, that several worthy merchants and other substantial tradesmen, who use the Exchange, were pleased on Wednesday last, to make a very handsome collection for their relief, which they then order'd to be equally distributed by proper officers.

A noted woolen draper in town, this week, lost his coachman, his daughter having run away, and committed marriage with him.

LONDON OCT. 11. Last Tuesday two of the Stokes Bay merchants were attached by the Government for near 20,000 £. each, upon information of frauds committed by them; and, for want of sufficient bail, were next day sent to Winchester Goal under a good guard of dragoons. This has put our smugglers into a terrible fright, and every one is providing for his own safety.

PORTSMOUTH OCT. 14. Last Sunday, a woman big with child, dropt down, and dy'd in the street of Golport. It seems she came from London in a waggon, and had taken little or no sustenance on the road, and having no money, no body cared to take her in; so that the poor creature perished purely through want and inhumanity.

The account by post from Scotland, take notice of the defence made by the Glasgow prisoners; They all alleged, amongst the rest, that the city of Glasgow during the unnatural rebellion, has exerted themselves for the service of the Government; and that particularly some of the prisoners had given eminent instances of their loyalty to his Majesty, To which it was answer'd by the Earl of Isla, "That if the inhabitants of Glasgow, or even the prisoners, had assisted in subduing his Majesty's enemies, sure they had not thereby conquered his Majesty, and acquired a right to assume regal power, and spurn at his authority when they pleased; to rob his subjects, to break his peace, to attack his troops, and cloud and ruffle the tranquility of his Majesty's serene reign; but that they and others, by their example, must be taught, they to yield obedience for once, does not exempt them from the proper correction of the law, when they shall dare thereafter to attempt any thing in opposition to it." The Criminal Council sat on the 4th instant at eight in the morning till six next morning.

LONDON OCT. 16. A gentleman travelling lately at a very considderable distance from his own home, had the misfortune to be thrown off his horse just at his entrance into a small village, and was so stunn'd with the fall, that he lay as dead. The people of the place came to his assistance, took him up, and put him in a warm bed, where having brought him a little to himself again, he desired a surgeon might be sent for, upon which the Parson of the parish came to let him blood, and searched to see if any bone was broke, at the same time acquainting him they had no other surgeon. The gentleman in a few hours, being somewhat easier, desired the people about him that some body might come to write two or three letters for him to his friends, to acquaint them with his condition, upon which the Parson of the parish was again sent for, as the man that could write the best of the parish. The next day the gentleman recollecting some proper remedy for a bruise, desired it might be fetch'd at the apothecary's for him. They told him they would see if the Parson had any such thing for they had no other apothecary among them, and the good man coming to visit him that day, found him in a fever, and exhorted him to expect the worst that could happen. As soon as he was gone the patient order'd a lawyer to be sent for from some town on order to make his will, but they fetch'd the Parson back to him, assuring him that he understood the law as well as the Gospel, and they had no other lawyer come into the place for these many years, and he accordingly drew up the will. Besides these good offices he was very diligent in praying by him, discharging all duties of a Pastor, and took so much care of his patient, that he sent him home in perfect health.

LONDON OCT. 19. On Friday last the gentlemen of St. Oliver's Southwark, distributed a considerable sum of money among the sufferers by the late fire on London Bridge, which was raised by a voluntary contribution among themselves and the neighbouring parishes; at which time 17 persons whose circumstances were narrow, had their whole losses made up to them; and twenty one others, whose losses amounted to the sum of 1755 £. 7 s. and 6 d. received 3 s. in the pound, they being better able to sustain there respective losses.

LONDON OCT. 21. We have an account from Taunton-Dean, That the weavers have rose in a body, to the number of 1500, and committed sad outrage for 3 or 4 miles round that town, and coming with a design to plunder the same, the combers joining with the town people, were equal to 'em in number, engag'd and routed them, making 30 prisoners, 6 whereof were ringleaders and sent to goal, and the rest bound over. That several hundred were very much maim'd and one killed.

LONDON NOV. 6. On the 28th in the night-time, 5 convicts for transportation in the city goal found means to make a break in the wall, and 4 of them made their escape; but Long Will, who was convicted on his own confession for stealing linen from the hedges while drying being an uncommon size, stuck in the hole, not able to go forward or backward, tho' naked; but one of them having some remmorse of conscience, return'd back again before daylight and wak'd the jailor, who found Long Will fast in the hole, and with much difficulty got him out, but not without the loss of a good deal of skin.

We hear a melancholy account from Devonshire, viz. That Sir William Pole, a member of Parliament, having a fine pack of dogs for the fox, some days ago, in chasing one of those creatures 9 or 10 miles over the downs very close, bay-yard at last betook himself to the cliff and rocks next to the sea, when his horse in full speed ran off a precipice near 300 yards high, and were both dash'd to pieces.

LONDON NOV. 11. On Monday last Captain Stackpole one of the persons lately taken into custody for inlisting men for the service of the King of Spain, was committed to Newgate.

LONDON NOV. 20. Yesterday 49 convicts under sentence of transportation were put on board, for the American plantations.

LONDON NOV. 30. On Friday night last come on a tryal before the Lord Chief Justice Raymond, between one Pierce plaintiff and an eminent Quaker at Chelmsford defendent, for a criminal conversation with the plaintiff's wife. It was proved and admitted that the Quaker and Mrs. Pierce, did lie together in one bed; But it appears that Mr. Pierce, the husband, in whose name the suit was carried on, was now absent in the East Indies, and that his wife carried the Quaker to a house of evil repute, whereupon the jury gave a verdict for the defendent.

The Scotch mail that was expected in last Friday, did not arrive, the floods being out in a violent manner between Newark and Grantham; insomuch that the post-boy narrowly escaped himself, but his horse and bag of letters were lost.

LONDON DEC. 1. The following tryal lately had at the Old Bailey, being very remarkable for the propiety of the evidence. We desire our readers to accept of it word for word, as we find it publish'd in the sessions papers.

Jane Johnson alias Price alias Pierce, of Bishopsgate, was indicted for stealing a pettycoat, three mobs, a sausnet-hood, and a child's frock, the goods of Jane Benson thus desposed: Mary Lee was my lodger, and the prisoner having some acquantance with her, came to see her now and then; and so it fell out that she came that day as I was tending a child; and the child was a little cross vixen thing, and it had befoul'd itself lamentationly: So says the prisoner to me, Mother Benson, says she, you look as if you was very weary and sleepy; I would have you go and take a nap, and lay the child by you, and I will wash its things the while. And so I went; but when I waked, I found that this wicked jade was gone, and my cloaths were gone too, it put me into a strange conformation, for I never respected she would serve me so. The next witness deposed to the effect, My name is Mary Lee, and tho' I say it, there is never a woman in the parish, that takes more care for an honest liverlyhood than my'self, I turn my hand to any of thing to get a penny: Sometimes I sell things in Leadenhall Market; and sometimes at another. We market women are up early and late, and work hard for what we have: We stand all weathers, and go thro' thick and thin. It is well known that I was never the woman that spared my carcass; and if I spend three farthings now and then, it is nothing but what is my own. I get it honestly, and I so not care who knows it; for something to cheer the spirits, between whiles, and keep out of the wet and cold; alackaday, I would never do: We should never be able to hold it, we should never go thro stich with it, so as to keep body and soul together. But as for this Jenny Johnson the prisoner, she coming sometimes for a quartern to the same shops that I made use of, we now and then had a dish of cheer together and so we became pretty well acquainted; whereof she came to see me two or three times; and of all the times in the world, she happened to come that day as my landlady lost her things. Now after that she comes to me at a certain place, and there we had two or three quarterns of such simple stuff as we poor souls are glad to drink. And from thence we went to another friend's house, and there truly she would needs treat me with a quartern of right French brandy; whereof I wondered at it, because we had had but very indifferent market that day. Oh! says she, I do not want for money; I have got above a crown in my pocket; and so we went to another friend's house and another, and another to that; and so by way of discourse about this and that and t'other; and talking about my landlady, and how she lost her things, and all that; Why says Jenny, says she, as for your landlady's three mobs and a handkerchief, I sold them all for a shilling. The jury acquitted her.

LONDON DEC. 10. Last Saturday morning the wife of Mr. Clarke, a clock-maker in Fetter Lane, having been at Clare Market, and returning home, a country cart which was at a shop next door in Portugal-Street, unloading goods, was set on running by one of the horses taking a sudden start, and was carried upon the pavement, where the cart squeezed the said unfortunate gentlewoman against the wall, and broke one of her legs and an arm before any help could be got, and bruised her in such a misarable manner that she expired in a few minutes. Her corpse was carried home in a chair to her husband and four children. The coroner's inquest having sat yesterday upon the body, brought in their verdict, accidental death.

LONDON DEC. 10. An odd sort of cheat was put in practice some days since, upon a woman that lets lodging in Red Lion Street in Holbourn: A young gentleman who lodged in her house being indisposed, went out of town for the air, with design to stay about a month; there came in his absence, three persons to the landlady, pretending to be his relation, and gave a very particular account of his sickness and death at Kickmansworth in Hertfordshire, the place he had told her he was going to. The woman being thus deluded with the story delivered them all his effects, and suffer'd them to take possession of everything belonging to the supposed deceased, to the value of about 200 pounds; and in four days after, the gentleman came to town, when to his infinite surprize, he found his lodging entirely stripp'd, and himself robbed of all he had.

LONDON DEC. 16. The Loving Brothers, Capt. Watson, from London to Figora, was at anchor in the hurricane last Tuesday se'nnight between the Nore and Margate, but soon parted from her anchor, and run upon the red sand; and was judged by the crew to have bulged, who took to their boat, but had the misfortune to break the oars; they afterwards kept driving at sea till Thursday, when the Sarum, an outward bound East Indiaman took them up, the mate and sailor, and a passenger died in the boat. The ship floated and was found by some fishing smacks, and by them towed up the river; and on Tuesday the gentlemen that shipt the goods in it, had a meeting, gave the three masters of the fishing smacks who brought her in 300 £. for their salvage and the goods, she being very rich, and a handsome gratitude will no doubt be given by the owner of the said ship.

1726

LONDON JAN. 3. Friday last a journeyman to a harness maker, in Swallow Street, being put in to St. James's Round House, for assaulting a woman, hanged himself dead in a few hours after.

Last week several felons on the common side of Newgate had form'd a design to escape, having furnished themselves with files, saws, and other implements necessary for such an enterprize, but were discovered by some of their fellows, and the principal contrives of design were laid in irons, and put into the dungeon.

There is advices from the country, that in several places, the stage-coaches, post boys and passengers, having been stopp'd by the floods, caus'd by the late great rains, and many of the places the roads are entirely wash'd away.

LONDON JAN. 18. On Friday last the Grand Jury for the city of London made the following presentment, which was order'd by the Court forth with to be printed and Publish'd.

We the Grand Jury of the City of London, sworn to enquire for our Sovereign Lord the King, and the body of the said city, at the Guildhall, London on Wednesday the 11th of this instant January, Anno Domini 1726, and in the twelfth year of the reign of our Sovereign Lord George, King of Great Britain, &c.

Imprimis. We present, as a grievous nuisance, the great number of beggars, shoe-cleaners, and other idle and wandering persons that daily frequent and pester the publick streets of this city, to the great disturbance of the citizens, and all other persons passing to and fro through the said streets upon their lawful occasions; The said beggars, and other idle wanderers, interupting and stopping such persons for to give them alms, and pretending to sell some trifling thing for to cover their asking for alms; and who daily do molest the shop keepers and inhabitants of this city, by standing or lying continually at their doors, and disturbing them and their customers in their traffick and business. Which great numbers of beggars, shoe-cleaners, &c. both men and women with their young children, if not timely prevented, may become a heavy charge at the inhabitants of this city; The said number having of late greatly increased in this city, as we apprehend, from the care and diligence of his Majesty's Justiced in the counties lying round about the town, by putting the laws in execution against such strollers and beggars, and in setting them to work, which so affrighten them, that, rather than comply with the law, they quit their parishes and fly to this city for shelter; and through the great remissness and negligence of the constables and beadles of this city, by not apprehending and seizing such idle vagrants and wanderers, and not carrying them before proper magistrates, to be dealt with according to the law. We therefore humbly recommend to the Honourable, Court, that such effectual measures may be taken for obliging the several parish and ward officers in this city to be diligent in the apprehending and seizing all such beggars and wanderers, and to carry them before the magistrates of this city, that they may be sent to their proper parishes they belong to, or the House of Correction in this city, to be punish'd according to their deserts. And as we doubt not the care and readiness of the worthy magistrates of this city to put the laws in execution against such vagabonds, so we hope, from the methods they shall take to oblige the inferior officers of this city to do their duty herein, the growing nuisance may be redress'd.

Dated at the Sessions-House at Justice Hall in the Old Baily, this 14th day of January 1726.

LONDON JAN. 18. Yesterday the sessions ended at the Old Baily, where two malefactors, viz. Samuel Sells, late a summoning baliff at Enfield, and John Mattocks a victualler in Newgate Street received sentence of death for a robbery on the highway near Shacklewell.

John Moor, convicted of a notorious riot and assault in the house of Mr. Hall a victualler, at the end of Princess-Street near Stock-Market, in opposing a peace-officer, and firing a pistol whereby a person is dangerously wounded, was fined 50 £. order'd to remain two years in Newgate, and afterwards to give security for his good behaviour for three years.

LONDON JAN. 18. A footman for a violent assault upon his mistress by running after her with a blunderbuss, to extort money from her, consented for transportation.

LONDON JAN. 22. On Saturday morning last between five and six (when the watch were gone off) some rogues broke into the house of Rt. Hon. Lord Chief Justice Eyre in Holborn-Row, Lincoln-Inn Fields, and they stole two cases of silvershafted knives, together with his lordship's hat and gloves, &c. that lay on the table.

LONDON JAN. 25. Last night the clerks of the Admiralty sat up all night, to send orders to the guard ships, to impress men to fill the complement, and this day the board of Admiralty sat to grant commissions to sea captains, in order of augmenting the Royal Navy in the Mediteranean and the Baltick, the better to prevent a new war, and the King has promised to assist the Dane and Swede, against the Muscovites in the case of a new war should happen.

LONDON FEB. 5. From Hull, that on the 28th of January a fire broke out in the night, at Mr. Waller's in this town; the family (tho' all in bed) were saved by ladders; The house was burnt down, and some adjoining houses much damaged, but by the use of three engines that play'd upon the fire, further mischief was prevented. Last Thursday one Derfley was committed to Newgate, for endeavoring to prevail with one Loyd to rob and murder Mr. Bampston, that lately kept the Oxford-Arms Inn in Warwick Lane, who is the said Derfley's kinsman, and to whom he had been exceedingly kind.

BRISTOL FEB. 5. Last week one George Pruett, of Horfield, near this city, was found dead in his bed, with his brains beat out, and three stabbs in his body. How this fatal accident happen'd is not yet known, but a kinsman of his (we are inform'd) was to be his executor, has been examin'd before a justice, but don't hear that they can prove any thing upon him.

They write from Marlborough, that some men are employ'd in digging and clearing the old Roman Well near that place, at the charge of the Earl of Hefort, on account of some pieces of antiquities expected to be found therein.

LEICESTERWORTH IN LEICESTERSHIRE, FEB. 7. Were found lately in this field, by two men digging of clay, 60 silver, and 8 or 10 copper medals, of the Roman coin; the silver ones being about the bigness of a six-pence, but much thicker, and the copper very near as large as half a crown, but above twice as thick: When the silver medals were made clear, the impressions appear'd very plain, and they are of Julius Caesar, Trajan, Vespusian, &c. but the copper ones were much defaced.

LONDON FEB. 7. From Porthmouth letters of Feb. 1. This place is like to be the scene of naval business and news for some time. The six guard ships here have orders to get their highest complements of men, to be dock'd and made ready for the sea with all possible dispatch; To this purpose they began to impress men here last Wednesday, and pretty well clear'd this and the neighbouring towns, and all the merchant ships here that day; and the next morning several crews were sent on the same business to the Isle of White, Southampton, Lymington, Pod, &c. have required 2,500 men more than they had, it will be some time before they get so many.

LONDON FEB. 8. A footman of Mr. Lamb at Hackney, having been on horseback on an errand, upon his return home went to set up his horse in the stable, and was there surprized by some rogues, who cut his throat, and broke his scull in several places. The coachman happening to go into the stable some time afterwards, found him lying at the point of death with a bloody hammer near him. It is known that he had a watch and four guineas about him, which the villains robbed him of. He died the next morning having laid all the time speechless and insensible. We hear, his Majesty will offer his most gracious pardon to any person concerned, for that they discover their accomplices, so that they be brought to justice: and that a reward of 50 guineas will be offered besides.

Mr. Ford, a young gentleman that was to have gone super-cargo of an East India ship lately sail'd for India, having absented himself, and been advertised in the news-papers, was, on Thursday last, about one in the morning, found laying across the channel of Bow-street, Covent Garden, in the agonies of death, by a watchman. When he was taken up, he cried, Dan Nelly, how could you serve me so? and expired.

Last Friday the coroner's inquest sat on the body of Mr. Grower, killed by Major Holby at the Castle Tavern in Drury-Lane and brought in their verdict wilful murder.

Also the same night the said Major was apprehended in Golden Square and committed to New-Prison, in order to his further examination.

Last Thursday about two in the morning the Earl of Hilborough coming in a chair up Piccadilly, with one footman before him, was set upon by two foot robbers, one of whom presented a pistol to the foremost chairman's head, who retiring knocked the villain down. Upon which my Lord come out of the chair, and drew his sword;

when the other rogue fir'd, and shot one of the chairmen, near the left shoulder; the shot came out, and re-entered his left breast, and penetreated between the flesh and breast bone, and lodg'd near the right pap. The rogues made their escape, and the wounded chairman was put under the care of Mr. Kirkham, an eminent surgeon.

A Kirk preacher in the country between this and Glasgow having been accused of adultry, the matter is examining into by the brotherhood, and notwithstanding he was catch'd in the fact, 'tis not doubted but he will be clear'd by the-means of a deritable fellow-feeling.

LONDON FEB. 22. On Saturday a private centinel of the Second Regiment of Foot Guards having been whipt there several days, pursuant to his sentence at the Court Martial for striking several times in the guard room at Whitehall the Rt. Hon. the Earl of Albemarle, his colonel, then on guard, was drumm'd out of the regiment with a halter about his neck, and, we hear, he had received sentence of death, but that the same was mitigated at the request of the said noble Lord.

LONDON MARCH 12. On Monday night and Tuesday morning last the Spring tide was so high in the River Thames, that many score acres of land were over-flown, 'tis said, it has not been known to rise so high for these twenty years past.

LONDON MARCH 12. A fortnight ago Mr. Charles Howard, keeper of Hampton-Court House Park, who is famous for taking and removing red and fallow deer from the forest, chase, park, or paddock, to another, did, by his safe and excellent method take and remove from Dawley Park in Middlesex, thirty one loads of deer, being upward of four hundred, to a park of Charles Eversfield Esq; at Horsham in Sussex very safe, the likes was never seen in that county before.

This week the said Mr. Howard has taken and removed eleven waggon loads of deer from Watlington Park in Oxfordshire, to a new park lately made by Governour Pitts at Swallowfield in Berkshire, without the loss of one deer.

LONDON MARCH 19. On Friday night about 12 a clock a terrible fire broke out near the Hermitage Bridge, which in six hours time, burnt about 80 or 100 houses, and 5 or 6 ships.

LONDON MARCH 26. On Wednesday, the thrice notorious robbers and murderers, mention'd by name in his Majesty's late proclamation, viz. William Blewer, Emanuel Dickenson, and Thomas Berry, who were apprehended in Holland, were brought over hither on board the Delight sloop, Capt. Taulor, from Rotterdam, which came to her mooring off S. Katherine's: They were in custody of three of his Majesty's messengers, an they were handcuff'd and double iron'd, and had a Dutch guard besides. They seem much harden'd in wickedness to a surprizing degree, and put on an air of unconcern, and even of mirth, seeing a press-gang at S. Kathrine's, they jocularly call'd to them to put out, and impress them for his Majesty's service. A file of musketeers were sent from the Tower to receive them from on board, who in two boats, one each side of that in which the messenger carry'd them, went with them through Bridge up to Wesminster; where being examined before Justice Blackerby and Justice Chalk, they were committed to Newgate, whither they were brought under guard the same night between eight and nine o'clock, and chain'd down in the condemn'd hold, from whence they will be carry'd to be try'd at Kingston Assizes, which begin the 20th instant.

DARTMOUTH MARCH 29. Yesterday came into the harbour a yacht under Dutch colours, the better to decoy the pilot boat on board; The yacht men had Dutch caps on their heads, and by their disguise impressed 7 or 8 seamen for the service, and carried them away to Plymouth.

LONDON MARCH 29. On Thursday night between 11 & 12 a dreadful fire broke out (as we hear) at a sail-maker's near the Hermitage, Wapping; which burnt very fercely all night before it could be extinguished, and consumed according to computation, about 100 houses, besides several ships, which laid on the shoar, the tide being out.

LONDON APRIL 2. The Neptune galley of Bristol, Capt. Cumby, bound from Leghorn to London, founder'd 120 leagues to the westward of Lisbon, the people were saved by a French ship from Martinico, and carried to Nantes, which fortunately came by as the Neptune was sinking: She was very rich, her cargo consisting of 50 tuns of fine marble, 1500 barrels of raisons, 15 buts of argol, 30 hogsheads of capers, 400 barrels of anchovies, 150 chests of soap, 10 tuns of brimstone, 180 chest of wine, 45 jars of oyl, 100 parcels of goods, 18 bales of silk.

LONDON APRIL 9. The Comptom Indiaman from Fort St. George, brings advice, that the pyrates at Madagascar had used the natives in so barbarous a manner, that it occasioned their rising upon them; so that they were all distroy'd by them except 12 who made their escape up in the country where they are likely to spend their time very indifferently.

LONDON APRIL 12. Thursday last a single highwayman, well mounted, robb'd 5 coaches on Hounsloy-Heath, taking a considerable booty from the passengers.

LONDON APRIL 16. A farmer who had newly received 30 £. was attacked by three highwaymen near Weybridge, but he had so hid his money that he carried it safe off, and the rogue got but half a crown of him.

On the same night the same week a rogue convey'd himself into a house in Clifford-street near Burlington-Garden, in which the Hon. Mr. Cornwallis, brother to the Lord of that name, had lodgings, and attempted to break into Mr. Cornwalis's chamber, he was heard, and the family being alarm'd, he took up stairs into the garret, and from the window he got over the houses and made his escape, leaving his shoes behind him in the entry.

LONDON APRIL 16. Yesterday was se'nnight Mr. Ferguson, a pensioner of Chelsea College, and formerly a servant in the Royal Scotch Greys, was murdered by two foreigners (said to be cooks) in the Five Fields; who quarrelling at an ales-house, and he upon the patrol being called to appease them, one of them stabbed him in the left pap with a case-knife and then ran away; the other was taken and committed to the Gatehouse.

The coroner's inquest having sat on the body of the above Chelsea pensioner, have brought in their verdict wilful murder.

Yesterday was se'nnight a fire broke out at a place called Feltham near Hounslow, by which three houses were burnt down. 'Tis said to have been occasion'd by a maid throwing out a basket of ashes in a yard adjoining the dwelling-house.

LONDON APRIL 26. Yesterday the Court of Admiralty was held at Old Baily, for the tryal of offences committed on the high seas, within the jurisdiction of the Admiralty of England, when Capt. Jeane, of Bristol, was try'd for the murder of his servant, in the most barbarous manner heard of, about two years ago, in a voyage from Carolina to Bristol, and being found guilty, he received sentence of death.

Letters received from Lisbon say that a ship was arrived from the Coast of Africa, the master whereof reported, that the English fort at Gambos in Africa was blown up, the magazine by accident taking fire; and that several persons were killed thereby.

LONDON MAY 5. The report of the condemn'd malefactors in Newgate that was to have to the King's Court yesterday was put off till this day.

LONDON MAY 5. Two of the said malefactors under the sentence of death died yesterday in the condemn'd hold within an hour of one another; viz. Thomas Wood condemned for the murder of Mr. John Hiyers, and Jan Varwick condemned for felony and burglary, who were immediately carried into the place call'd the Pump-House, for the coroner's inquest to sit upon the bodies. We heard the former show'd, to outward appearance, grave prominent contrition all the while he was in the said goal, for the part he acted in that barbarous murder, saying in the effect of his being intoxicated in liquor, begging mercy of God for so heinous a crime, owing the justice of the Court a condemnation, and his sentence wishing he might only live off the sentence of the law should be executed upon him for a terror of others.

LONDON MAY 7. The Baltick Squardron were arrived at Copenhagen, several sodomites convicted and order'd executed, and a dozen others committed for sodomy.

LONDON MAY 14. A servant maid belonging to a person of distinction in Chelsea, has been committed to the Gate-House Westminster, for secretly putting a quantity of Spanish flies into some ale, and giving it to a glazier, her sweatheart, by way of love powder, whereby his life is in great danger. And another woman, who was assisting in the mischief, is bound over to answer it at the sessions.

They write from St. Albans, that some days since an old woman of the Parish of Burnt-Pelhath in that county, was by vertue of a Justice of the peace, apprehended for a witch, but being brought, in order of her commitment, before another justice, when several gentlemen were in company, he acquitted her at first sight, have the opinion of all the gentlemen to back him, That she was too homely for a witch. The report, however, was immediately spread about the country, and it being the opinion of the learned, That none but the young and the handsome are capable of being witches, it is said, that thereupon several young pretty ladies of the said parish, were so alarm'd, that they absconded upon it, as apprehensive of being taken up for bewitching several of the King's subjects.

LONDON MAY 14. Last week a gardner at Elton in Kent, bought a piece of ground of a widow neighbour; and two days after pulling down an old shed, that was on the ground, in digging up the earth he found 2 earthen pots full of silver, and a small purse in one of the pots full of gold, in all to the value of about 200 £. It being noised about by one of the gardner's servant, who assisted him in digging, the woman who has 4 children, lays claim to the treasure, and they have begun a law-suit about it.

LONDON MAY 22. The press for seamen continue still so hot, that many who had protections, and a considerable number of watermen belonging to the Fire-Insurance-Office, who on that account used to be excepted to sea service, have been taken up. 'Tis talk'd that 4 regiments are soon expected to Spithead or Portsmouth from Ireland, in order to embark with a detatchment out of the foot guards, on board Sir John Jennings squadron, who is now equipping with more than ordinary diligence.

LONDON JUNE 7. They write from Fort William in Scotland, that tho' the garrison there had kept the Highlanders very quiet, and had prevented their committing any violence for almost all the year, yet a few nights before, 50 or 60 of them fell upon and destroyed the salmon fishery, belonging to the Duke of Gordon, being set on, and supposed, by certain persons who maligned the same. They staved and turned adrift all the boats, and cut their nets, and beat the fishermen who endeavoured to with stand them, in an outragious manner. A night or two after the mischief, a gentleman in the same neighbourhood had 12 of his calves killed by some of the same sort of people who cut all their throats, and left them dead on the place: They were in hopes the garrison at Fort William would be able to take some of the offenders.

From Devizes, that they had a violent storm of hail and rain, which in a small time, made a great flood, some of the stones measured 4 inches about.

From Stroud, that there fell hail stones which measured 6 or 7 inches round, and that the damage done to the windows, &c. in said town amount to 100 £.

From Preston upon Stower, that Mr. John Smith had 4 cows struck dead with lightning under an elm tree in his yard, the bark of the tree being like dried hops, and broke off in several places.

The savage boy that was taken last winter in the forest of Hamelen, walking upon his hands and feet, running up the trees, and feeding upon grass, and was presented to the King of Herenhausen, is brought over here; and yesterday se'nnight was carried into the drawing room at St. James's to be viewed by the whole assembly. He is supposed to be about 15 years of age, and is under the care of Dr. Arhurtnot.

LONDON JUNE 18. An unlucky accident happened at Lesingham, on Tuesday morning the 7th instant, which had like to have proved fatal. One Richard Lane, a widower, who had courted a gentleman's servant of this town, but the maid for some time past having slighted him, and declar'd she would not marry him; he seeing the girl come from a fair which was kept at Ingham the day before, behind a young man, took an opportunity to lurk about her master's house in the night, as soon as the maid open'd the door in the morning, the said Lane enter'd the house (the rest of the family being in bed) knocked her down twice, and then took a knife and cut her neck in several places; and had cut her from ear to ear, had she not happen'd to put her hand to her throat to save herself, which the villain cut to the bone. The family being alarmed, the rogue fled, and warrants are issued for apprehending him, but as yet is not taken.

LONDON JUNE 29. On Friday last died in his country house in the town of Highgate, Mr. Medez de Costa, one of the oldest Jew merchants in this Kingdom. In the reign of her late Majesty he advanced several large sums of money upon the Government's security, for the support of publick credit. His body, according to the Jewish custom, was the same night decently interr'd in the Jew's Burying-ground at Mile End.

LONDON JULY 2. They write from Canterbury, That a Scotsman having projected a leather boat, to be carried in a hankerchief, in which he lately went off to sea at Deal near a league, to the amazement of the spectators, came last week to that city, to shew so great a curiosity; and last Friday in the afternoon being the time appointed to make his experiment, at Coal Harbour, a neighbouring river, abundance of people assembled on the occasion; but were unluckily disappointed by the following accident, viz. The projector being on Coal Harbour Bridge blowing up his boat with a pair of bellows, where some of our chief magistrates, as well as citizens were assembled, and being much crowded, the middle part of the bridge fell in, containing about 6 yards in length, and 3 in breath, by which means about 5 men, women and boys tumbled into the river, as well as the projector and his boat; and tho' it was two yards to the water, and pretty deep, yet, by good providence, all got safe out, suffering no other hurt, than being extremely surpriz'd, well duck'd, and the loss of some hats, wiggs, &c. The projector said, it was an English trick; others in return, took him to be a conjurer. Several waggons loaded with hay pass'd over the said bridge a few days before very safe; The bridge was made of timber, and boarded, with rails on each side which still stand.

Last Friday about ten at night, two sharpers seeing a boy and a man carrying a couple boxes to the Saracen's Head Inn in Friday Street, one of the villains stopp'd without the gate before them, and said I suppose you want the book keeper. Yes, reply'd the man. He is not here, said the fellow, but is just now gone to the White Swan at the lower end of the lane, lay down your things, step thither, and call him. The poor man very innocently complies, lays down the boxes, and orders the boy to stand by them. Soon after he was gone, says one of the rogues to the boy, run after your master with all haste, and give the book keeper this penknife, for a token or else he won't stir. The boy obeys, and so the coast being clear, the rogues march'd off with both the boxes, in which were goods of considerable value.

LONDON JULY 9. The Surat Merchant, Capt. Audiber and an English ship, having arrived lately at Lisbon from Leghorn, was fired at from the Tower and obliged to put out to sea, persuant to a late order there about ships coming from places, where, are reported, some had died of the plague; but our merchants have received letters from Leghorn of a fresher date than the coming away of those ships, which contradict that report, and say it was utterly groundless, they being absolutely free there from any pestilential distemper.

LONDON JULY 18. They write from Dublin, That Capt. Moses Newland was drawn, hang'd and quarter'd at St. Stephen's Green, persuant to his sentence, for inlisting men into foreign service. He was guarded to the place of execution by a troop of horses; and died like a soldier: His quarters were delivered to his friends to be buried.

A woman that for 17 years hath gone in men's apparel, was convicted to the value of 10 d. by the name of George Kelf, alias Cole.

LONDON JULY 18. On Saturday night the sessions ended at the Old Baily; where 8 men and 1 woman received sentence of death for the following crimes, viz. Peter Piercy, for murder, Edward Reynolds and Thomas Smith, for robberies on the highway; Richard Hinton,

Thomas West, John Brakes, and William Flowers, for horse-stealing; John Claxton for returning from transportation; Mary Stanford, for privately stealing some guineas from a gentleman. The last pleading her belly; and was by a jury of matrons, found to be not quick with child.

Margaret Clap, convicted of keeping a disorderly house in Chick Lane, for the entertainment of sodomites, was sentenced to stand in the pillory in West-Smithfield, to pay a fine of 20 marks, and to suffer two years imprisonment.

Thomas Brown and Benjamin Mackintosh, being convicted of sodomitical practices, they were sentenced to stand in the pillory; the former on Moorfield, and the latter in Broad St. Giles's each to pay a fine of 10 marks, and both to suffer a year of imprisonment.

Moll Blewit, widow of the late infamous William Blewit, and Moll Arnold, wife of Quilt Arnold, clerk of the papers to the late Jonathan Wilde, being both convicted to the value of 10 d. for robbing of one Edward Havley; the Court order'd special care to be taken of them, in order to their transportation.

We hear by letters from Portsmouth on the 14th instant that the day before a boat laden with passengers for the Isle of Wight, was overset by the dock-wall boat running foul of it. The waterman and one passenger were drowned, and the rest had met with the same fate, if several wherries had not come out immediately, and took 'em up when nigh expiring; They are now in a fair way of recovery.

LONDON JULY 26. Yesterday Joseph Cutler stood in the pillory at the end of Shooe-Lane, in Fleet-Street, pursuant to his sentence at the last sessions of the Peace at Guild-Hall, for endeavouring to extort money from a shopkeeper in the said street threatning, in case of refusal, to swear sodomy against him. The populace express'd an uncommon abhorrence to the crime, by pelting him with stones and filth, that he bled pleantifully, and fainted away on the pillory, and was carried off for dead.

On Wednesday last, a man of 80 years old, and a woman of the same age, and upwards, enter'd together into the Holy State of Matrimony, at Chelsea Church, And the week before, a man of 105 years of age was married to a woman of 40, at the same church.

LONDON JULY 28. The S. Sea Company have letters from the Greenland masters, that they have taken seventeen whales, and are yet fishing.

LONDON AUG. 4. One of our Greenland ships brought a seahorse as far as the Orkney, which was so tame, that it would follow the men about the deck; but was killed by one of them, who the master had disobliged. It is said to be one of the fine creatures in the watery element; so that the publick has lost one of the greatest curiosities that, perhaps, were ever seen in this nation, by the folly of a sailor.

LONDON AUG. 6. There is brought in one of the Greenland ships the head of a sea lion, of a large-size, which is look'd upon as a great curiosity, the like not having been seen in this country: It is presented to Sir Mane Sloene.

At the Assizes at Lincoln, a petition was signed by 500 glaziers, farmers, &c. setting forth the hardship, on account of the price of wool, was offered to the Grand Jury for concurrence in applying of Irish wool and yarn, but the Grand Jury declined meddling with it, and left it to themselves to apply for relief.

SOMERSETSHIRE AUG. 6. There lately happened near this place the following accident viz. As one Thomas Seldon was riding along the road, the horse startled threw him off, and trod upon his breast; however, he got up and ran after the horse a little ways, and fell down dead.

LONDON AUG. 8. By the Cape Benda galley, lately arrived here from Angola in Guinea, we have advice, that a few days before they set sail from Angola, the mate and two men belonging to another of our gallies, had murdered their captain on shore, and buried him in the sands, and made their escape upon the country to the natives; It is pretended this was occasioned thro' a jealously of the captain's carrying on shore several parcels of coral, belonging to the ship, which sells there for a great price, for which the men, 'tis said, would be accountable out of their wages.

LONDON AUG. 13. There are fifteen Jews and their family's arrived in London, having escaped from the inquisition in Portugal, with one of the officers and have brought with them 60,000 pounds in ingots.

BRISTOL AUG. 13. This morning about 500 weavers assembled together without Lawford's Gate, and rescued two of their trade, who were taken up by the justices warrants the night before and afterwards dismantled the house of Mr. Edgar, on St. Philip's Plain, and he and his wife narrowly escaped out of a back window: After which they proceeded to the house of Stephen Faihout, on the Castle

Ditch, where they forced open his door got into the house, broke his China ware, a fine clock, carried away a silver tankard, broke the windows, and did very considerable damage. About 3 o'clock they march'd thro' the city into Temple Street, where they were joined by a great many more, and they proceeded to Bedminster, a mile out of the city, into the County of Sumerset; where they enter'd the weaver's houses, cutting to pieces the goods in the looms, and burning them into the street; and when they had done, they return'd thro' the city to the place of the first rondezvous, which is in the Suburbs, but in the County of Gloucester. Mr. Littleor, the Adjutant General Will's Regiment, offer'd to assist the civil power, and had order'd a sufficient number of soldiers, who were ready, but none being required, were dismiss'd.

OXFORD AUG. 17. A few days ago the following accident happen'd in a village near this city. A dog-keeper, who had the custody of a gentleman's pack of hounds, went 8 miles upon some business in his neighbourhood, where he was kept two days longer than he at first design'd so that the poor creatures were full 3 days without food, upon his return to see how they did, he entered the yard where they were confin'd, they fell upon him, and tore him to pieces, before anyone come to his assistance.

GLOUCESTER SEPT. 5. They write from Cardiffe, that this day John Humphrey of Bonvilstone, a notorious villain is to be try'd there, who has already confess'd several inhumane murders, robberies, rapes, &c. viz. Stealing from his uncle a Blacksmith, with whom he work'd, several sums of money, which led him to commit the following barbarous rapes and murders, namely, Mary Mills, whom he ravish'd and murder'd, and afterwards robbed the house; Mary Nickol, whom he strangled, and afterwards robb'd the house, Elyzabeth Thomas, widow, who he ravish'd and murder'd, and then took away some silver, &c. He also ravish'd and robb'd a servant maid, when he was on the road, and one Smith's wife: He likewise broke open the house of Mary Evans, of the parish of Lancarvan, and robb'd her, and then ravish'd her. He robb'd one Morgan Evan, of the parish of S. Nicalas, of the highway, of 3 £. 1s. Mary John of Bonvilstone, single woman, he ravish'd and afterwards cut her throat. He further confesses, that he had perjur'd himself, by falsely accusing William Miles, and Thomas Rees, of Bonvilstone aforesaid, by charging them with being concerned in the several murders, they being innocent of the same.

CAMBRIDGE SEPT. 24. There have been a great many robberies committed this Stourbridge-Fair, several upon the coaches between Barnwell and the fair, and some even in our streets; but two of the gang are apprehended, and committed to our goal, one of which calls himself Blewit, the other Hearne. The old trade of stealing dead bodies newly buried, is taken up again, one of those bodies being found concealed in a pit, 'tis suppos'd the old offenders this way, which were transported are return'd.

LONDON OCT. 1. Not long ago, a poor blind man, who sell wallnuts, being accompanied by a young fellow from the market, was robbed by him near Lord Albemarle's Park: But the blind man coming afterwards to the same market went into the publick house, where he told his loss. Upon which, everyone expressing their abhorrence of such a villain, the old man distinguish'd the voice that had demanded his money; and upon getting a warrant, the young fellow own'd the fact, and was committed to prison.

They write from Sutton in Hampshire, That there has been an incredible deal of mischief done by the late high winds, hail, and rain, which has rooted large trees, blown the leads off of churches, quite destroyed all the orchard-fruit that was not already gathered in, and raised the waters to such a height, that a great deal of mischief has been done by the flood.

LONDON OCT. 8. On Saturday last, a melancholy accident happen'd at the seat of Sir John Shelly Bart. at Mitchel-Grove in Sussex where Sir John, his Lady and Mr. Shelby, his brother, after having diverted themselves with fishing, rode together in the park. The Lady's horse taking a sudden fright, ran away with her between two thorn bushes, that Sir John and his brother could not readily pursue. After much search about the park, the unfortunate Lady was found by her husband lying on the ground, with her face dreadfully cut: Surgeons were sent for from Chicheller, and all possible means used for her recovery, but on Monday morning she expired. She was daughter to Sir Thomas Scawen, one of the aldermen of this city, and sister to Thomas Scawen of St. James's Square, Esq.

LONDON OCT. 8. We hear, That tomorrow morning early above 70 convicts under sentence of transportation in Newgate will be shipped for the American plantations.

On the 21st past about 4 in the morning a vessel of and from Swanswich, Capt. Viviun master run on Goodwin Sands, and was lost;

the boy, that could not swim is drowned; The boat broke, loose, and the master and two men swam to her; who being at sea, a boat went out and brought them in the same day very much spent.

FROM GLASTONBURY OCT. 8. Last Saturday one John Walters, of Street, eat 120 hens eggs 3 pounds of bacon, and a twelve penny loaf, in an hour and half, at the George Inn of this place; and, besides making such a luscious meal gratis, won a wager of 50 guineas.

In Northampton-Street, Woods Clefe, (a woman called Mother Hubbards) who-is above threescore, hang'd herself till she was black in the face, her tongue hanging out of her mouth above an inch and a half, cold, without pulse, nevertheless, by the help of bleeding she is come to life; her melancholy is imputed to the undutifulness of her children.

NORTHAMPTON OCT. 11. Last Wednesday one Osborn, a butcher of Towchester, going to carry rent to Sir Verney Cive, was robbed near Foster's Booth at noon day, by two highwaymen, who left him bound hand and foot, and his neckcloth tied so hard, that had not a treveller come soon by, he would not have recovered; The butcher made affidavit of it before a Justice of the Peace, in order to sue the hundred, and swore they took from him 80 £.

BATH OCT. 13. Yesterday a new and extraordinary entertainment was set on foot for the diversion of our polite gentry; and what should it be but a match at foot-ball, play'd by six young women of a side.

DORCHESTER OCT. 15. There is a remarkable piece of villany discovered in the Parish of Nettlebury in this county, viz. A clerk to a Presbyterian Synagogue, who had constantly attended the service of the Saints in that place, found opportunities to turn the Tabernacle into a bawdy-house, and so many years cohabited with his wife's sister, even in the very vessel from whence his master rour'd forth his instruction to his flock. He carried this work of iniquity on so long that eight children were begot by him, one of which is now ten years old, but the rest were barbarously murder'd; five of them he threw down the meeting-house well, and two he drowned in a pond. The whole scene lay undiscovered till brought to light in this manner; The rogue's conscience becoming a little flexible by the load of guilt that lay upon it, he fancied the last murthered infant appeared to him, which terrified him so that he immediately disburthened himself to his bedfellow, whom was his servant, and then gave him a shilling to lock up the secret in his own breast; but the young man finding it so troublesome, and dislodged it before a magistrate; upon which, and other circumstances, the clerk and his sister-in-law were committed to this goal but to give the devil his due, the preacher himself is cleared from having any handling in these matters.

LONDON OCT. 18. Yesterday a gentleman accidently passing by, observ'd a woman scrambling at the rails of the Church Yard of St. Andrew's Holbourn; upon which he sent for the sexton to let her out; and suspecting she had got in upon some ill design, ask'd her what business she had there; she answer'd, Dear Sir, I am just come to life you may feel my hands which are yet cold; and so they were, she having it seems, gone in with a funeral, and fallen asleep in some corner: Says he again, what have you in your pocket? she answer'd, I have a little gold and silver, and plumbs too; all which was true. Upon further enquiry she appear'd to be a woman that had suffered great losses, which disorder'd her senses; She was last night comfirm'd in the work-house for her own security.

LONDON OCT. 20. From Guildford. There being 3 women working in a field, saw a rabbit, which they endeavour'd to catch but could not, they all being with child at that time, one of the women has since by the help of a man midwife been deliver'd at several times, of something in the form of a disected rabbit, with this difference, that one of the legs was like onto a tabby cat, and is now kept by the said man midwife at Guildford.

Yesterday at Guild Hall, at sessions of Oyer & Terminer held by adjournment from Old Baily, John Harwood & Mary his wife, were tryed upon an indictment for keeping a disorderly house in entertaining sodomites, and knowingly and willingly permitting them to commit the detestable sin of sodomy, it was fully prov'd by four or five unexceptable witnesses that sodomites used to meet there, and practiced divers sodomitical obsenities, and sometimes in Mrs. Harwood's presence, and that she abetted such practices. The defence consisted in producing many persons on their reputation, but the only material circomstance in their favor was, that there was no proof of the latter part of the indictment, viz. The commission of the gross act of sodomy: And thereupon they were both acquitted, but were admonished by the Court to reform their behaviours and not suffer such practices in their house for the future.

LONDON OCT. 26. On Monday last William Paradise was committed to Newgate, being charg'd with robbing John Antif Esq; of a guinea and some silver last Sunday on the road to Hounslow.

The same day Thomas Hyde, who receiv'd sentence at the last sessions in old Baily, for horse-stealing died in the condemn'd hold at Newgate.

EXETER OCT. 29. Last week one White, a weaver of Crediton desiring his wife to lend him a pen knife to pair his nails, on a sudden cry'd out, Damn it, let it go all together; and with the same ripp'd up his own bowels. He languished three days under the care of a surgeon, and expired without any apparent remorse, the coroner's inquest brought in their verdict, Felo de Se. He was Sunday buried in a cross road, according to law, and now the vulgar will have it, that a spectrum, in the shape of that unhappy person, has appeared to many; and, 'tis certain, that a young woman of his neighbourhood was to be scar'd and afright'd by his pretended shadow, that she presently took to her bed, and died in two days. The rumour of this appearance is spread all over the country.

A Gentleman of this town having purchased 10 tickets in the State Lottery, presented one of them to his clerk, which it come up a prize of 1'000 £.

LONDON NOV. 5. Last Friday se'nnight, late at night, a duel was fought in the Meuse between Mr. Smith, formerly a West India merchant, & Mr. Walpole, a gentleman of Ireland, wherein the former was mortally wounded; but made shift to walk to the E. Cardigan's Head a tavern over against the Meuse Gate, where he died soon after; the latter, we hear, is since dead. The next day the coroner's jury sat upon the body of the deceased, and examined two witnesses in relation to Mr. Smith's death, who have deposed, that they saw the deceased engag'd with a tall thin gentleman near the pond in the Meuse; that they made violent passes at each other; that one of the contestants said, "Damn ye, now you have it;" but cannot say to which of them it was that used the expression, that soon after Mr. Smith sat down on the bench, &, the other retired, Mr. Smith's sword was bloody, & the edge hack'd in many places. The inquest adjourn'd till late night for further evidence.

Mr. Emery, who kept the Cardigan-Head Tavern at Charing-Cross & his son, are both dead, since the said Mr. Smith returned to the house after he had have received his death wounds, having each of them taken a fever, by the hurry and confusion they were put into on that occasion.

LONDON NOV. 5. They write from Torrington in Devonshire; that the 23d past, a small vessel was run on shore by a storm, near Radflow, having fifty stout men on board, who all saved their lives; 14 of them went to a miller's house, who kindly entertained them all night, and lent them all dry cloaths he had in his house; but in the morning they were so ungrateful, as to march off with the miller's garments, and their own. Two were afterwards apprehended, and committed to Launceston jail; and one of them made oath that they were all enlisted in Ireland for foreign service.

LONDON NOV. 8. We hear that Mr. Charles Buggs of Coventry, has found out a sure and safe method of curing the gout, rheumatism, dropsic and consumption, in a way never yet practiced before. That he cures the gout by a plaister, which draws out and dischargeth all the gouty matter so gently as not to break the skin, but carries it quite off by sweat and persperation in six or seven days. That he has very lately cured vast numbers in the city and country. That many of the cures being so surprizingly great were proclamed at the Cross in Coventry on the market day, before Thomas Lawrence Esq; Mayor, and the Aldermen, and vast numbers of spectators and patients cured by him, which being fully proved, a diploma as Dr. of Physick was granted him out of the Court of the Board Bishop of Litchfield and Coventry.

LONDON NOV. 12. His Majesty, out of his Royal bounty, hath been graciously pleased to give the sum of 500 £. towards defraying the great expences of printing 10,000 copies of the New Testament in Arabic, for the use of the poor Christians in Syria, Palistine and other Eastern Countries.

LONDON NOV. 22. On Wednesday morning about 80 convicts under sentence of transportation, were carried from Newgate to be shipt off to Maryland.

LONDON NOV. 24. They write from Grenoble, by the way of Paris, That a gentleman in that neighbourhood, riding out with his servant and happening to benighted, he went to a lady's house about two leagues from thence, who had that very day received 15,000 livres of a Notary at Grenoble, and desired the favour of a bed. The lady at first made some hesitation, but had too much compassion to turn her unknown applicant to shift in the dark. The gentleman and his servant were admitted; and between twelve and one o'clock at night when the family were all in bed and asleep, the house was attack'd by four rogues, who knock'd at the door, and demanded immediate entrance, threatning, in case of refusal, to cut their door in pieces with their axes. The servants refusing to open the door, they went to work accordingly. The lady taking it for granted the stranger she had admitted was at the head of this design went to his chamber, and begged him to spare her life, and take her money: But the gentleman being told the reason of her fright, got up and ran to the door with his servant; and being provided with pistols, fired through the holes which had been made with the axes, killed two of them upon the spot, and mortally wounded another. The fourth who made his escape, has been taken since and appears to be the very Notery that had paid the lady 15,000 livres, who came with the villains.

LONDON NOV. 24. They write from Dunbarton, Nov. 8. That on that day John Smith, from the Parish of Rosneath, was committed to the tolbooth there, for the murder of his sister and wife, both with child; which he effected by throwing them down into the riverlets of water, and holding their heads therein till they died. The said murders he at first denied, but afterwards confessed before several magistrates and signed a confession thereof in a fulled manner.

LONDON DEC. The Russians who design, it seems, to have a mind to take from another nation the character of being the Cascons of the North, threaten the world with vast projects both by sea and land, which are meer rhodomontadoes, and therefore without taking notice of them, we shall observe, that the letters from Petersburg confirm the design of the Czarina to go to Riga, and that the troops on that side are to be reinforced with several regiments, but upon the design they cannot tell. They add, that the Czarina and her Poles are likely to come to a rupture about the Dutchy of Courtland, that Princess Having declared, that she will never suffer the Poles to put in execution the decree they have passed in their last Diet at Grodno for dividing that Dutchy into Polatinates after the death of Duke Ferdinand, till they have previously given her satisfaction on the pretence of her neice the Duchess Dowager, and reimbursed the charges of the late Czar in relation to that country, which demands and petitions amounts to several million, and exceed by a great deal what that Dutchie could be sold for, if it were exposed to sale.

1727

BRISTOL JAN. 7. A barbarous murder was committed last Tuesday, by one Henry Brookman, (an idle fellow about 18 years old) on the body of Mary Coff, a Quaker, who was found in the Meeting-House last Wednesday with her throat cut from ear to ear. It happen'd that one of the neighbours seeing the said Brookman coming from thence, caused him to be apprehended upon suspicion, and being brought before the Justices then sitting, they immediately ordered him to be search'd, and found a bloody knife, which prov'd to be the poor woman's; That he first knock'd her down, then search'd her pocket, found therein 18d in money, and the knife with which he cut her throat, he was thereupon committed to Ivelchester Goal.

LONDON JAN. 13. On Tuesday night a grenadier of the foot guard, who had been dismissed from the employment of doorkeeper to the Phenix-Gaming-House in the Hay-Market came to the said place, with a bayonet stabb'd his successor thro' the heart who died immediately.

LONDON JAN. 18. Last Monday night about 7 or 8 rooms over some stables in Fuddle-Dock fell in, whereby several persons were buried in the ruins; 3 women & 3 children have been taken out dead, and 'tis fear'd that some more have perished in that sad accident.

WORCESTER JAN. 19. Last Thursday one Colley was committed to our castle, for attempting to murder his father, by cutting his throat, and afterwards stabbing him in the neck; and he had undoubtedly killed him on the spot, had not his sister interposed, whereby she received a wound in her arm. 'Tis said he is mad; be that as it will, there never enter'd into prison a more resulute ruffian, ten men being little enough to fix on his irons. He continued some time after that, belching out such shocking excrations, as ever scared the most abandon'd wretches in the prison. His father is in a fair way of recovery.

ROCHESTER JAN. 31. Yesterday a most lamentable accident happen'd at Mr. Forsyte's brewhouse in this city, occasioned by the inconsiderateness of one of the servants, who was at play with a little boy that frequented the brewhouse, and being wanted to mash, since the little child on one side of the mashing-tub, who unfortunately fell in and pull the man in with him: The boy was scalded to death, and the poor man in such a manner that he languish'd till this morning before he died.

LONDON FEB. 1. On the 28th of last month a ship called the St. Paul, Capt. Henry Peters, bound from Bordeaux to Hambourg was lost in Bigberry Bay near Dartmouth. Her cargo consisted of 53 tons of wine, 30 pipes of brandy, 40 casks of sugar 11 casks of indigo, 40 casks of razins, and 3 tons of turpentine.

LONDON FEB. 1. William Morrice, Esq; High-Baliff of the city and liberty of Westminster, hath obtained his Majesty's leave to go to France, to visit Dr. Atterbury, the late Biship of Rochester, his father.

FALMOUTH FEB. 11. Yesterday arrived here a ship in 14 days from Gibraltar, whose commander reports, That the Spanish army was advanc'd within reach of the cannon on Willis's Battery; that they had not made any attack for the want of their heavy cannon, which the wetness of the weather had retarded the getting to them; that Admiral Hopton had landed his soldiers, in numbers about 600; and that his ships were drawn into shoal water in a line; that two Spaniards who us'd to bring bread to town, returned from thence, had been hang'd by order of the Count de las Torres; that great numbers of soldiers having deserted from the Spanish army, and order has been publish'd, by beat of drum at the head of every regiment, forbidding both officers and soldiers saying, that the taking of Gibraltar was impracticable, on pain of death; and requiring them to encourage one another in believing they should become masters of the fortress.

LONDON MARCH 2. This morning a poor aged woman, destitute of a lodging, and all other necessities, died under a tree in St. James's Park, where she had wander'd about a day or two.

This day arrived a mail from Lisbon, dated the 2d of March N. S. by which come advice, that the Durfley galley man of war, Capt. Purvis, arrived there the day before 48 hours from Gibraltar, and brought the following account. That the Spaniards having erected a battery within half cannon-shot of the works of Gibraltar, the Governour sent to know the meaning, and being answered, He should have it from the mouth of their cannon, the English fired at them, and did great execution; the Spaniards returned the fire, and began to bombard the town. They had dispatched 2000 foot and two battalions of horses to lie to the N. E. of Willis Battery, so near as the cannon from thence could not be brought to bear on them, on which the Durfley galley was sent round the point, and drawing but little water, she came within reach of them, and before dark, obliged them to retire back to their camp, leaving near 600 men dead behind them; the Spaniards deserted in great numbers to the town, as had about 400 Swiss. Admiral Wager arrived with a squadron the second of February, O. S. and hostilities began the 11th; the Spaniards and garrison had continued firing at each other 36 hours, when the Durfley was dispatch'd thence with this account.

LONDON MARCH 6. About 3000 men, mostly sailors, have been impressed for his Majesty's service, and put on board ships of war in the Downs &c. to man Sir John Norris's Squadron.

LONDON MARCH 9. Last week the son of a late forfeiting South-sea director won upwards of 50,000 £. and a certain chocolate-house, a noble Earl lost 20,000 £. of the money.

NORTHAMPTON MARCH 10. Last night our Assizes ended here, where a great deal of business hath dispatched at both Nifi Prius and Crown Bars. One cause was tried between the Lord Halton, Plaintiff, and Lord Goring, defendant, about the property of some wood ground, but a mistake appearing in the proceedings, the plaintiff consented to a nonsuit.

NORTHAMPTON MARCH 10. Four persons received sentence of death, viz. William Tinsey for a robbery on the highway; William Godman for house breaking in the day time; William Richardson for horse stealing; John Driver for stealing some shaloon from the tentery: Godman and Driver were reprieved.

LONDON MARCH 13. Last night the fine statue of the King on horse back made by Mr. Nost and set up in Governour Square, was very much defaced by some villainous persons yet unknown, the left leg being torn off at the thigh and laid upon the pedestal, one rein of the bridle almost cut through, the sword and truncheon wreck'd off and carried away, the neck also hack'd as if they design'd to cut off his head, and a most scandalous label was left at the place.

PORTSMOUTH MARCH 15. Last Friday a Spanish vessel from Bilboa, bound for London, by contrary winds was obliged to put in here at Spithead, and being ignorant that the hostilities were begun between Great Britain and Spain, she hosted Spanish colours, which being perceived by Lieutenant Orelen of the Bedford (who was going with some of the ships company in one of his Majesty's hoys to impress men out of the homeward bound ships) he immediately went on board, took her as a prize and brought her into the harbour, she is loaded with Spanish wool and Iron.

The following melancholy accident happen'd on Monday last in the afternoon, viz. Twenty of the Prince Frederick's men, who had assisted in rigging his Majesty's ship Lyon in this harbour, were returning again on board their proper ship when the boat overset, and 14 of them were drown'd besides two women who were going on board to see their husbands.

LONDON MARCH 15. Died at Kensington, in a good old age, the profound mathematician, Sir Isaac Newton, Knt. President of the Royal Society, and Master-worker of his Majesty's Mint in the Tower of London.

Yesterday a considerable number of large brass cannon and mortar-pieces, with their carriages, was shipped on board the transport ships in the river for Gibraltar; and utmost diligence is used for dispatching those ships, which will be ready to sail in a few days.

LONDON MARCH 18. At the Assizes at New Sarum for the County of Wilts, the three following malefactors received sentence of death, viz. William Merick, upon the Riot Act, for assembling together with other persons in a riotous and tumultuous manner, and committing many notorious riots at Bradford and other places, threatning to pull down houses, and compelling people to give them money; and Edward Williams for burglary; and Ambrose Duford for felony; the latter reprieved.

William Towsend, for attempting to commit buggery, was sentenced to suffer three months imprisonment, to stand in the pillory, at Westminster, to pay a fine of twenty marks, and to find securities for his good behaviour for three years.

LONDON MARCH 19. Yesterday several of the debtors in the Gatehouse Prison, Westminster, were discharged from their confinement and debts, by the Westminster Wardmate, or Christmas Jury; who applied a great part of the money collected from the inhabitants, as usual, at Christmas, for that good and charitable work; and did, at the same time give the poor objects some money to relieve those necessaries.

LONDON APRIL 6. The Ipwich Stage Coach going from London, was attack'd on Monday about 5 in the morning, between Stratford and Ilford, by one highwayman; four men were in the coach, two of whom on one side he robb'd; but going to the other side, and leaning into the coach to rob the other two, a man on the coachbow knock'd him down off his horse, with an oaken stick. He was immediately seized, and tied hand and foot, put into the coach and carried before a Justice of the Peace, and sent to Chelmsford Gaul. He had 3 pistols about him, all loaded, he said he was a butcher, and that he lived in Southwark.

We have account from Rumford, which tho' something out of the way, may be depended upon for truth; on Tuesday morning a highwayman attacked a stage coach in that town about five a clock in the morning, and making a little more noise than ordinary, waked an inn-keeper, who apprehending what was the matter, call'd up two drovers that lay in his house; they glad of the jobb, run out almost naked, one with a poker, and the other with a pair of tongs, being the first thing they could meet with; he with the poker came up with the highwayman first, and asking what was the matter, the fellow very readily told him, he had robb'd one of the coaches, upon which he up with his poker, and knock'd him off the horse, and recovering himself, the drover serv'd him so the second time, and the clapping in with him, bound him, put him into the coach and convey'd him to Chelmsford, where he lies confin'd into goal.

LONDON APRIL 8. Rice Jones (said to be one of those cheats that have lately cheated several unwary farmers and gentlemen of considerable sums of money by drawing them to taverns, and by slight of hand exchanging bags with them, leaving the country men copper for gold and silver) was lately apprehended and committed to the Gatehouse, Westminster, being charged on suspicion of robbing Thomas Haynes of 60 £. in gold and silver.

The said Jones is also detain'd on oath for robbing a country man of 60 £. in gold and silver.

The same Jones is also detain'd on oath for feloniously taking from Abraham Barker 100 £. and upwards.

HIGHWORTH APRIL 8. A substantial farmer, who rented about 150 £. per annum in our neighbourhood, and was to have been married to his sweetheart on last Sunday, went into his barn and hang'd himself the Friday before upon receiving a message from her that she would not have him; and she sending it only in jest, to obtain a little more courtship, is now ready to make away with herself for her folly.

LONDON APRIL 8. George Webb, committed for leaving his family was ordered to remain in custody.

LONDON APRIL 8. At the Assizes at Exon for the said city and the county of Devon, Nathaniel Langley for the murther of Daniel Palmer of Broarlist, William Hall for felony, William Molland for burglary, Richard Edwards, Samuel Hutchinson & William Tipling, for the highway were convicted.

Mary Haddon, convicted for assaulting and beating her husband & being a disorderly woman was discharg'd by proclamation.

At the Assizes at Stafford, one William Cole was try'd for high treason, in having in his possession a dye for coining shillings; and tho' a great amount of bad money was found under his shop floor, he was acquited by the jury, to whom he appeared, that the dye but impurfectly resembled a shilling on one side, it having the letters Geo Dei Gratis, instead of Georgius: and he having brought divers persons to his reputation, and none appearing to accuse him of endeavouring to put off bad money.

OXFORD APRIL 10. A tumult happened lately at Heddington, a little village within a mile of this city, occasioned by a quarrel between some gowns-men, who went thither to a bull-baiting, and the country people. The former having sent for assistance to the University, were soon increased to a number of about 1,000; when a dreadful conflict ensued, wherein some were maim'd, some carried off dead, and all the windows in the village were demolished; and had they not been prevented by the proctors, their rage had been more mischieveous.

Tuesday morning Mr. Darby, son of Mr. Darby one of the secondaries of the Court of Common Pleas, was found murder'd and robb'd in his chambers in Hare-Court in the Temple.

On Wednesday the coroner's inquest sate upon the body, but could make no discovery of the murderers. It appear'd that he had been shot in the head, and 'twas thought the bullet lodg'd in his skull; he had two small bruises, one on the fore part and the other on the back of his head; his scrutore was broke open, and several things were lost out of his chambers; The jury was likewise inform'd, that he had received 1400 £. but Saturday to pay for a purchase he had made, which money was missing, and one of the company that left him the night he was kill'd swore he had a diamond ring on, which was not on his finger when found dead next morning. The coroner having made an order for his burial, adjourn'd the jury sine die, to wait for further evidence, if it can be procured, relating to the barbarous action.

LONDON APRIL 15. A young woman, who had been apprentice to a mantua maker near Fetter Lane, who afterwards put on men's cloaths, and went by the name of Tom Shammy, and became servant to a noted tavern near Temple Bar, was last week brought to bed of a daughter.

On Monday last a little boy of about 6 years old, that was heir to an estate, being in fear of correction for some fault, threw himself out of a window two stories high, at his mother's house in the Broad Way at Westminster, and expired in about two hours after.

LONDON MAY 2. On Sunday in the afternoon, Mr. H. Fisher an attorney at law, was committed to Newgate by Sir William Thompson, upon a violent, suspicion of his murdering Mr. Darby, Jun. on the 10th of April at night. When he was apprehended, there were found upon him two rings (which the diamonds taken out) and a mother of pearl snuff-box, which belong'd to Mr. Darby. At his examination, he confess'd that about the latter end of the week that Mr. Darby was murder'd, as he was passing through Lincoln-Inn Fields, about four in the afternoon, he took up under the wall of Lincoln Inn Gardens, a white paper parcel, in which were contained the goods before mention'd; together with a gold watch which he believ'd did belong to Mr. Darby, as appeared by the publick advertisement; but that he was afraid of discovering the same, lest he should be charg'd with the murder; that the diamonds he sold for 10 guineas to a jeweller in Patter-noster Row, and pawn'd the watch for nine guineas to a person at a Brasier's in Bond Street, sold the gold chain and gold swivels to a person in Lombard Street, and that he had discharg'd several debts, and bought things with the money. He deny'd the knowledge of Mr. Darby's murder, and said he was at a billiard-table in Duke Street St. James's at the time the fact was committed. First he said he was at play with the boy of the house, then he said 'twas with the master, and at last he cou'd not be sure whatever 'twas with the boy or master: However, they were both sent for to come before the recorder, they cou'd neither of 'em be found that day, but yesterday they came to Sir William and made affidavit, that he was not at their house that evening at all. It was deposed by some persons present, that Mr. Fisher was an acquaintance and companion of Mr. Darby, that the night he was murdered, Mr. Fisher came not to his lodging till one the next morning; That a porter coming about eight to acquaint him with Mr. Darby's fate, he shew'd not a due concern thereas, but shut himself up in his chamber for some hours. Mr. Willoughby his landlord, a gentleman of worth and reputation, made oath, that the day Mr. Darby was murder'd, Mr. Fisher borrow'd of him 2 s. 6 d. to pay his washerwoman, and was much necessitated for money; that having after that great reason to suspect him, from several odd circumstances, he caused his scrutore to be open'd in his abscence last week, and found therein a brace of pistols, a vizard mask, a dark lantern, and a pair of lace ruffles (which ruffles two persons made an oath did, as they believ'd belong to Mr. Darby). A woman made oath that she saw a person very much like Mr. Fisher hovering about the deaceased's chamber a little time before he was murder'd. Such a suit of cloaths as the person that was seen hovering late at night about the chamber wore was found in his lodging, and there were several spots upon the coat which was carry'd to the scowerer, but by what seem'd to've been us'd about it he cou'd not say whether 'twas blood or not. There were many other strong and corroborating circumstances to tedious to be her related. He sign'd his confession in the presence of Sir George Cooke, the Lord Finch, and several other persons of distinction.

LONDON MAY 23. The following account comes attested by the Captain's affidavit from Antegoa, dated March 17, 1726-27. Thomas Gallaspy, captain of the Fair Parnelle sloop; bound for Antegoa, set sail on the 7th of May before from Cape Coast-Castle in Africa with 120 Negroes on board & at three in the morning, June 8th, in about 482 leagues west from Cape Coast having a fine breeze at N. E. with a square sail, and main sail set; the sky being fair and clear a violent whirlwind came so suddenly upon them, that before they could get their main sail down the sloop overset; 95 Negroes who were under the hatches were drown'd, one, who was become a helper to the cook escaped the sea, to suffer a more ling'ring fate; two and twenty of the Negroes were dead before; Finding it impossible for them to right the vessel, about nine the same morning twelve white men and a black quitted her; betaking themselves to their boat; without oars, masts, sail, rudder, or any instrument, without a morsel of food, except a drown sow, or a drop of fresh water, keeping near the sloop they found five or six bottles of a'rack in a case; by what afterwards broke off the sloop they made four wretched paddles, a mast, and a sail, the last thing they pick'd up belonging to the vessel was a compass; in this miserable condition they steer'd away for Cape de Verde Islands: but on the 13th of June they alter'd their course; and stood away east for the main land: on the 3d of July they discovered it; on the 4th, ten got on shore at the mouth of Cobblee River in Africa, three of the company being dead in the passage by hunger, and the inexpressible hardships they met with; of these ten, seven died by the latter end of September; what become of the other two the captain has not thought fit to tell us; on the 14th of December the captain got back to Cape Coast Castle; and on the 10th of February he arrived in a very weak condition at Antigoa; from whence, 'tis likely we may in a short time have a much better account of so extraordinary an affair than the imperfect one already published.

BRISTOL JUNE 5. They write from Gibraltar, of the 13th past, That the Spaniards have done more execution against the outworks and fortifications of the town and batteries the 7 preceding days than had since the siege began; and that the garrison had not been wanting in making a suitable return from 100 good cannon and mortars, which dismounted the guns of several of the enemies batteries, and much annoy'd their trenches, and must needs have kill'd abundance of men. It was computed that the Spaniards fired near 4000 shot a day for several days together; but by their flack firing afterwards, 'twas believed abundance of their fine brass guns were overheated, and render'd useless. That Willis's Battery was a great gall to their camp and trenches; for which reason they kept a battery of 14 cannon and another 6 mortars, continually playing upon it. Our gunners on this occasion had behaved themselves with such bravery and expedition that the Lord Portmore their Governour distributed abundance of gold among them. A deserter from the camp inform'd them, that on their being reinforced with six battallions of regular troops, the Marquis de Torris had ordered all the scalling ladders to be got in readiness for a general storm; which the garrison was in no fear of, being well provided to receive them.

BRISTOL JUNE 10. We hear an account by a small coaster from St. Ives, in Cornwall that a few days since, the fishermen discover'd to the westward of that place a large Virginia ship, overset as is suppos'd which they towed in to St. Ives, and upon searching her they discovered she had had a full lading of tobacco, which was all spoil'd and wasted by the water; in her cabin they found three dead men, and several others lash'd to the sheets on the deck, (on which the grass was about 5 inches long) and going to heave the bodies over the ship they drop'd to pieces, being so very much decay'd, by which 'tis conjectur'd she must have been lost about 5 or 6 months, in searching her they could find no papers, to discover where she belong'd to; she is a New England built ship, and suppos'd to belong to London. 'Tis thought to be the same wreck as was discover'd off the west of Ireland about 6 or 7 weeks since, by several captains of the port, particularly Captain Fry who was very near to it.

LONDON JULY 10. A sad accident happened on board the Charlotte Yacht, upon saluting his Majesty, where, in charging a gun, the powder took fire as they were ramming it in, which tore off the arm of one of the mariners, and blew out his eye, so that the poor man died immediately.

LONDON JUNE 11. Yesterday one Elizabeth Archer was by Sir Thomas Clarger Bart. committed to Newgate for the murder of her bastard child, by burying it alive in a garden at Burton, at the Parish of Hanbury, near Burton, in Staffordshire; from whence she made her escape to London and had concealed her self at a house near Tyburn Road, where she was discovered & apprehended. Yesterday morning she sign'd her confession of the fact before Thomas Clarger, and is to be removed to Stafford to take her tryal at the ensuing Assizes there. Her mother is a prisoner in Stafford Goal, on suspicion of being a confederate with her in the murder.

LONDON JUNE 15. Yesterday soon after three of the clock in the afternoon, Mr. Crew one of his Majesty's messengers, arrived here with this melancholy news, that his Majesty, our late most gracious Sovereign King George, departed this life, at two o'clock last Sunday morning, at Osnaburg, of a fit of an apoplexy, Sir Robert Walpole, who first received the news at Chelsea, sent an express with it to the Prince and Princess of Wales at Richmond; Their Royal Highness immediately came to London. And in the evening Privy Council assembled at Leicester-House, and declared his Royal Highness George Prince of Wales, King of Great Britain, France and Ireland, &c. and signed a proclamation for his being proclaimed as such this morning at the accustomed places, and with usual solemnity.

The proclamation is as follow: Whereas it hath pleased Almighty God to call to his mercy our late Sovereign Lord King George of blessed memory, by whose deceased the Imperial Crown of Great Britain, France and Ireland, are solely and rightfully come to the high and mighty Prince George Prince of Wales; We therefore the Lords

Spiritual and Temperal of this Realm, being here assisted with those of his late Majesty's Privy Council with numbers of other principal gentlemen of quality, with the Lord Mayor, Aldermen, and citizens of London, do now hereby, declare with one full voice, and consent of tongue and heart, publish and proclaim, That the high and Mighty Prince George, Prince of Wales is now, by the death of our late Sovereign of happy memory, become our only lawful and Rightful Liege Lord. George the second. By the Grace of God King of Great Britain, France and Ireland, defender of the Faith &c. To whom we do acknowledge all faith and Constant Obedience, with all hearty and humble affection: Beseeching God by whom Kings and Queens do Reign, to bless the Royal King George the Second, with long and happy years to reign over us.

Given in the Court of Leicester House, this fourteenth of June, 1727. God save the King.

LONDON JUNE 16. We hear that his Majesty King George was very much indisposed after he landed in Holland, thro' the fatigue of his passage by sea, but being very desirous to finish his journey without making any considerable stay upon the road, he travelled after of the rate of a hundred and fifty miles a day, and would not take regular rest or refreshments; on Thursday he was very ill again, on Friday something better, and eat his dinner heartily; but afterwards grew very ill, and was blooded upon the road; on Saturday he reached Osnaburg, where he died about three o'clock in the morning at his brother's palace, The Duke of York.

Yesterday about noon his present Majesty George the Second, was proclaimed King of Great Britain, France and Ireland, at Leicester House, Charing Cross, Temple Bar, Cheapside, and the Royal Exchange, with the usual solemnity, the Prime Minister of State, and a great number of the nobility and gentry attending on that occasion with the King's heralds, and furservants of arms in their proper habits, preceeded by a detatchment of horse and grenedier guards: When they came to Temple Bar the gates being shut, were upon their knocking at them, order'd to be open'd by the Rt. Hon. the Lord Mayor, accompanied by the Aldermen and Sheriffs in their robes; and at night there were bonfires, illuminations and other rejoicings thro' out this city and suburbs.

LONDON JUNE 24. We hear that nothing but the English tongue shall be spoken at Courts, unless by those who do not understand it.

LONDON JULY 15. The last letters from Gibraltar by the Lyne man of war gave an account that the beseigers, in April last were about 15,000, but by sickness, fire and desertion, were reduced to under 7,000; that the garrison lost two officers & 107 men, a third by griping of the guts and bloody flux, and 6 deserters, that there was now sick of distemper, and of their wounds, 177, and 4,900 men in the garrison in good health.

There is undoubted intelligence that Henry Fisher, the supposed murderer of Mr. Darby, who escaped from Newgate in May last, was lately seen at Bilboa in Spain, by an English gentleman who knew him, but had not heard of the crime imputed to him: Fisher told him he was forc'd to retire to Spain on account of debt.

PORTSMOUTH JULY 29. A merchant ship bound for Philadelphia had several Palatines on board: It happened a Swedish ship laden with Norway goods, saw her at some distance, and mistook her for a Turk, imagining the caps of the Palitines were turbants; it surprised the Swedes, so very much, that they immediately drop'd anchor, and left the ship every man of them, and went a-shore, at a place called Little Hampton in Sussex, between Arundel and Shoreham, where they offered a reward to any who would convey them safe into an harbour; but in the interim, some fishermen comming by the Swede, and finding no body on board, they took her as a wreck and brought her into the harbour. The master of her is since come thither, but the fishermen keep to the ship, and will not suffer him to come on board.

PORTSMOUTH AUG. 16. Last week at noon, a boy about 10 years of age went with some others to swim, in a place called Mill Laste near Gosport, where he was unfortunately drowned.

Yesterday a woman of Gosport, as she was riding a little way out of town, unfortunately came by a gate where a team of horses were coming thro' and the fore horse unluckily running up against her, beat her off, & afterwards trampled her to death.

LONDON AUG. 16. On Tuesday night last, between 10 & 11 o'clock, Mr. Rambouilet Lieutenant of Granadiers, and quartermaster of the First Regiment of Guards, was set upon by five foot robbers in York Street, near St. James's Square, three of them keeping their pistols presented at his body, while the others took from him a diamond ring, a broadpiece, two guineas and a half, some medals, and a silver watch, together with his hat, periwig, & cane, and then commanded him to kneel on the ground while they got off, which he did and one of the villains turned back sudden and cut him on the head with a hanger, in a barbarous manner, tho' he did not attempt to rise, and then they all went off together.

LONDON AUG. 17. We have certain advice from the west, that the most notorious Roger Johnson who some time ago broke out of Newgate with Fisher, has lately been in the west, and committed great frauds, one of which was at Shaftsbury, in Wiltshire, where he, together with Fisher, or some other person, defrauded a shopkeeper of a large sum of money, and was pursued & taken the same day, but before assistance could come, he got off with the booty.

LONDON AUG. 26. On Wednesday an experiment of proof of several new mortar-pieces was made on board the Shoreham man of war, at Woolwich, before several of the Lord Commissioners of the Admiralty, and many officers of the Ordinance, who were after elagantly entertained on board at dinner by Capt. Long the commander.

On Thursday night a fire broke out in a barn joining to the town of Gravesend in Kent, (in which some people lay who were employ'd in gathering hops) which consumed half the town on the Westside: The steeple of the church, which was built of wood, was burnt down, and the church much damaged.

Letters from Newark in Nottingshire informs us, That after the late election for members of Parliament was over, the mob rose in a tumultuous manner, broke the windows of several houses, and committed several other disorders; nor could they be dispensed by reading the proclamation until some troops were sent for, who seized the ringleaders, who are now in custody.

LONDON AUG. 26. On Thursday one Stewart Dormer, a prisoner in the press yard side on Newgate for misdemeanor, stabb'd another prisoner in the belly, with a case knife, insomuch that his life is thought to be in great danger, and Dormer is put into the condemn'd hold, and chain'd.

LONDON AUG. 29. Extract of a letter from Graveland. The desolation here is hardly to be express'd; about 250 houses lie in ashes; The Church Steeple, which was of timber, is burnt, and whatever within the church was combustible; So that all that remain are naked walls: the largest and best half of the town is destroyed; several hogs, cows and horses were burnt to death though the fire broke out in the dead of night, when the whole town almost were asleep, not a single soul, praise be God, has not been kill'd or hurt. The fire was occasioned by a spark falling from a pipe, among some corn in a barn near the Church, and not by any person's lying in the barn, as had been reported; We were ill provided for such a visitation, having but one engine in the town and that unfit for service it having been so play'd these 3 years; what added to the calamity, was our not blowing up the houses, which if it had been done in time, as it ought to have been, and in such a case in the practice, a multitude of houses might in all probability have been saved; The houses being insured, our people perhaps did not take to much pains as they would have done had the loss wholly fallen upon themselves: The sum fire office is in for about 9,000 £. and another office much more. The whole damage is computed to be upward of 2,000 £. sterling.

EXON SEPT. 10. We have an account from Wiveliscombe in Sumersetshire, of the following barbarous paricide, viz. One Fitbal, son of an honest farmer of that place, who had deserted from the regiment quarter'd here, and being protected and concealed by his parents till they had accommodated the matter of his desertion, and procured a discharge, being, the 27th past, got much in liquor, and upon return from a ramble, demanded of his mother some ale; upon which she making some hesitation least he should be intoxicated, he took up an axe, and therewith by several blows cleaved his mothers skull, and as she lay weltring in her blood, he punched her with the handle of the axe till she expired: The horrid wretch was soon after seized, and committed to Ivelchester Jail.

LONDON SEPT 19. Some days ago 121 persons perished by fire in a barn at Burwell near Cambridge, where a puppet-show was acting.

LONDON SEPT. 21. Yesterday morning a youth about seventeen years of age, apprentice to a sawyer near Puddle Dock, walking up a plank from a lighter with a large piece of timber on his shoulder, and his foot slipping, fell down and the timber upon him, by which he was so bruised, that he died on the spot: The coroner's jury have since sat upon him, and brought in their verdict accidental death.

They write from Peterborough, that two dragoons, quarter'd in that town, being got into a farmer's wallnut tree, gathering the nuts, in the middle of the night; and the farmer hearing them, went out with two servants well arm'd with sticks; whereupon a battle ensued, and the dragoon's were so beaten, that one of them is since dead, and the other is hardly recovered.

LONDON SEPT. 21. Some mischief was done on Tuesday at the horserace at Barnet, by some horses running away with their riders against a gentleman's coach with that violence, as to overturn it and break one of the wheels; but we do not hear of any limbs broken.

One Mr. Ryley a gentleman of Oxfordshire, between 70 and 80 years of age, going to walk in a little paddock by his house, was lately kill'd by a large stag that was kept in the same.

LONDON SEPT. 23. On Thursday was burnt, at the tobacco grounds in Cupid's Garden in the presents of several officers belonging to the East-India Company, customs, and inland duties, thirty eight chests of damaged tea, and five chests of damaged coffee.

LONDON SEPT. 30. Last Thursday a person stood on the pillory over against the Royal Exchange, for about three quarters of an hour: As he concealed his face, and the name of the offender not being affix'd on the pillory as usual, we cannot with certainty give further account of him.

LONDON SEPT. 30. One day this week, the Northampton Stagecoach coming to London was robbed by two highwaymen, who took about 60 pounds from the passengers, who were Mr. Davidson, a gentleman belonging to the Earl of Strafford; a clergyman, and two women, whom the villains used very barbarously.

LONDON SEPT. 30. A live rattle-snake brought over by a surgeon from the West-Indies, was last Wednesday carried to the college of physicians in Warwick Lane. Being the day of the quarterly feast: We hear it was offer'd to an eminent member of the college and a great vertuoso, but being a dangerous creature he had no mind to it: However before it was carried away they made the following experiment, they got a dog to be drawn by a string backwards & forward over it, the snake being thereby provoked bit him by the leg, and he swell'd and died immediately: They made use of another dog in the like manner, and he being also bit died in a few moments: Then they opened one of the dogs to search into the manner of the operation of the poison that's so violent and quick an account of which we have not yet heard.

LIVERPOOL OCT. 6. On the 3d instant, a ship of about 150 tons belonging to London, Capt. Gale commander, laden with lead and tann'd leather. For Leghorn, was lost on a sand bank near Hayley

Lake, It was coming from Danpoole (without a pilot) with a design to lye in Haley Lake, parts of the wreck is put on shore.

LONDON OCT. 6. About a fortnight ago, a footman was taken up by the watch at an unreasonable hour in women's apperal for which, and creating a disturbance in the street, he was carried to the Gate-House, but was discharged the next day without bail, by a certain gentleman who was pleased at the same time to bind over the honest watchman to Hick's Hall: However we are assured a Complaint will be made above of this very extraordinary piece of justice.

LONDON OCT. 6. This morning the Otter sloop arrived at Deptford with a great number of pirates on board, taken in the West-Indies.

LONDON OCT. 7. Yesterday was landed at the Tower from on board his Majesty's sloop Otter, John Ashley an Englishman; John Prie of Guernsey; and Martinique, a Negro man, charged with piracy on the high seas; they were carried to Doctor's Common and examined, and afterwards committed prisoners to the Marshalsea.

Yesterday morning early before day-light, above 70 convicts in Newgate under sentence of transportation, with near 30 others brought thither from country goals, were ship'd off the America.

LONDON OCT. 12. Yesterday the park and tower guns were fired at the King's and Queen's coronation, the bells rung, and the flags were display'd thro'-out the city and suburbs, and the night concluded with bonfires, illuminations and drinking their Majesties, and Royal Families and other Royal healths.

They have begun in the suburbs of London to beat for volunteers to man the ships daily put into commission.

LONDON OCT. 14. The other day two dragoons were committed to Southampton Goal for ravishing a couple young girls who they met with a little way out of town; They were first discovered by an old woman, who seeing their wicked design, called some people to her aid, and they took the fellows in the very act; and what is more surprizing, one of them was so flagrant in his villainy, that the girl seized being to young for him to execute his design on, the ravisher drew out his knife, and was going to rip her open, in order to gratify his outragious desire.

LONDON OCT. 18. Extract of a letter from Shire-Drain in Lincoln-shire Oct. 16. An eel was taken in this drain of so monstrous a size, that I thought the particulars of it might be worthy communicating to the publick in your paper. It was taken by William Townshend. The length was 7 feet 4 inches and a quarter; 'Twas 2 feet 6 inches round the belly; the fat taken out weigh'd 16 pounds and a half; length of the ears was 8 inches; water taken from the bladder was 3 quarts and a pint; and the weight was 65 pounds. In short, it was the wonder of all that saw it.

LONDON OCT. 28. Yesterday noon, one Mr. Trunkett, a jeweller, who had lately lost considerably by stock-jobbing, hang'd himself in the cellar at Robin's Coffee-House, in Exchange-Alley, as soon as discover'd, he was cut down, but too late to recover him.

On Tuesday night at the theatre in Drury Lane, a gentlewoman who sat in the pit to see the play, fancying saw a smoke issue from under the stage, and thinking fire perceived the smell of fire, happening to declare these thoughts aloud, at the same time endeavering with great precipitancy, to get out of the house, all this gave such an alarm, as threw the numerous audience into confusion for about the space of half an hour, in which time much mischief was done, and one woman big with child was press'd to death; but upon a strict search no signs of fire appeared, the terror was stop'd at length, and the rest of the play was acted out without interruption. (King Henry VIII)

Our homeward bound Turkey Fleet are arrived safe in the Bay of Gibraltar, the want of which place, if it should be given up, or else demolished, would be a great inconvenience to that trade.

LONDON NOV. 2. On last Sunday night, a Gravesend boat was overset in coming from London, whereby Mr. Dunning, a pewterer at Greenwich, with several other persons were drowned.

The next day a pleasure-boat was overset in the Thames near Whitehall, by which one person on board the same was drowned, and all the rest were saved by timely assistance of boats upon the river.

And yesterday morning a carman had the misfortune to fall down, his foot slipping under the wheel of his own cart at Salt-Petre Bank near Smithfield, and was kill'd on the spot.

LONDON NOV. 7. On Sunday morning, about five of the clock, a violent fire broke out at the Crown Tavern in King Street by Guild-Hall, which soon consumed the said house, and 3 other adjoining, and damaged several others: It began in a room below stairs; but how is not certainly known. Mr. Fisher the master of the house was at Croydon, Mrs. Fisher got into the yard, and by breaking a window at Jack's Coffee-House was taken in there; A drawer and a nurse escaped with some plate by the back door into Cateaton Street; The cook maid leap'd out of a window three stories high and broke an arm; as did Mr. Taylor, brother to Mrs. Fisher, who also broke his leg and thigh, and was so bruis'd that his life is despaired of: The house maid, one of the drawers, and a boy, perished in the flames, and several parts of their bodies have been since found in the rubbish.

On the same day about the same time, another fire broke out in a smith's house in Grob Street near Criplegate, which consumed part of the same. It began in the garret, where a bed-ridden woman lay, who was burnt to death.

LONDON NOV. 9. Yesterday died Mr. Taylor, clerk of the committee of the East India Company for buying, and brother of the mistress of the Crown Tavern near Guild-hall, of the hurt he received by leaping from a window of the same house, at the late dreadful fire there.

We hear that two certain noblemen have laid a very great wager upon two cooks dressing a bill of fare; the one Mr. Red, a Scotsman, cook to his Grace the Duke of Hamilton (who is reckon'd as much a master of his business as any we have in England, and has lately been offered very great encouragement) the other Mr. Bruce, a foreigner, who is also reckoned very famous.

LONDON NOV. 10. One James Huges, a swordsman from Northern Ireland, being come over with a number of his gentlemen, on purpose to fight the noted and admired Mr. Edward Sutton, pipamaker from Graveford, for a considerable sum of money, several persons of distinction have laid extraordinary wagers, on the side of the said Mr. Sutton, and we hear the conflict is to be decided on Monday next at Mr. Stoker's Amphitheatre. Each person is to be on stage between the hours of two and three, and to play or pay. It is thought there are wagers to the value of two or three hundred pounds depending on the battle.

FALMOUTH NOV. 16. Some days past, about 500 tinners went to Padflow, and took from thence what corn they could find designing for exportation, and last Thursday and Friday they did the same at Gweege. On Tuesday about 1,000 came here &, took away what they could get. On Wednesday to our great surprize about 300 more, most on horses, came hither armed with clubs; they filled our streets, and cryed aloud, We come for corn, and corn we will have; adding, the merchants have no commission from the King to send it to their enemies. The commander of the company of invalids joyn'd with the merchants, and made them retreat, but could not force them out of town till they had search'd all the warehouses; they took from hence, and in the neighbourhood about 2,000 bushels of salt, &c. The proclamation was read to them before they dispersed, that had they been fired upon, as some advised, they would have laid the town to ashes.

FALMOUTH NOV. 16. They write from the inland parts, that grain is so very dear every where, that it is almost next akin to a famine; and that some places the farmers being threatened by the women to have their sacks cut if they held it at so high a price, had occasioned some abatement; but the labouring people being sick in great numbers, so, little corn was brought to market, that it has risen to 7 s. 6d. a bushel.

LONDON DEC. 16. They write from North-Yarmouth, They have been grievously afflicted with the new distemper, which carried off above 400 persons in that town in seven weeks but was much abated.

This morning about 50 convicts were conveyed from Newgate on board a vessel in the river, well mannacled, for Maryland.

LONDON DEC. 16. Yesterday a gentleman bowl'd from Highgate to London, (which is 4 miles) for a wager of 50 £. which he was to perform between the hours of 7 in the morning and 5 in the evening, at 100 bowls: He had an artful contrivance of bowling in a through of 100 yards in length, which was removed, after each throw to the place where the bowl stop'd; by which means he did at 82 bowls, and by 4 o'clock.

LONDON DEC. 20. We have a comical account from an alehouse at Wapping kept by an airy widow. A lewd surruping tar-jacket coming into the house, called for a pot of stout, drank to the landlady, and perseived her to be brisk and airy, thought her also to be right for his turn, began to be very sweet upon her, and needs must bee feeling towards that which modesty forbid him; She perceiving his drift said, Since you are despos'd to be merry, if you please, Sir, w'll draw lots, whether you shall feel me or I feel you, which being agreed on, it was his lost to feel her; whereupon she immediately up with the tongs and broke his pate, making the blood fly about his ears: She then asked him whether he had felt her, and how he lik'd that sort of feeling? This put the poor tarr into such a consternation, that instead of making a reply, he took his heels, and ran out the door faster than a bankrupt before 6 serjeants, leaving the scot on chalk. 'Tis verily believed, but few such landladies are to be found in the hundreds of Wapping.

LONDON DEC. 23. Our merchants have advice, that two English private traders, from Bengal attempting to deal with the Arabians those wild people, upon some words arising fell upon them and wounded the crews, running away with most of the cargo. The one was commanded by Capt. Hill, and the other by Capt. Douglas.

1728

LONDON JAN. 6. The Cary Capt. Barns, arrived in Virginia the 19th of November, about 30 leagues eastward of Cape Henry, she took into tow a wreck, being called the Lever, of Liverpool, Robert Lawrence master, bound from Antigua to Liverpool, and carried her into Virginia; she had no masts, boats, anchors, nor any manner of movable, above deck, they being without doubt washed away.

An Abstract of the project and proposal for the encouragement of the seamen of the Kingdom.

I. All seamen who enter voluntarily into the Kings service, shall begin wages from the day of their entry, provided they appear within fourteen days on board the ships, and besides, shall have conduct money.

II. They shall have two months wages advanced to them.

III. They shall have 4 s. a month added to their present wages, if they be able seamen, or inferior officers; and 2 s. a month if they be ordinary seamen, or able bodied landmen.

IV. Masters or owners of merchant ships, shall not give above forty shillings a month wages to their common seamen.

V. Seamen who enter voluntarily into the King's service shall be paid two months wages every six months, till the final pay of the ship.

VI. When a voluntary seaman dies, wages shal be forthwith paid to his executors, without staying for the pay of the ship.

VII. Only press'd men shall be turned over from one ship to another. Voluntary seamen shall be exempted from it, except in case of extreme necessity.

VIII. All petty officers and preferments in the ship shall be given to voluntary seamen only.

IX. When any ship is paid off, every voluntary seaman, who desires it, shall be protected from pressing, for a month.

X. If any ship is fitted out at one point, and laid up at another, the voluntary, who lives near the first port, shall be allowed conduct money.

XI. Seamen who desert, shall forfeit no wages but what are due in the ship they desert from, the law punishing desertion with death.

XII. The treasurer of the Navy shall pay the wages to the seamen themselves if they are present, and not their creditors; and no letters of authority shall be in force, but what are attested by the captain of the ship, Commissioner of the Navy or the Mayor of a town.

XIII. All seamen however may dispose of his ticket, which shall be paid to a lawful purchaser, even though the party should desent afterwards.

XIV. If any seaman applies for his wages after the ship's books are made up and closed, he shall be paid within a month after application.

XV. A seaman who has served the King voluntarily 20 years, and is not under fifty five years of age, shall be for ever protected from being press'd, shall be free from all parish offices, and shall be admitted into Greenwich Hospital, preferable to any other.

XVI. If a land officer enlist a seaman, upon proof made that he is a seaman, he shall be discharged.

XVII. Governours, Ministers, and Councils in foreign ports, shall subject poor straggling seamen, at the allowance of 6 d. a day, which shall be repaid them of the Navy board; and shall send the said seamen home in the first ship.

XVIII. Masters of ships, homeward-bound, shall be obliged to receive all such seamen, and bring them home, the Navy Board allowing them 6 d. a day for their passage and subsistance.

XIX. Foreign seamen, having served three years voluntarly in the King's ships, shall be allowed the privilege of Englishmen.

To all which we think, should be added in XXth place, an article for the better usage of our sailors on board his Majesty's ships, by the commanders, against some whom there has been lately, and still lie heavy complaints.

LYMINGTON JAN. 10. The Beaver Capt. Matthew Smith, is arrived here in 27 days from New-York bound for Amsterdam; They received much damage in her passage, having been forced to fling part of the cargo over board, and her boat and all things on her deck were wash'd away.

LONDON JAN. 11. By a ship arrived in the river the 8th instant, which left Gibraltar the 1st of December, O. S. The master thereof reports, that there was an order come from Madrid, for the Spanish troops to withdraw from before that place; and that they were treating for the hire of ships to transport them to Barcelona.

LONDON JAN. 30. The Anne, Capt. Cooke, bound from Malaga to London, was lost the 8th past, within 3 leagues of Port Croix in Britany, in France; part of her wreck and her cargo, with the mate and two men were saved but the captain, 9 sailors and an officer from Gibraltar were drowned.

We hear from Cambridge, that by the great rain they have had in the neighbouring counties about fifty thousand acres of land Bedford Level is under water.

One John Gretton was killed by one Whitaker, his antagonist, at a boxing match at Stoake's Amphitheatre, near Islington: They fought for 25 minutes with amazing vigour and agility, till at length the battle issued in a defeat of Gretton, Whitaker having just strength enough remaining to raise his bruised body upon his knees to give a blow, whilst the other lay incapable of lifting either hand or foot, nor would he bleed upon opening a vein, which was done immediately upon the stage. So that our polite country men, who honoured this battle with their presence had the high diversion of seeing a man beaten to death by one of his own species. This Whitaker formerly beat the renowned Venitian, for a large sum, and Gretton had formerly beaten Whitaker.

LONDON FEB. 10. The ship Prince of Wales, Capt. Raglesfield, which some time since took in her loading at the city of Hambourgh, a sea port in his Majesty's German Dominion on the Elbe, was lately drove into Harwich by contrary winds, having many passengers and valuable cargo on board, bound for Philadelphia in Pennsylvania; which seems to shew that great benefits may accrue to this Kingdom by the advantageous privileges said to be granted for the opening a door to commerce in and to his Majesty's said Dominion.

A farmer in Islington, living near the hole in the wall, who was to have done penance in the Church there tomorrow, persuant to his sentence, for begetting two bastards on the body of a very near relation, dy'd suddenly in his chair last Tuesday.

LONDON FEB. 15. On Tuesday one French a centinel in Colonel Short's Company in the Second Regiment of Foot Guards, was drumm'd out of the regiment with a rope about his neck, for picking pockets in the Mall in St. Jame's Park.

The same night, between twelve and one on the clock, as Mr. Cane attorney at Law, who lodged in Salisbury Court, was going thro' Castle-Yard in Holborn, in a hackney coach, accompanied by one of his tenants, a country farmer, he was set upon by two robbers who holding each a pistol to his breast, demanded his money, watch and rings. He gave them 10 shillings in money, and a silver watch, but had the good fortune to save 60 £. which he had just received of his tenant, besides rings, &c.

The same gentleman was set upon last week in Fleet-Street, but came off without damage.

LONDON FEB. 16. A few days since a poor woman, who was lodged on Elbow-Lane, near Thames Street, being in great want, kept with-in doors till she dy'd, with hunger; her daughter being present fell into fits, and her spirit being sunk with want she dy'd presently after.

LONDON FEB. 18. On Saturday morning last a French merchant in Hanover Street cut his throat in several places and died immediately. What could induce him to commit this suicide is not yet known: He was an old bachelor of 80 years of age, whereby it is thought that love was not his predominate passion.

LONDON FEB. 19. Last Saturday a cause was try'd at Wesminster, before the Lord Chief Justice Raymond, wherein Capt. Thomas Smith (master of the ship Beaver from New-York) was plaintiff against George Dent an officer of the customs, defendent, for seizing and taking 5 barrels of beef and pork out of the said captain's ship, under colour of several Acts of Parliament as being more than was necessary for the said ships provision in her said voyage, from New-York for London: It appeared, that the reason of so much beef and pork being left, was from the shortness of the ships voyage, she having by the favour of the winds and of the weather, arrived here in about five weeks; though it appeared the provisions laid in was but ten barrels of beef and pork, which was reckoned sufficient for ten weeks; and it appearing to the Court, that the time making such voyage is very uncertain, and that it is used to take three months provisions for such voyages; the Court directed the jury to find for the plaintiff, damages 15 £. being the value of the five barrels of beef and pork so seized, besides cost of suit.

LONDON FEB. 24. The insolence of the street robbers is arriv'd to such an amazing pitch, that the like hath not been known in memory of any man living, who every night perform in fact what the comedians of Lincoln-Inn Field only represent in Farce; and by the accounts of one of the gang who has been apprehended, their project have equall'd if not exceeded those of the players, 70 guineas it seems was found in his purse, being his just dividend, or share of the booty they had met with in their midnight occursions: Several gentlemen having been atack'd and robb'd in the Hackney coaches, and others on foot in the high streets of the city, insomuch, that we are inform'd his Majesty hath been pleas'd to declare, the same shall be taken into consideration by the Council.

LONDON MARCH 2. The Endeavour Capt. Raynolds, which sail'd the 20th of December for Virginia, on the 13th of January, being in the latitude of 46 degrees and 40 minutes, a clap of thunder, with lightning, split the main top mast in pieces, struck off the check and wooldings of her main mast, struck down 12 men on the deck, went down the larboard pump, which it split to pieces, and entered a chest with arms in it, which was between decks, blew up a cartrige, and melted some of the arms in the chest; the ship received so much more damage thereby, as obliged the captain to desert from executing the voyage; and on the 25th past she got into Plymouth to refit. A ship which was in company with her when the aforesaid accident happened, received much damage also, and had three men killed.

LONDON MARCH 5. Letters from Lord Portmore, dated Gibraltar, Jan. 16. There is advice, that Count Monemar had march'd off all the battalions that were employ'd in the seige of that place, and sent away his artillery, ammunition, and warlike stores, and pull'd all batteries to pieces.

LONDON MARCH 12. A certain person having yesterday the curiosity to hold a conversation with a female prisoner thro' a chequer door, in the postern of Newgate and attempting a greater intimacy than was strickly decent, before that he could recover his hand from the bottom of the door, his new acquaintance robbed his head which before seemed not over-well furnish'd, and he went away swearing and cursing without his hat, and vowing revenge, pretending to be a keeper of Birdwell, but proved to be only a servant to a small officer of that house.

Six insolent debtors, who had been long confined in Newgate, were yesterday set at liberty by means of part of the King's most gracious bounty, given for that purpose last Lord-Mayor's day, when their Majesties honour'd the city with their Royal presence at dinner.

The same day a foot-race was run for 10 guineas a side, from Tyburn Turnpike to Acton, and back again, being about 12 miles, between two running-footmen, one belonging to Lord Gallway, and the other called John Heath, alias Yorkshire Tom. The race was run in an hour and two minutes, and Lord Gallway's footman beat the other by about 70 yards, tho' the odds were laid 3 to 1 against him.

LONDON MARCH 12. On Tuesday last one Smith, a glazier, in King Street Golden Square, being mending the outside of a window up two pair stairs, fell to the street, and broke his thigh bone in 2 places, and the glazier's knife he had in his hand, run near 3 inches into his scull. He languished till Thursday, in a very miserable condition, and then died.

LONDON MARCH 13. On Saturday last about seven in the evening, several stage-coaches going to Hampstead were stopp'd, a little beyond the Half-Way-House, by two highwaymen who rifled the passengers.

One of the waiters at the White's Chocolate House in St. James's Street, coming from the bank on Wednesday last, whither he was sent to receive money, in a hackney coach, dropt several bank notes to the value of 369 £. in the hackney coach while he discharged before the same was missed: But luckily for him, some time after, a gentleman going in the same coach, found all the said notes lying upon the step thereof, which he took care of, and upon enquiring who the coachman set down last, went to White's and gave the same to the waiter for the right owner.

LONDON MARCH 14. Yesterday came on at the Excise Office a great trial before the Commissioners (being the first that yet hath been of that kind) between the King plaintiff; & Joseph Mason, a distiller in Southwark defendant, pursuant to a late Act of Parliament for inflicting a penalty of 500 £. upon any that shall bribe or corrupt an officer belonging to the revenue: The trial lasted about three hours; and, as many thousands, including officers and other that pay duty there for several commodities, were solicitious to know the issue, there were some hundreds present to hear the decision, the Councils for the King were Mr. Serjeant Darnel, & Mr. Filmore; Councils for the defendant, Mr. Serjeant Comyns, & Mr. Bootle: After the full hearing it appear'd that the distiller had given the officers a considerable sums of money at _____ _____ and also a note under his own hand of 60 guineas, which was produced, for procuring him a blank permit, which he might fill up at liberty, proportionably to the goods he should run, and so defraud the King of his revenue. The crime being plain he was order'd to pay the penalty of 500 £.

LONDON MARCH 16. Thursday last four private centenels of the Second Regiment of Foot Guards, according to the sentence of the Court Marshal, and another was to have the same number of lashes, but being old and thin skin'd, he came off with only 56 lashes.

Last Saturday died at his father in Holbourn, the Rev. Mr. Hughes, son of the Rev. Dr. Hughes. It is remarkably that this young gentleman was married to a young lady of a considerable fortune two or three days before he died, but being taken ill on his wedding day never bedded with her: He was a young gentleman of fine parts and is greatly lamented by all that knew him.

LONDON MARCH 16. Sunday in the afternoon a melancholy accident happened: Two boys one an apprentice to a shoe maker in Milford Lane, the other an apprentice to a cooper in Blackamoor Street, went from the Belfry of St. Clement's Church, to turn the Sance Bell, and standing upon the ledge without the steeple, both fell into the church yard: The former dash'd his brains out, and the latter received no damage by the fall, except one little bruise on the side of his head, he walks about, and is very cheerful; and what is very surprizing, he remembers his being let blood, which was done by a surgeon, who accidently came by as he fell, at which time he was, by everybody, supposed to be dead; he says the other boy's foot slipp'd and finding himself falling he caught hold of his legs to save himself, and pull'd him after him.

Yesterday Alexander Gibson, a grenadier in Col. Stewart's Company of the Second Batallion of the Third Regiment of Foot Guards, was tied to the Serjeant's Halberts in St. James's Park, and received ten lashes from each of the six drums that mounted guard, and is to receive the like punishment the next guard day, as we hear, for extorting money from a gentleman when on duty.

On Thursday last the body of a boy unknown, about 13 years of age, was thrown on shore by the tide within the flood-gates of Chelsea Water-Works, suppose to have the Thames 6 weeks or a month at least: It being in the Parish of the St. George's Hanover Square. The body was carried to the Black Boy by the turnpike near Duke of

Buckinham's, where the coroner's inquest sat upon it yesterday. He had on a black waistcoat, bound about the skirts, a coarse blue jacket, and a pair of rid breeches with white metal buttons; and had in his pocket only a farthing in money, and several boy's play-things.

LONDON MARCH 16. Yesterday between 1 and 2 in the morning, a servant maid to Mr. Cunningham, a linen-draper in bed in the back parlour, was kill'd by the back part of the house falling upon her; the son of Mr. Cunningham, who is about 8 years of age, being in bed with her at the same time, was very much bruised, but is likely to recover.

A day ago one Mr. Meale, a cheesemonger, over against the playhouse in Drury Lane, leaving a bag with 224 guineas in it, upon the desk in the Computing-House, while he went into the shop; upon his return miss'd the same to his great surprize, as no person could go in or out without being seen: But it seems, the bag being somewhat greasy, an hungry dog had snatch'd it up and run off with it, dropping it by a cobler's stall in Princess-street, who seized the same, and hearing no immediate enquiry after it, e'en paid away 14 £. of it among his creditors, and spent some of it feasting his family upon his good luck, and all of them talking freely and rejoicing publickly, it soon came to Mr. Meale's ears, who came to the cobler and found his bag and all the guineas, excepting the few disbursed by the cobler, as above. Upon this, Meale declared, that he had intended to offer a reward of 20 £. for the same, and therefore presented the cobler with about 6 £. more, besides what he had expended, and so they parted well pleased on both sides.

LONDON MARCH 16. Yesterday Charlotte Tales, daughter to the late Hackney writer, in Matre-Court in Fleet-Street, being disordered in her senses, flung herself out of a window in Gray's Inn Lane, three stories high, and died immediately.

The same day one Harvey, who kept the Hat and Feather Alehouse in St. Martin's Lane, and stood indicted on account of the prosecution of Henry Wilcox, for pretended robbery in the street, but absconded, was seized by Mr. Chambers, tipstaff to the Lord Chief Justice Ramond, by virtue of his Lordship's warrant.

LONDON MARCH 19. We hear, a project is on foot for preserving his Majesty's ships of wax and merchant ships, that make voyages to the West Indies, from being rotten or wormeaten so soon as usual by six years, and for abundance less expence that the common way of cleaning ship's bottoms, &c. And that a patent is to be granted for that purpose.

LONDON MARCH 23. By letter from York, there is advice, that on Saturday the 4th instant, at Mr. Brough, a master bricklayer, and master joiner, with five labourers, were at work in the cellar of a new house that was just finishing near Micklegate Bar, the whole fabrick fell upon them, and crush'd some instantly to death; among who are, Mr. Brough and one labourer, and 'tis thought, the others, being much bruised, cannot live.

LONDON MARCH 28. On Saturday inst. 2 women went to a certain justice of the peace and under pretence of getting a warrant against some ruffians that had assaulted them; and as the justice was writing the warrant, one of the women stepp'd into the room to him, pretending to give him a more particular account of the story, and watching her opportunity, stole his gold watch and chain, which hung near him on a hook by the chimney piece, and got clear off with her companion before the watch was miss'd.

LONDON APRIL 2. On Saturday evening about 7 a-clock Mr. Sainthill, a noted surgeon in Bread Street, was attacked between Hamstead and Halfway House, by two highwaymen, who robb'd him of a piece of gold and some silver, but two gentlewomen who were in the coach with him were robb'd of much greater sums, having deliver'd up their purses with all their contents upon demand of the rogues, who carried away a great booty thereby.

LONDON APRIL 6. Letters from Gibraltar, by way of Holland, advises, That the Spaniards have withdrew themselves from before that place, leaving only a guard near the mills, and a certain tower called Devils Tower, as also two squadrons to prevent any communication between the town and the continent.

One day last week a comical wedding being made up at a brandyshop in the Mint, the loving couple went to an alehouse and sent for the parson to stitch them together according to the laudable custom of that place, but the poor man not having money enough to defray the expence, his loving wife, after the ceremony, and a cann or two of flip, persuaded him to let her carry his coat to pawn, which he consented to, she bid him good-bye softly, and the poor fellow has not since heard of her, or did he ever see her before, insomuch that he was obliged to pawn his waistcoat to pay the reckoning.

LONDON APRIL 6. They write from Tetbury in Gloucestershire, That as they were burying a corpse in the Meeting-House there, the grave being dug very near the pillar sunk into the grave, and the whole gallery fell down, but of the great number of people that were therein and under it, only two or three were slightly wounded.

'Tis written from Salisbury, That one Smith, condemned at the last Assizes there, being order'd for execution as last Tuesday the hangman went to him, and in discourse with him, happening to tell him that his family were all rouges, that he had hanged his father and his brother and was the next day to hang him, Smith swore he should not, and immediately with amazing violence seized him and dash'd out his brains against the wall.

LONDON APRIL 11. On Tuesday last the Assizes ended at Kingston, when four men and one woman received sentence of death, the latter for the death of a bastard child, by cutting its throat with a knife; two of the men for robberies committed in St. George's Fields, and the other two for burglary.

Yesterday morning a journeyman pewterer, after drinking largely at a brandy shop, going to take water at the Old Swan, fell down the stairs, broke his arm, & tumbling into the Thames, was drowned.

LONDON APRIL 13. Last Monday night a person having been drinking a little too much with an acquaintance in Westminster, returned home towards the Royal Exchange fell down near Temple bar, and was help'd up by a stranger, who seemingly out of kindness got a coach and put him into it, getting, in soon after himself, accompanying him as far as Cheapside Conduit, in which time he found an opportunity if rifling his pockets, taking from him a good hat and peruke; and had the cunning to put his own on the man's head.

LONDON APRIL 13. Last Sunday the boat at Jeremy's Ferry in Hackney River, was, by the rapidity of the stream forced on a pile and overset, whereby 3 persons were drowned.

Last week a coach was overset in the way to New Market, by the waters; A waggon near Stony Stratford, and some rich goods spoilt; and two horses drowned at Bury.

FALMOUTH MAY 11. The tinners are exceeding troublesome strolling daily from place to place in the adjacent parts, and commiting great disorders; last night, about 100 of them were at Flushing, on the other side of our river, opposite to us, searching for corn, and we hourly expect them here, except their scouts deter them, by apprizing them of our preporations to receive them. The company of soldiers, which lately came hither, have been on duty all this day, and we are mounting four pieces of cannon on the Strand.

BEECLES IN SUFFOLK MAY 12. Last night a melancholy accident happen'd in our river: Thirty young men & women sailing in Sir. Edmond Bacon's pleasure boat, the main sheet fasten'd, and a sudden gust of wind arising, the boat was overset, and 7 men & 8 women perished, the rest being saved by two men who were then fishing near the place.

LONDON MAY 21. Yesterday nineteen condemn'd malefactors, viz. sixteen men and three women, were executed at Tyburn, being carried thither in seven carts. Just before they came to the tree a party of foot guards took a post round the same, with their muskets loaded, and bayonets fix'd to the muzzles, which prevented all riots &, disorders. Nichols, one of the prisoners, broke his halter upon being tunn'd off, but he was tied up again, and suffering with the rest.

LONDON MAY 23. Yesterday one Willis, who keeps the Appletree Alehouse over against the end of New-Bond Street, in Oxford Road, sent a porter, commonly known by the name of Yorkshire, to a friend with a gallon of brandy, who meeting with the wife of one Major, with whom he had been well acquainted, they went together into a private place in the Fields, and drank so freely of the brandy, that they were both found dead drunk; the woman died in that condition, and Yorkshire being made sensible at what had happened, by being taken into custody, got out of the top of the house into the next, and so made his escape.

LONDON MAY 25. On Thursday last a boy riding a horse in Lincoln's Inn Fields, the horse flung him, and his foot hung in the stirrup; the mob running to save the boy frighten'd the horse, who ran away and dash'd the boy's brains out against the ground.

LONDON MAY 28. On Sunday last a boy swimming in Hackney River, near Jeremy's Ferry, being in great danger of drowning, a person went into the river, to his assistance, but both were unfortunately lost.

PORTSMOUTH MAY 30. Yesterday morning the Plymouth man of war a 4th rate, of 60 guns and 365 men, Capt. Robert Mann, commander, The Anglesea a 5th rate, of 40 guns and 110 men, Capt. Samuel Chadwich; the Southampton, Capt. Edward Brooke, and the

Happy sloop, 114 tons, 8 guns and 60 men, Capt. Douglas, all bound for Jamaica, weigh'd anchor from Spithead, but coming little wind they anchor'd again at St. Helen's: The wind this day coming to N. E. they all weigh'd again, and got under sail for Jamaica: The happy sloop, being a light vessel, and a good sailor, is to make the best of her way, Having a packet for Admiral Hopson; the Southampton is to remain as a hulk in Jamaica, being fitted for that purpose. On the arrival of these ships at Jamaica, Mr. Potter will be removed from being Naval Officer there.

LONDON JUNE 1. Edingburg May 13. We hear from Angus, that the Laird of Briggs and Finhaven happening a quarrel, the Rt. Hon. the Earl of Stratmore with whom they were in company, running in between them to prevent any mischief, received a wound from the latter, of which, we hear, he is since dead, and that a warrant is granted for bringing up prisoner hither that unfortunate gentleman by whose hand the unlucky accident happened.

The interview between the King of Prussia and Poland, occasioned great speculations in most of the Courts of Europe. The Russian's fleet is said to consist of 45 ships, of the line of battle, 19 frigates, and a great number of gallies, and other flat bottom'd vessels, fit for transporting troops.

LONDON JUNE 1. The South Sea Company are hiring ships to go to the Coast of Africa, to purchase Negroes, to be carried to Jamaica, in order to supply the Spaniards.

Mr. Matthews, is sworn in Bookseller in ordinary to his Majesty.

A few days ago a fire broke out at the Half-Moon and Rummer alehouse in New-bond Street, by which three women and two children, who lodg'd in the garret, were misarably burnt to death; A man and a child were saved getting out at the top of the house, but the poor man is run mad, having a wife and another child among those that perished in the flames.

On Saturday Mrs. Hipworth, at the Three Rings, in Piccadilly, having been much troubled with a pain in her stomach and side for some time past, sent for a surgeon to bleed her, which he accordingly did, and as she was bleeding very freely, a living animal, about an inch and a half long, with several legs, came out of her vein, thro' the orifice: The animal is still alive, and has been seen by several eminent physicians.

Yesterday the bodies of the five persons burnt to death by the fire which happen'd at Mr. Willson's house, the sign of the Rummer and

Half-Moon in Tyburn Road, last Wednesday night, were dug out of the ruins, in order to the coroner's enquiry. We hear that a little before the dreadful misfortune happen'd three rude fellows came into the house in a disorderly manner, and being refused such liquor and attendance as they required, they went out, demanding Mr. Willson, saying, he should repent of it before the morning, and soon after the house was in flames. There had been no fires lighted in it that day by any of the inhabitants.

LONDON JUNE 8. On Monday night last about 11 o'clock a Mr. Wheeler master and owner of a ship being on board with his mate near Horsley Down, and both being in liquor, some difference arose between them, and in a scuffle they both fell into the Thames and were drowned.

BRISTOL JUNE 13. Last night arrived the Kertlington, Capt. Pitt, she came away from Jamaica the 27th of May thro' the Gulph. A Spanish privateer of 8 guns, and full of men, attacked her off the Havanna, and after near half an hour's engagement, boarded her by beat of drum with about 40 men; the Kertlington's crew being but 17, return'd to their close quarters, and the first kill'd was the drummer, and in little time they killed all that boarded her; having only two of their own crew wounded, who lost their fingers; they found twelve muskets, one blunderbuss, &c. on deck; two of the enemy who fell, lived half an hour, they were Frenchmen. The privateer (which was a sloop) upon this bore away, but in appearance had scarce hands enough on board to hoist her sails; her crew was composed of all nations. The Kertlington persued the sloop, and gave her three broad sides, with three chain shot in each gun; and continued chasing her as long as her guns could reach her. They apprehended she came out of Havanna.

LONDON JUNE 22. We see by this mail several regulations made at sessions, among others, that the conference shall be held where is no seat higher or lower, and at which the Plenipotentiaries are to place themselves as they come in, their domesticks are to wear neither sticks or swords nor any fire arms either open or privately, on pain of being turned out of the city; they are not to be out late at night, and if they commit any crime to have no protection from their masters from being published according to law.

CANTERBURY JUNE 22. We hear that on Monday in Whitsom Weck there was caught between Hockenbury and Stile Bridge in Kent, a fish 30 feet long, with a large head, two feet like a man, and of leaden colour; and no man that has yet seen it can tell what kind of fish it is.

LONDON JUNE 26. A paragraph having been inserted in several newspapers, giving an account that Miss Spence, a young lady of about ten years old was inoculated for the small pox about four years ago, and has nevertheless had the distemper lately in a natural way; whereby it is generally understood, that tho' she had undergone the aforementioned distemper by inoculation, yet that did not prevent her having it again in the natural way; it is thought proper to state the fact truly, which is as follows: An attempt was made to give Miss Spencer the small pox by way of inoculation about four years ago; but it is certain that such an attempt did not take place in any respect whatsoever, she continuing in perfect health from that time without complaints or appearances of the illness at all, till she fell sick lately of the small pox of which she recovered.

LONDON JUNE 29. We hear from Gloucester, that at Arlington in that said county, there fell a storm of rain in the 19th instant, which caused such a dreadful flood, that in the space of half an hour, it carried away more than 50 loads of stone and gravel, some of which stones were judg'd to be about 300 weight, and fix'd in the road, which the violence of the flood tore up, and drove down the highway, not much less than a furlong; in our common field the mould of several acres was entirely carried off. About a mile distance on each side of the town was very little ruin.

LONDON JUNE 29. Thursday the felons in Newgate under sentence of transportation, to the number of 117, were shipp'd away for the American plantations. Abundance of their acquaintance attended to pay them complements of a good voyage; wishing themselves no worse off in the end.

REDING JULY 1. On Wednesday last we had a terrible storm of thunder and lightning, in so much that it tore the stocking and shoe off a boys leg, that was keeping of sheep near that town, and kill'd his dog that lay by him. It enter'd several houses in that town, struck a screen chimney-piece in one and severed the posts of a bed to pieces in another.

LONDON JULY 2. On Saturday last died John Lawrence, of Barns, Esq; son of Sir John Lawrence, formerly Lord Mayor of

London, and being opened, about 100 stones were taken out of his kidneys, two of which were surprizingly sharp in size.

LONDON JULY 4. Letter from Oxford advice, some poor labourors employ'd in building a new church in that city, being in great distress on account of their wages not being lately paid them, the Rev. Dr. Hole, Rector of Exeter College, sent them 100 £. to expedite so religious and necessary a work; The said gentleman is also intent upon some other charitable benedictions.

THUMBRIDGE WELLS JULY 4. Yesterday it rain'd almost all day, and this day we have had very severe showers, with lightning and thunder. About noon a boy of about 10 years of age, playing upon the common, was killed by the lightning; he looks freshly and much the same as before; the only mark is a round hole, seemingly cut out from the crown of his hat, and his hair is singed.

LONDON JULY 9. Letters from Wales tell us, That during the late flood in the River Dee, a fisherman got into his corrocle, (a sort of British canoe) with a design to cross the river between Farm and Holt, but his wife apprehending his voyage was only to the next alehouse, persued him with so much haste, that she came as he was putting off from the bank, and got hold of the corrocle, which was overset by their struggling, and both of them, together with their child were drowned.

LONDON JULY 13. Last Wednesday between 7 and 8 o'clock in the evening Mrs. Jones wife of Mr. Jones in Salisbury Court, dropt down dead, being with child, a surgeon was immediately sent for and open'd her, and her male child liv'd some time after her.

LONDON JULY 16. Yesterday was held a session of the High Court of Admiralty at Justice Hall in the Old Baily, before Sir Henry Penrice, Judge of the said Court, Baron Carter, and Mr. Justice probyn, when John Prie was arraigned on two indictments one of felony and murder, and the other for piracy; and after a long hearing was found guilty of both.

The evidence against him was John Ashley, who deposed in substance as follow'd: That in April of 1727, he went upon business on board the sloop Young Lawrence, burton about _____ tons, of which Michael Danzel, or Dolzel was then master, which sloop was then lying at anchor near Eustacia, an island to the westward of St. Christopher's in America; that then the prisoner John Prie, who was a sailor on board her, (her crew and the master, being only five) enticed him to come on board again, and join with him in running away with the sloop; that accordingly he went on board again, soon after which the mate came on board, much in liquor, and gave directions for sailing away; which done, he got into the boat which was on deck and fell asleep; that then Prie with a cutlass, was going to kill him, but the captain awaked, and asked him what he was going to do, he said, nothing, and privately slung his cutlass overboard; soon the captain went to sleep again, when Prie, with an wood axe, knock'd him on the head, and said to Ashley, he had done his business; but some remains of life appearing, and he groaning, another with an axe beat him on the breast till he expired; that they flung him overboard, after taking his buckles out of his shoes, his gold ring from his finger, and what money he had in his pockets from him, (which were particularly mention'd in the indictment) and going into the cabbin, they burnt all the papers, and ransack'd it, which done, they chose one of the crew for their commander, and went to the French island of Guadelupe, where they sent their new commander ashore to get more hands, but he not returning so soon as they expected, they were afraid he had discover'd them, and therefore stood away for New-England, which they over-shot, falling in with the land about Cape Sables; then they resolv'd to go to Newfoundland, where arriving, they wooded and water'd, but under great terror of mind, believing every ship the saw was a man of war; in fear of which they departed, and made for the British Channel, in the Chops of which they met a vessel, to whom they gave some cocoa for some provisions and water, and getting in sight of the Isle of Guernsey, they hover'd so long about for the opportunity to go on shore, as to give cause to the officers of the island to suspect their being on a smuggling account, who set off, seized, and brought them into the island; and examining them, Ashley made a confession of which they were clapped into goal, but one of them broke out and escaped; the two above mentioned were brought over to the Marshalsea, together with a third, who was a Negro, and who soon dy'd there. The vessel when run away with, had on board 30 hogsheads of sugar, some cocoa and other goods.

LONDON JULY 20. Latter end of last week a proclamation was published, requiring quarantine to be perform'd by all ships and vessels coming from the Levant, the isles of the archipelago, Zant, Venizi, Cephaatonia, S. Mauro, and any of the adjacent islands, or any of the ports or places of the Morea, into Great Britain, or the Isles of Guernsey, Jersey, Alderney, Sark or Man.

OXFORD JULY 27. This day the most infamous rogue, William Colear was brought hither from Newgate, by Habeas Corpus, in order to be try'd at the Assizes here on Wednesday next: It is remarkable, that his grandfather, his father, and 3 brothers have all been hang'd here, and 'tis said he is charged with near 20 robberies & burglaries.

LONDON JULY 30. Yesterday about one in the morning, a plaisterer in East-Smithfield, meeting in Cornhill a person who had been sometime in his debt, demanded the money, upon this, the other person, put his hand in his pocket, drew out a penknife, stabb'd him, and made his escape.

On Friday last, ladies going in a chariot from Beckenham to Bromley, were robbed by a single highwayman, who took from them about 3 £.

Last Thursday night Mr. Edward Warner, an ivory turner, in Gunpowder-Alley, Shoe Lane, as he was at work in his garret, had the misfortune to be bit in the hand by his own dog, who was mad; after which the dog leaped out of the window and breaking three of his legs, was caught and killed, and his liver broiled and given to Mr. Warner, who ate it. But his hand growing worse, he set out last Saturday night for Gravesend, to try the benefit of the salt water.

Last Friday morning the hostler at the White Lyon Inn Spittle-Square; was found dead on the stairs, his neck being dislocated: It is said he went drunk to bed, and is supposed to have risen in the night, and have stumbled down the stairs.

A few days ago a boy was found lying in a chest in Moorfield among the old goods, set out there for sale. It seems he was a poor friendless creature who had wander'd to town and having liv'd a long time without lodging or food, got into the chest for want of better shelter. He was discovered by a groaning, and brought so low by continuing without sustenance, that he was not able to eat. About a day or two after, he was found dead in another chest in the same place.

LONDON JULY 30. Last week a woman who hast pick'd oakum for the dock yard, brought thither her bundle as usual, but she had not been there long before she dropt down dead, though the moment before she seem'd not the least disordered, but was joking and laughing with the rest of her companions.

LONDON JULY 31. From Warwickshire, That at Hampton in Arden a cow hath lately brought forth a calf with two heads, two tails, and (as appeared upon opening) two different hearts, and the body of a very large and uncommon size. This hath occasioned many a weighty speculations among the vulgar, who all agree to be ominous, but they cannot agree for what.

From Northampton, that a young lad asking a countryman what he should do to be talk'd of after he was dead, was answer'd, that he might go and hang himself, upon which, the lad went into the barn and did as he was advised.

LONDON AUG. 1. On Tuesday last the body of a new born male infant supposed to have been strangled, was found in a beast box in Mary Bone Fields, having a very rich lac'd cap on his head, and his feet tied.

LONDON AUG. 1. Yesterday in the evening a poor waterman sailing down the river in his boat, ran her against the rudder of a West Country barge which was likewise under sail, and running forward to clear her, fell overboard and was drowned.

Yesterday morning about 11 of the clock Mr. Evershed a grocer, near the end of Bermondsey-Street in Southwark, was found dead in the cellar of his own house, no person being in the house but the maid, who going down into the cellar, found him lying dead on the ground, very bloody, and a pistol by his side. We hear he went out in the morning about 6, returned about 9 in a violent agony of passion, and went down into the cellar, where he committed this horrible fact.

On Tuesday night last Capt. Deval and Mr. Godfrey, a mate to Mr. Putland, surgeon to the Second Regiment of Foot Guards, having been drinking together, some difference arose between them in their return home, so that in Southampton Street near Covent Garden, they fought a duel. Mr. Godfrey received several wounds, one of which is tho't to be mortal; he was carried to his house in Exceter Court in the Strand, and Capt. Duval was confined in Covent Garden Round-house till last night, where he was committed to Newgate by Justice Vaugham.

On Monday night about 10 a clock, a fire broke out in an outhouse belonging to Mr. Aldridge at Acton, which consumed his dwelling house, two barns full of corn and hay &c. and was not extinguished till five the next morning.

The Lord of the Admiralty having order'd the Durfley Gally, Rey, and Scaford men of war, which were station'd upon the Coast of England, for foreign service, four other men of war are appointed to see that all ships coming from places infected with the plague, perform quarantine.

LONDON AUG. 6. Yesterday John Mitchel, who lived in Rose-Street near Soho-Square, was committed to Newgate by John Ellis Esq; for stabbing his wife in the left breast, with a knife, on which wound she died instantly.

On Sunday last a man was found dead, lying between the parishes of Acton and Turnham-Green, with his head in one parish and his feet in the other, which caused a great dispute between the two about burying him.

On the said day the body of a man with a rope round the middle, in gray stockings, and shoes with silver buckles in them, the rest of the body being naked, was drove ashore at Todd's Wharf near Westminster Bridge, supposed to have laid in the water many days; he was exposed to publick view in St. Margaret's Church Yard.

LONDON AUG. 8. They write from Manton in Rutlandshire, of July the 30th, that on Sunday before a dreadful fire broke out there, which in a short time consumed 11 dwelling houses, besides barns, stables, &c. 'Tis said to have been occasioned by some fire which a careless man was carrying from a neighbour's house, at a time when the wind was high, and blew part of it onto some thatch.

The Anne-Galley, of London Capt. Sparkman, from Jamaica, with 250 Negroes on board, was taken off of Cape Taberon on the west end of the Island of Cuba, on the 12th of June last, by a Spanish privateer sloop of six guns and 65 men belonging to St. Jago in Cuba, they stript her crew naked, and treated them barbarously; but four of the crew, viz. George Fox, John King, Joseph Vaugham, and Adam Sewel, who were ordered by the Spaniards to carry the boat with goods to the privateer in the dusk of the evening, they found means to get away with the boat, where they were two days and nights, without any provisions or water; and they met with a French ship, which took them up, and treated them with great humanity, and carried them into Donna Marie Bay in Hispaniola, where the Rippen and the Bredah men of war were watering, in order to come to England, and who brought these four men to Portsmouth.

On Monday last a youth of about seven years of age, was drowned in a pond near Marybone, as he was washing himself; he was son in law to Mackdonnell, one of the gentlemen of the guard, who lived in Lancashire-Court by Bond-Street.

LONDON AUG. 24. On Saturday night last his Excellency Coffan d. Choja Ambassador extraordinary from the Bashaw, Dey and Divan of Tripoli, arrived here from Weymouth with upwards of 20 persons in his retinue. The presents which his excellency set out with from Port Mahon for his Majesty, were twelve of the finest Barbary horses that have been seen, four whereof died in the voyage, one lyon, which died, eight antelopes, five died and two young ostriches. His Excellency was conducted to town by Jezrrel Jones, Esq; at whose house in Fetter-Lane he is now entertained. On Tuesday his Excellency delivered his credentials.

LONDON AUG. 27. On Tuesday last as a little girl, six years old belonging to an alehouse man in the strand, was going to school, a woman pick'd her up, and gave her a cheesecake, telling the child she would carry her to her room, and dress her very fine, which she did, by stripping off its clean frock and clean cap, &c. and putting on some ragged things in their room; but before she had finished dressing her, she was seiz'd and committed to Newgate, and will be try'd for this piece of civility to the child next session at the Old Baily.

LONDON AUG. 31. On Thursday last was shipped by an eminent merchant of this city, on board the Francis, Capt. Samuel Cary for New-England 15,000 common prayer books, which were wrote for thence, there being a very great demand for them in that province.

LONDON SEPT. 5. We have advice from Virginia, of the Mary, Capt. Charmock, being arrived there from Jamaica. In her passage she had been taken by a Spanish privateer, which was carrying her away for Havanna; but part of the Mary's crew, which were on board the privateer found means to surprize the Spaniards, at High Mass, it being one of the grand festival days, and secured them; but finding they had not sufficient provisions to carry both ships to Virginia, they contented themselves with retaking their own.

LONDON SEPT. 5. We learn from Londeniere, a little village in Normandy, that a young man of about 25 years, being passionately in love with a young woman of the same village, and having been unsuccessful in all his efforts to prevail on her, made a eunuch of himself, thro' dispair, with a razor, and gave himself also several cuts in the arm, but immediately taken care of by an able surgeon, he is now perfectly recovered of the cruel operation.

LONDON SEPT. 5. A very fine statue of his present Majesty King George II in Roman habit, eight foot high, is just finished, at Mr. Pitts a statuary, at the Golden Head at Hyde Park Corner. It is done by the direction of a French gentleman, who intends to set it up at Plymouth in Devonshire.

This morning advice came, that a vessel with 15 passengers on board sailing from New-Castle for Scotland, was cast away, and all wherein drowned, except two men and a boy, who were saved by swimming to shore.

LONDON SEPT. 10. On Thursday last a very lamentable fire broke out at Hickley in Leicestershire, which consumed almost sixty houses, and many ricks of corn and hay, to a very considerable damage, and the utter ruin of many families.

Last Wednesday an unhappy accident happen'd at Sir Creel Bishop's at Pareham in Sussex; the undertaker of his park, and two other men got into a boat on one of the ponds, playing with one another, overturn'd the boat, and they were all three drowned.

They write from Anstell and Dennington, two villagers the hither part of Yorkshire, that on the 29th ult. a sudden shower of hail fell, the stones of such a bigness, and greatly surprized the inhabitants. They add, that about an hour before a wirlwind happen'd which considerably damag'd several dwelling houses, & barns, but the greater lost fell among oats, barley, and other grain in shock in the fields.

LONDON OCT. 4. Last week a noted Quaker, who would come himself to town to fetch a doctor for his sick mistress he knock'd down the constable of the watch who was sent for to qualify the outrageousness of his spirit: But being carry'd to the Gate-House, he had coolness enough next morning to send his mistress's gold watch to the pawn-broker's, to free him from his bodily restraint.

Princess Amelia has been to view Mr. Allen's stone quarry on Clerken Down, also his new invented engine, which with the help of one horse will carry four tons weight of stone two miles to the river side.

LONDON OCT. 5. On Wednesday night, a gentleman crossing Bloomsbury Square, met two young sparks, who took from him his hat and peruke, which they gave to a boy they meet immediately after, and made him go after the gentleman and return them, and tell him, they had only been trying to practice upon him, in case necessity obliged them to take up the business.

On Saturday last George Dewing, late keeper of the correction at Halstead in Essex, was committed by Anthony Collis, Esq; to the County Goal in Essex for the barbarous murder, committed on a travelling woman, his prisoner; we hear, that after he had murdered her, he cut out her bowels, and with a clever chopt her in pieces. This wretch was condemned at Chelmsford in March last, for murder of a bastard-child begot upon the body of one prisoner, whom he used with unheard barbarity; he afterwards obtained his pardon, and pleaded the same at the following Assizes.

LONDON OCT. 8. On Thursday night, about eight o'clock two little boys attempting to rob a chandler-shop in Buckingham Court, Charing-Cross. The woman that kept it, had just shut her door and gone over the way. Being dissapointed there, one of them lifted up the sash of the next house, and cut one of the window curtains close to the rod, while the other stood watching at the court end. They got away with their booty by darkness of the night.

Last Friday evening, a child between three and four years old, being left alone in the room, of an apartment of Mrs. Letirange at the picture shop in Theobald's Row, he got to the window, and found a bottle full of liquid that is used in their trade, and drank it, and died in about three hours after.

The same day the borough constable had 16 persons before the Justice Nichols that they had taken out of disorderly houses; when before his Worship, they proving profligate, and people of no character, the justice committed them to Bridewell.

A youth of fifteen years of age, son of Mrs. Parson at Dowgate-hill, that was knock'd into the Thames by a cart last Thursday se'nnight, at Bear Key, and drowned, was yesterday taken out of the river, to the great satisfaction of his mother and relation.

Last Wednesday night, two gentlemen were robbed between Hampstead and Highgate, of about 15 s. each and a gold head cane.

They write from Bristol, that last week about 500 weavers rose without Lawford's Gate; where they seiz'd and burnt about 30 looms; and from thence went to Chewmagna, Pensford and Keynthan, in which compass they destroyed a great many more looms and one house.

LONDON OCT. 8. On Saturday night inst. several gentlemen talking together in Cavendish-Square amongst whom was a country gentleman just off a journey; a person well dressed came up and beckoned to him, they went together and turning the corner, when the new acquaintance claspped a pistol to his breast, and robb'd him of his money; on his return he told his friends what had happened; They persued the villain and took him robbing a woman, and secured him that night, and on Sunday he was committed to Newgate.

Thursday night a little boy was found hid in Sir Robert Walpole's house in Chelsea. He has own'd that he was to have let in some rogues when the family were all in bed, to rob the house. He has promised to discover several of the gang.

Last Wednesday night, a hackney chair was stopt in Golden-Square by three footpads, two of them laid hold of the poles, and the other told the gentlewoman that he wanted to speak to her. One of the chairmen seized the villain, and two ran away; as did also the third, leaving the lappet of his coat in the chairman's hand.

Last Thursday night, three men, well dress'd went into an alehouse near Church-Lane S. Giles, and called for some brandy, but before they had drank it, a person whispered the master of the house to get a constable; the three fellows apprehending danger, made their escape without paying their reckoning; one of them was Norton, a noted street robber.

LONDON OCT. 8. Last week a man well dress'd, came to an eminent doctor of physick's house in the city, and enquired for the doctor. The servant told him he was not at home; upon which he said he would stay: At that the servant let into the hall, and went about his business. In about half an hour he knock'd; and the servant coming, he told him, it might be long before the doctor returned, and he would call him again another time; so away he went. It seems he had made use of his time; for the doctor had had a new beaver hat come home that morning, and left it in the hall, which the gentleman took, and left one not worth a groat in the room. The parlour door happen'd to be lock'd, which saved the plate, &c. which no doubt he had a design upon. He very likely had a companion without.

On Tuesday night a woman and a boy got into the house of Mr. Gerrard, a salesman at the Three Colts, the corner of Eastcheap; his daughter hearing a noise called out Mary (thinking it was the servant) whereupon they went (having a dark lanthorn) into the room, the boy with a pistol, and the woman with a penknife, threatning to murder her if she made any noise, or refused to shew where the plate and other things of value were. Under this terror she then got up, and conducted them to several chambers, the shop and kitchen; in this last place they were packing up what they got; but remembering they had left something above stairs, the young woman was ordered to go up with the boy, and bring them down: When she had got into the chamber, she fastened the boy out, threw up the sash, and cried out thieves; this awakened Mr. Gerrard, and he making the like outcry, they made off immediately out of the garret window (at which they had enter'd the house) with about 40 £. value of plate, leaving the other good behind them.

LONDON OCT. 17. We hear from Mortdider, that a farmer's son of a village near this place, going to see a young woman, who was with child by him, made her believe that he would conduct her to a place where she might remain 'till after her lying in: the young woman followed him, but on their entering into the wood, he knocked her down with a hammer, ripped open her belly, and afterwards betook himself to flight.

Many of the gentry and principal inhabitants of the villages about London, are going to associate, to concert measures for suppressing of robbers; and we hear some further rewards will be offer's for apprehending them then those already order'd by law.

LONDON OCT. 26. They write from Newbury in Berkshire, That on Tuesday last one Mrs. Gray a widow woman who lives in Tatcham Parish, being gone to borrow a thimble at a neighbour's a large sow in the meantime enter'd her house, where her two children being in bed on a ground floor, the sow reach'd over the biggest child, and eat the face of the other quite off, together with the flesh of one of the shoulders, the unhappy mother coming home, beheld the sow sucking out the child's brains, who was then dead. The beast has been since burnt to ashes by order of the magistrates.

LONDON NOV. 2. About a fortnight since, a baker's boy in Fetter-Lane playing with a young woman flung some salt in her eyes, and to take off the smart they wash'd it with cold water, which in the opinion of the surgeon who was afterwards sent for caused the salt to penetrate more into her head, insomuch that on Sunday last she died; After feeling the most racking pains, one of her eyes being quite perished, and had so inflam'd her whole body, that her nose had a hole broke out in it, and it had penetrated into her brain.

Yesterday morning between seventy and eighty felons were brought from Newgate, to go on board one of the merchant ships, in order to be transported to America.

LONDON NOV. 8. The six celebrated beauties that are painting by Mr. Jervase, the King's principal painter are, we hear, the Lady Harvey, Mrs. Pulteney, Miss Searriot, Mrs. Talbot, of Brook Street Hanaver Square, Mrs. Keyte, and Mrs. Oldfield.

LONDON NOV. 9. The wild youth, (as he is commonly called) who was in keeping at Bone End in Hertfordshire, went away from thence about a fortnight ago; whether he is yet found out we are not inform'd, but he was missing four or five days after, and several persons were got out all over the country in quest of him; 'twas thought the fool (who now comes under that denomination by all that know him) got into the woods, of which there is great stores in those parts; but he is not like to be so well provided there as he was before.

LONDON NOV. 21. Last Thursday a trial came on at the Common-Pleas, between the overseers of Glerkenwell, and a gentleman's footman of Lincoln's Inn, relating to a bastard child that was still born. The former had obliged the latter to pay them 13 guineas and a half; but the Court made them pay his money back besides charges.

LONDON NOV. 23. On Thursday a dresser at one of the Playhouses, dropp'd down dead as she was coming through Duke Street, in Lincoln's Inn Fields.

LONDON DEC. 7. Yesterday came on the Court of Common Pleas, Westminster, a trial between Mr. Butler of Portsmouth plaintiff, and Capt. Delgarnoe, captain of the South Sea Castle defendent, for that he ty'd up the plaintiff, whipp'd and used him in a most barbarous manner on board the said ship, and set him ashore at Guinea; the action was laid for 1,000 £. and the jury gave the plaintiff 500 £. damages.

LONDON DEC. 8. A few days since, a live camelion, brought over from Barbary by Capt. Spilman, and which is estemm'd a great rarity in this part of the world, was shewn by Mr. Michael Heathcote to her Royal Highness the Princess Amelia; her Majesty and other Princesses having seen one sometime before.

LONDON DEC. 9. A woman in Newport-Market, being young with child, had a rat thrown in her face, in jest, by another woman: The pregnant woman instantly claspp'd her hand to her mouth, and upon her delivery since, the infant has a strong resemblance of a rat about the mouth, and the under part of the face.

LONDON DEC. 17. St. James's Park is ordered to be taken particular care of, with respect to the cultivation of the trees, and grass-plots, and also the graveling the walks, all which is to begin soon after Christmas, that nothing may be wanting next summer, to make the same delightful to their Majesties.

The British nation have so great a regard to seamen and seafaring-men, and so desirous to have them home, to be ready on occasion to serve their country; that all men of war, when they are abroad, have orders to receive them on board, and bring them home: And to encourage the merchant ships so to do, they are allowed by Act of Parliament, for every man six pence a day, till they are put on shore in England.

From Windsor we have the following story, a young gentleman of Bristol being in love with a fair Quaker of that place, who was somewhat cruel to him, he took place in a stage coach for London, and about Slough he took it into his head that the coachman design'd to murder him that night, so that he hired a person to guide him to Windsor; he went into the inn, where having supp'd; after some discourse, he suspected and charged him with the same design, after which he went to the Thames a little distance from the bridge, pull'd off his cloaths and drown'd himself; seven guineas were found in his pocket but his body is not yet recover'd.

LONDON DEC. 17. 'Tis wrote from Edinberg, That a gentleman traveling to the south, was attack'd on Soutry-Hill by two fellows armed with bayonets, who desired him to serrender his purse; but the gentleman putting his hand beneath his Joky coat presented a pistol, and asked them, whither that or his money was fittest for them? They earnestly begg'd he would spare their lives, for necessity had forced them to it, and they had never robb'd any, save one countryman an hour before of 26 s. 8 d. The gentleman put them to this delemma, either to receive his bullet, or cut an ear out of each other's heads, the last of which with sorrowful hearts they performed.

LONDON DEC. 21. We hear the oppressions and miseries Mr. Castill, a debter in the fleet, suffered through the cruel dispensations of his creditors, is since deceased; we hear also, that there are more in the Poultry Compter above 120 confined debtors, most who are languished for want; and for some time past numbers have died through indigencies or tedious confinement; so that the survivors have no other hope left, than that the Legislature will consider their deplorable condition, and pass an act for their relief.

LONDON DEC. 22. We hear that at the last feast of the company of grocers and apothecaries, one of the fraturnity devoured a meat tongue, an udder, half a pig, one duck, and a sufficient quantity of apple-pye; and wash'd the same down with a gallon of port wine.

1729

LYMINGTON JAN. 10. The Beaver Capt. Matthew Smith, is arrived here in 27 days from New-York, bound to Amsterdam; she received much damage in her passage, having been forced to fling part of her cargo over board, and her boat and all things on deck wash'd away.

LIVERPOOL JAN. 18. From Capt. John Ree, who arrived here a few days since from Africa, but last from Fyall, we have the following account; That about the 10th of May last, on the Coast of Africa, in his passage from the Leeward, he put into Little Mezurada to get rice, and there stayed a day or two and sailed for Gallanas, where one Thomas Kirkham came to him on the 26th of May and gave the following melancholy relation. The Queen Caroline sloop from Bristol, Capt. Halladay, in her trade down the coast, had been at Bonana Islands, and Sierra Liona, and had taken on there 20 young Negro men, each not past 20 years old: At the Island he took a black Grometto, in order to help him in his trade for some rice at that island. On his arrival at St. Pauls he sent his mate, boatswain, and three more hands ashore in their boat along with the black to procure rice, but he run the boat into the river, where the Negroes on the shore endeavoured to take them prisoners; They defended themselves as well as they could, but the mate and one more being killed on the spot, the rest with the boat were seized; next morning the Grometto, with a canoe and 4 or 5 blacks went on board the ship, and told the captain that his boat was fully laden with rice, goats, and would be soon with them. The captain grew jealous, but concealed it, and took this fellow into the cabin, and treated him; after which the black went upon deck and persuaded the purchased Negroes to rise (they unfortunately being without irons) which they agreed to: One took an iron bar out of the fire hearth, with which he killed the captain, and all the rest were soon murdered, except a boy, who warded the blow off his arm (which they broke) but the pain flung him into a swoon, and they thinking him dead flung him overboard, and by accident into the canoe, which, when they hove up the ships anchor fell asturn. The boy continued in her two days, when he was taken up by some Negroes at Cape Mount, who carried him to the Kings house, where he was taken care of, and there the said Kirkham saw and had the foregoing relation from him. The sloop was carried to a place called the bar, about 18 leagues to the windward of the Gallenas: They turned all the Negroes ashore; and landed all the cargo at the black fellows house, Two white men, who lived near him, went off in the night and weighed the sloops anchor, pretending they designed to carry her to the Bonana Islands or Sierra Liona, and there deliver her to the English for account of her owners, but on the 7th of June, Capt. Reed was at Bonana, and heard no more of her.

CANTERBURY JAN. 15. The middle of last week 26 persons, men, women and boys, being gliding on the mill pond the ice broke, & they all drowned.

LONDON JAN. 21. There have been published here a genuine account of British captures, made by the Spaniards, since the last seige of Gibraltar commenced: An abstrack of which is as follow viz. Ships seized in several ports in Spain 14 —— ships taken at sea by Spanish men of war and privateers, in Europe 32 —— ships taken in America 51 —— In all 97.

On Sunday Mr. Airs an eminent wood-munger at breakfast in perfect health, rose up, when on a sudden he cried out, Lord have mercy on me; how a man ought to be prepared for death, and dropt down dead immidiately.

LONDON FEB. 15. Last Sunday night the corpse of Mr. John White, age 104 years, was carryed from Pauls Alley in Red-Cross-street, and Buryed at St. Giles's Cripplegate. It was attended to the grave by eight men of 100 years old; six to bear up the pall, and two to walk before.

By Letter from Colraine in Ireland, Feb. 1. We learn that multitudes of people are preparing to transport themselves to America; we are assured a Popish Priest and most of his Irish congragation are getting ready to go; and this humour prevails thro people of all persuasions; even the Quakers as well as the rest.

LONDON FEB. 18. There was launched at Chatham the Royal Sovereign, a first rate man of war, carrying 100 guns and 780 men; which reckon'd one of the noblest ships in the Royal Navy.

Last Wednesday night about eleven o'clock, one Jackson, a slaughter-house butcher, was attack'd in Lincoln-Inn-Fields near the watchhouse by two footpads; but making resistance one of the villains whistled an immediately two more came up, when they beat him, and kicked him so violently that he lies dangerously ill. They robbed him of about three shillings; but a gentleman appearing with a light they made off.

And on Friday a miner on Mold Mountain, long employ'd in winding up the bucket of ore, was entangled in the ropes, and thrown down the lead-pit, being 150 feet deep. He was taken alive, none of his limbs broken but his body and ribs crush'd to pieces, so he died in a few hours.

On Sunday night last, William Sparrow and George Gayley, who were under sentence of death at Newgate, for robbing on the highway, made their escape out of the said goal, by taking up a plank in one of the new cells, where they were confined, and getting between the joist into a hole underneath, that was almost filled with rubbish, throw into it, near the foundation was laid; and then found means to dig a hole thro a brick wall into an uninhabited house, and so got out at a window into the street. The person who were sent with search warrants in persuit of them, got some information of the former and traced him to a little cottage in Lambert Marsh, where a woman of the house inform'd then that Gayley and his wife were there on Monday night and fry'd some liver and sweet bread, and told her he had broken out of Newgate; but that as soon as he had refresh'd he went away.

LONDON FEB. 18. A reprieve went down to Hertford on Sunday for Lawrence Richards, a farmers son, who was to have suffered on Monday with Luke Horsfall and Henry Gandry, who were then excecuted pursuant of their sentence.

CANTERBURY FEB. 18. Yesterday Elizabeth Pilcher of Buckland, was committed to St. Dunstans Goal, on suspicion of murthering her bastard child: It is said she has confess'd it was still born, and that she burnt it, being brib'd by the father for that purpose, to prevent discovery.

The same day Tho. Fox, an Irishman, a notorious offender (who formerly escaped as he was going to receive sentence at Hicks Hall) was retaken by virtue of a warrant from the Lord Chief Justice, and committed to Newgate. It is remarkable, that he had a cause depending in the Court of King's-Bench, against one Glass, another Irishman, for a debt of about 30 £. and just as the coach and horses in Old-Palace-Yard, by virtue of an escape warrant, and carried to Newgate.

LONDON FEB. 25. They beat up every day here for volunteer seamen to man the Kings ships now getting ready.

LONDON FEB. 26. The Commissioners for Victualling of his Majesty's Navy, have of late made a contract for 500 oxen and 2,000 hogs, which were begun to be kill'd on Thursday last.

LONDON FEB. 26. Last week about 50 persons, charg'd with several crimes, were carried to Newgate, partly from other goals, and partly by fresh commentments, in order to take their trial at the ensuing sessions in the Old Baily.

Several of the prisoners, more at this time than usual, who have been apprehended here, charg'd with capital offences and to be carried by Habeas Corpus, to be try'd at the ensuing Assizes in the respective counties where they committed the fact.

LONDON FEB. 27. A milk woman's daughter at Endfield, was buried alive there: When she was going to be interr'd some people at the funeral thought she looked fresh, and taking a looking glass, and applying it to her lips, they fancied they perceived a dew on it, as from breath; but the cruel mother mock'd and reviled them, and swore she should be buried, and so she was; but this coming to the ears of a man relation, he got the grave dug up, and the coffin open'd, where she was found with her knees drawn up, and nosegay in her hand bitten to pieces struggling for her life. A surgeon was sent for to bleed her but it was then too late.

LONDON MARCH 3. By the list of prisoners for debt in the several counties in England, there appears to be about ninety five thousand persons so confined.

LONDON MARCH 5. N. S. On the 18th past put in here one galleon (being a man of war of 50 guns) in very great distress for want of provisions, not having an ounce of bread on board her. She had been 84 days from the Havanna, she came from thence with 11 more men of war and 12 merchant ships, but parted from them near the Western Islands. 'Tis reported the fleet had on board 30 millions of pieces of eight in gold and silver, and 15 millions in effects. Just now we learn, that the Spanish Ambassador has by express, received an account of their being arrived, viz. 5 in Galicia, 2 in Ferol, 1 in Vigo, 2 in Porta Veura, the rest at Cadiz, and in sight of Port St. Mary's.

LONDON MARCH 10. Last Friday 200 £. was paid by Lord of the Treasury to the persons concern'd into the apprehending of Will. Maple and Thimothy Cotton, now under condemnation in Newgate for a robbery on the highway near Knights-Bridge. The constable who assisted at the taking then, was excluded from any part of the reward, for not appearing as an evidence at their tryal.

Forty eight convicts are ordered for transportation.

LONDON MARCH 12. On Monday 108 felons in Newgate, were shipped off for the plantations.

The next day, one Ferris an Irishman, and a woman, were committed to Newgate, being charg'd with high treason, in counterfeiting the current coin of the Kingdom.

BRISTOL MARCH 13. We have an account by coaster, Capt. Gough master, from Cork, that the Gibraltar, said to be bound from the Canaries to London, was beat to pieces between Cork and Kinsale, and that every soul on board her perished. There was the body of a person drove on shore, belonging to the said ship, (supposed to be a passenger) who, as it is surmised, seeing the imminent danger they were in, tied 50 pieces of gold about his waste, and with it a subscription in writing, requesting those who should take up his body, to bury it in a decent manner, and to apply that money, or part of it, to defray the charges thereof; it happened that two Irishmen, who were looking out for the wreck, took up the body, but instead of burying it, as requested, they left it on the sand, and after quarrel'd about the money, where one of 'em killed, and the other committed for murder.

LONDON MARCH 13. On Wednesday of last week an odd unhappy accident happen'd in Fenchurch-street one John Micour, a frenchman, who formerly serv'd his apprenticeship to Mr. Guy at the Swan Tavern in Cornhill, but of late has dealt himself in wine, brandy, rum and other liquors, and as he was hurrying along with a bottle of wine in his hand, he had the misfortune to run against a post, by which the bottle was broke, but with such an edge, that it cut into his belly through his cloaths, and tho' the wound was sew'd up by an able surgeon, yet he died in about twenty-four hours.

By letter from Jamaica we learn that the Spaniards took four ships in October last, belonging to the English merchants of the Havanna.

Extract of a letter from St. Ives, dated March 6. On the 6th instant we were surpris'd with the sad news of two or three hundred tinners being upon the road to our borough under the pretence of seeking corn; which obliged us to make such preparations to receive them, as the short notice we had of the coming, and the hurry and confusion we were in would admit of, in the space of about half an hour we got together a body of about 30 or 40 men armed with fouwling-pieces and pistols in the church yard, which front the entrance into the borrough. We were no sooner placed in the posture of defence, but they came in upon us according to information, and were several times desired to retreat, but to no purpose, they still pressing in upon us in a violent and furious manner, stricking with their clubs and all such as were in their reach, by which they broke the jaw-bone of two of our best men, and slightly busted others; so that we were forced from our security, to fire upon them, upon which two or three were killed, and several others wounded.

LONDON MARCH 21. Wednesday last, 400 barrels of gun powder were put into the store room in the White Tower of London.

LONDON MARCH 22. On Monday two gentlemen came to Fleet Prison, and accurately took account of all the prisoners names in the goal which the sum of 20 £. would discharge from their confinement; and we are credably informed, that the same was like to be done in the goals in the Kingdom.

LONDON MARCH 27. Yesterday Mr. Hayes, convicted of forging a bond for 350 £. stood on the pillory at Charing-Cross, and afterwards being placed in a chair upon the stage or platform of the pillory, a surgeon cut off his left ear, and deliver'd it into his own hand; an officer then took it from him, and held it up to the view of the crowd; and afterwards folded it up in a paper and put it in his pocket.

LONDON APRIL 5. The Duke of Wharton having been indicted of high-treason and required or summoned in four several counties to surrender himself and answer thereto, which having not done, he was on Thursday last declared publickly a traitor to the Realm, at the Court held for the County of Middlesex at Brentford.

LONDON APRIL 5. Yesterday about noon several of the lords Commissioners of the Admiralty waited on his Majesty with the measures they are taking to equip a sufficient fleet of ships for sea service.

LONDON APRIL 6. Letters from Musselbury, a port-town, 14 miles from Edinburgh, relate, that Mr. Alexander Macdonald, and Mr. George Riggs, two intimate friends, having words at cards, the latter took a knife, and stabbed the former six inches deep in the belly, of which he died on the spot.

LONDON APRIL 11. Last night orders were given for a commission to be prepared for Sir Charles Wager, to take upon his command a squadron of his Majesty's ships of war, design'd for the Mediterranean; and we hear that Sir George will hoist his flag on board the Cornwall.

LONDON APRIL 12. They are to work night and day at the victualing office on Tower-Hill in preparing provisions for Sir Charles Wager's squadron.

On Thursday last in the afternoon warrants for impressing seamen, were issued at the Admiralty Office, and the officers to whom they were deliver'd, used such diligence that night, that several hundred men were impress'd upon about the River Thames before next morning: Lieutenant Edwards of Oxford, commanded by the Lord Vere Beauclere, having in that time got near one hundred persons.

Great numbers of mariners do also enlist themselves voluntarily, on account of the encouragement given to seamen by the late Act of Parliament.

LONDON APRIL 18. Was interr'd at St. Annes Church, with great funeral decency the corpse of Mr. Wilson one of the masters of the pacquet boats; who, with two or three others, was lately drowned, as they were returning in a boat from on board the paquet in our bay. He was taken up by some of the King's officers, who saw the body floating near the piles, and at first took it to be a concealment of run goods. He had his cloaths and sword on, and his watch and money were found in his pocket.

LONDON APRIL 19. There was lately presented to her Majesty from the Royal Society, by Sir Han Sloane, a branch of one of the four great cedar trees growing in the Physick Garden at Chelsea, with 9 cones upon it; and we hear their Majesties will go the first warm day to see the said tree, which are allow'd to be the largest of that kind in Europe and not to be match'd nearer than Mount Libanus near the Holy Land.

The press still continues, taking all hands out of the vessels that come in the road. The captains of the outward bound ships, to prevent their men from falling into the hands of the press gang, let the pilots proceed with their ships as far as the Holmbs, while the men march by land down the country, and are fetched off by the pilots boats.

LONDON APRIL 23. They write from Bristol, that there has been a very hot press in the city for sailors, and that they had got upwards of 400 on board one of his Majesty's ship in King-Road.

LONDON APRIL 23. Yesterday in the evening came on a hearing before a committee of the Privy Council at White-hall, in relation to the difference between Governour Burnet and the General Court or Assembly of New-England, relating to his salary, council learned in the law were heard on both sides, and we hear it went in favour of the Governour and the same is to be reported to his Majesty.

LONDON APRIL 26. From the Cock-News-Letter, On Monday some persons coming up the river in a boat near Lee, discover'd a large fish coming out of a creek near the Blyth Sand, which one of them struck with a knife, upon which it made back, the tide going out they took this fish with 34 more, most of which were from 24 to 26 feet in length, making in the whole about 80 tons, and are thought to be worth 500 l. several of them are brought to town, and have been shewn as a sight.

On Tuesday last a great feast of the gardeners call'd florist was held at the Dog on Richmond-Hill, at which were presented about 130 in number; after dinner several shew'd their flowers (most of them auriculas) and five ancient and judicious gardners were judges to determine whose flowers excell'd; on that occasion two silver spoons and ladles were given to the gardners that had the best flowers; a gardner of Barnes in Surrey was so well furnish'd with good flowers, that the judges in the affair, ordered him two spoons and one ladle.

At the same feast a dish of garden beans, with bacon, was given to the society, by a gardner near Leatherhead, but he was no ways entitled the above plate, by reason he brought no flowers. The beans were full and big as common horse beans when out of the shell.

LONDON MAY 3. Last Thursday a marriage was solemnized at Edmonton Church between Thomas Jenkins, a servant to the Hon. Bryan, Fairfax Esq; about 28 years of age, and an old maid about 70 years of age, who has saved in her service 2000 £.

They write from Winchester on the 26th of last month, That on Friday last being St. Mark's Day, a most horrible parricide was perpertrated at a village called Dretford, near Waltham, within ten miles of that city, when a young gentleman about 22 years old, son of a very reputible person in that neighbourhood, returning from church, and having some words with his mother, fell upon her, and beat her head against the floor with such violence, that he broke her skull in many places, in which she instantly died, his father being present in the room, but being ancient and lame of his hands, could not prevent his sons execrable design; The murtherer was that evening brought prisoner under a strong guard to the Castle in Winchester.

We hear that several of the principal persons employ'd in the north of England, in making of hard ware of iron of all sorts, are applying for an Act of Parliament to encourage the importation of pig-iron from the plantations in America, where the same was to be wrought into pigg from the oar, and setting forth, that the same will not only be a great help to some hundred of families, but a means of saving the government some thousand pounds per annum paid to Sweden, Denmark and Russia for that commodity.

LONDON MAY 3. We hear from Gloucester the 26th of April last, That people die no faster there than usual; but 'tis very sickly in the country all around them; in one family, but one was left out of nine; and not above a mile distance from thence, three corpse, viz. the father, son and daughter, were brought all together to be buried last Sunday; and the man's wife died but a little before. The physicians here are of opinion, that the smoke keeps it out of town.

LONDON MAY 10. We have a melancholy account from Gloucestershire, that a contagious distemper rages there, which kills people very suddenly, and sometimes whole families die together, some by swellings in the throat and other parts of the body, which except they break, take people off in 24 hours: They have in the village of Ashton Underhill (near Tewkesbury) above 45 persons since Christmas last out of inhabitants, whose number did not exceed 100; these are found to be more that have dy'd in that place in twenty years past.

Most of the other neighbouring villages are in the same misarable condition, and that with poverty and sickness, the people are in the most deplorable circumstances, a few labourers are able to work, and these that do have double wages; the poor's rates are excessive, being above seven shillings in the pound in several parishes, which, together with the scarcity of corn, has driven the farmers to despair, that several farms in the rich country are left in the gentlemen's hands, and very few are able to pay any rent.

LONDON MAY 20. It is written from Jamaica, Jan. 16. That the week before a ship put in there, belonging to Mr. Hart of Londonderry, and bound from thence with passengers for Pennsylvania, having been 23 weeks at sea, in which time they were reduced to great streights for want of provisions, insomuch that 40 persons quitted the ship and went ashore at Porto Rico, an island inhabited by a fort of Spanish banditti: (how they received them is not said) it is added, that the ship was a mere wreck, and could not be made capable of putting to sea again.

By letters from Paris, dated May 11. We have the following remarkable story from a town in the lower Bretagne: That a damsel there having been abused by a young man in the neighbourhood, who promised marriage, and afterwards not only denied the promise, but also protested, that he never had any commerce with her; the poor girl began judicial process against him; but upon conviction whereof, in those cases, the man is to be tied up by the priest, or the hangman: But as the meeting of the State of Bretagne had been lately surpressed by the King's edict, the Lower Court had no power of life and death, so the lover was condemn'd only of 6,000 livres damages, the young lady, who was an only child, and of a good family, did not think this sufficient satisfaction; so that immediately after the judgement, she took a pistol, and went to find out her spark, and spoke to him after this manner: I am come, Sir, to oblige you to repair my honour, and do me justice, by marrying me; which of you refused, this instrument shall instantly put an end to your life. The young man was adroit enough to seize his mistress, and to disarm her of the pistol, which he carried directly to her mother; withal told her, that if she did not take care to prevent her daughter from giving him any further disturbance, he would sue her in a criminal process. The mother took the pistol, and assured the gentleman, that her daughter should never after give him any trouble; but as he turned about to go out of the room, the old gentlewoman discharged the pistol at him, and shot him dead on the spot; and as soon as she had done, went away with her daughter to the Isle of Guernsey, from whence she is soliciting her pardon, by the interest of some Lord in her neighbourhood.

LONDON JUNE 7. We think it will be a service to inform the publick, that there are abundance of bad Moidores pass'd in payment;

a merchant receiving 25 of them, and upon proving them, found they were not worth above 4 s. a piece.

SHEFFIELD JUNE 10. Between five and six this morning, it began to thunder, lighten, and rain here in a violent manner, and continued so till about two in the afternoon; which produced the greatest and most outragious flood that was ever known, vast green trees were brought down the River Dun from the adjacent parts; several bridges broke away, and the buildings, and the works upon the river carry'd clear off. One end of the Duke Norfolk's Hospital was destroy'd and born away. The carriage and four horses of one Loxley were carry'd over the hospital wall, and the horses all drown'd. The gate of the hospital were afterwards thrown down, with the greatest part of the walls, and part of the bridge. The chappel was two yards deep in water, the pulpit fill'd with sludge, and the furniture of the chappel and of the whole hospital wash'd away. So sudden and amazing was this storm, that from the moors the water roll'd down like the mountains themselves; cattle of all kind caught in angry torrent: and by a moderate computation the waters must have risen near the hospital (where the river Shelf and Sheffield Broke empty themselves into the Dun) four yards perpendicular in the space of six minutes. It was with the utmost difficulty people escaped with their lives, and only one man and woman was drown'd. Some children were wash'd away in their cradles, but were taken up again of a distance from town. The like was never known in the memory of man. Such fury threaten'd all before it; and without the testimony of many thousands presented, it is incredible.

LONDON JUNE 12. On Monday the 2d instant about 8 o'clock in the morning a fire happen'd to break out in an out-house at Sturminster-Newton-Castle in Dosetshire, which setting fire to the town did with the space of four hours consume and burnt to ashes sixty seven dwelling houses and a large market house, together with a great quantity of mercers and other goods, ten barns besides some stables and out-houses thereto belonging. The damage whereof at a moderate computation amount to thirteen thousand pounds and upwards, insomuch that many of the poor inhabitants are obliged to shelter themselves under hedges, the houses remaining being not sufficient to entertain them.

LONDON JUNE 12. Early on Tuesday a countryman (walking along Turnmill-street near Smithfield-Bars) dropt by degrees 10 guineas out of his pocket; of which a butcher following him took up five, and a woman four, which she gave to the same butcher, supposing them to be his, and accordingly he kept all the nine: But a girl pick'd up one, and gave it to the countryman, which was all he cou'd recover of the whole.

The beginning of this week, a poor woman in the borough, being suddenly taken with a swimming in her head, laid down on her bed and dy'd immediately: One of her children, a girl coming in soon after, seeing her mother lie dead, fell into such a passionate lamentation, that she expir'd also before she cou'd be recover'd out of her fit of surprize; and they were both bury'd in the same grave.

And on Wednesday the following being the 4th instant, a terrible fire happen'd at Hinistrid, a little town without four miles of Sherborne, which begun in a smith's shop, and consumed forty three dwelling-houses before it was extinguished, tho' not one person perished.

On Wednesday the report of the committee of the House of Commons was made relating to the Marshalsea Prison after which the house resolved, that the Attorney-General should prosecute John Darby, keeper of the said prisson, and William Acton, his deputy or lessee, for high misdemeanor, in the management of their offices; and that the said report (which contains circumstances no less shocking than those in the first) be forthwith printed and published.

LONDON JUNE 12. The bridge that is building between Fulham and Putney, is begun in the middle of the Thames, where the great arch of 28 piles, 14 to a side; The builders thought they should have driven the whole number of piles there by Saturday evening, but could not exceed 19, the ground proving harder than they expected, the rammer for driving them is 2,500 weight, and the piles are forced in nine or ten foot deep.

LONDON JUNE 14. They write from Bridgewater, that on Monday night last, or rather early Tuesday morning a terrible storm of thunder and lightning happened there, which lasted about three hours, and did considerable damage. Some out-houses adjoining to the ham house, belonging to George Doddington Esq; were set on fire by the lightning, which, if it had not been happily discovered by one Mr. Collins that was passing that way about three o'clock on Tuesday morning, that the large dwelling house had in all likelyhood been also burnt, and several people in their beds. Some more out-houses were likewise burnt not far distance from thence. A bull and four cows that lay under a tree were kill'd, and the tree much shattered. The mast of a vessel that lay on the key was split from top to bottom without further damage to the vessel. It broke a top window of Mr. Harvey's house to pieces, and had like to have thrown down part of the east end of the house.

WORCESTER JUNE 16. We hear an account from Suckley, seven miles of this city, that on Monday last a poor woman of that place went with her pitcher to a neighbouring uninhabited cyder-mill-house, where she knew they lay a hogshead of cyder; but there being no open way thereto, she endeavoured to force herself down thro' a hole in the loft, which being very small, she stuck by the ribs, and in struggling was sufficated, and lay dead undiscover'd till the next day, to the utmost surprize of the man that went into the millhouse.

WORCESTER JULY 3. We have an account from Parshort that a young man of that town last Saturday cut his throat for some disappointment he met from his father in respect of his solemnizing matrimony with a young woman of the place; and his tragical death had like to have been follow'd by that of his father, who took so much to heart the rash action of his son, so to throw himself into a moat, out of which he had never come alive, had not some kind neighbour timely plung'd in and drag'd him out.

PLYMOUTH JULY 4. On the 26th ult. a smuggling sloop the William of Guernsey, was brought in from Kelvestock Bay within this port, after a very great resistance from the crew, who, 'tis said, are all liable to be tried for their lives: The master, one William de Putron a desperate fellow attempted to fire on the officers, and snapped a pistol, which blew in the pan, but did not go off; whereupon the officers fired in their own defence, and shot him dead on the spot.

LONDON JULY 4. Last night about 11 a-clock, a fire happen'd at Potters-Butts near Angel, by the carelessness of the maid, who was going to bed, left the candle burning, which catched the bed and burnt the cottage house, and 6 more; some of the people had not cloaths left to cover them. One man pulled his thatch off from his house and lay upon it, thinking he could put it out by so doing, but burnt himself.

LONDON JULY 5. By a private letter from the Board of Industry, Capt. James Williamson commander, at Barbadoes, we have this account, That in her passage from Guinea, the slaves having contriv'd to rise upon the ships crew, and to that purpose made themselves master of the gunpowder, muskets, shots, &c. A Negro woman was seized in the fact (between decks) of conveying powder, balls, &c. thro' a hole in the partition between the mens and womens apartments; The master with the greatest difficulty, being able, after giving her several cuts with his cutlass, to bring her upon deck, finding her so mangled, that tho' her life might be saved, yet she would not be fit for the market, called a council, where they unanimously agreed to make her an example to the rest; Accourdingly they hosted her up to the fore-yard-arm, in view of the other slaves, whom they had disarmed and fired half a dozen balls thro' her body; the last shot that was fired cut the rope which she was strung up by; so that she tumbled into the sea at once; Which terrified the rest so, that they brought them to Barbadoes safe, without the least disturbance the rest of the voyage.

PLYMOUTH JULY 6. Last night an unhappy accident happen'd at a place call'd the Ridout (belonging to our fortification) John Bretton, a young gentleman, and a volunteer, who had belong'd to his Majesty's ship Phoenix, walking out with two boys of the town, was persuaded by them to go into the water, who after taking three or four steps (the entrance being very steep) was out of his depth, and lost immediately, there not being any body near enough to assist him but the boys, who were utterly incapable thro' the great surprize that attended them.

BRISTOL JULY 19. On Wednesday last the corpse of Cornelious Stephens, Esq; the noted beau, was interred in St. James Church, after lying in state at his lodging in Queer-Square, the corpse was attended with 12 coaches and six; and notwithstanding there were men on horse back to prevent the mobs from taking away the escutcheons. The hearse was soon dismantled of them. The mob was so great at the church, that the gentlemen and ladies who were to hold up the pall, and the rest of the gentry that attended the funeral, were obliged to keep in their coaches, and the corpse was carry'd in only by the underbearers.

They write from Stilltor-Green in Wiltshire: That last Thursday se'nnight Wm. Lynn, constable of that town, going to serve a warrant on Robert Milton, on the account of some scandalous words that had happen'd between him and a neighbours wife, Mrs. Milton, in her passion, catched up the knife, and stabbed the constable in two or three places, so that he died of wounds the Sunday following.

LONDON JULY 29. Yesterday at Mr. Westbrooke a surgeon in Dartmouth Street, Westminster, was comming to town from Reading in Berkshire in a coach and four horses, with his wife, mother and three children, near Colenbrooke, the horses being young to fright at two men riding on asses, and ran away with the coach, which at length overset; the coachman kill'd on the spot, Mr. Westbrooke's wife had her collarbone broke, and his mother one of her arms broke, and one of the children so bruised that it was at the point of death this morning, and Mr. Westbrooke was hurt in one eye.

LONDON JULY 29. On Friday night last John Raven, a cow-keeper at Hampstead, about 20 years of age, being light-headed in a fever, stole out of his bed, and got out of the house from his mother, who sat up by him, (but happened to drop asleep) and went over two or three fields without his clothes, to a deep well, where 'tis supposed he intended to drink, and tumbling in was drown'd, his body was next day found in the said well.

On Sunday night a child was drowned at Mr. Mawley's next door to the Dublin Castle in Slanhopt-street, Claremarket: The mother had laid it carelessly on the outside of the bed, and left a pail full of water and clou's near, into which the child unfortunately pitch'd head foremost.

On Sunday next Mr. Rayne, who lives at the Three Leggs in cloth-Fair, and Mr. Maynard a shoemaker on Ludgate-Hill, are to set out at 4 o'clock in the morning, and to walk forty miles out, and return again by eleven o'clock the same evening, for a wager of one hundred pounds, being 80 miles in all.

LONDON AUG. 2. One day last week a master of a ship arriv'd lately from Philadelphia going from Fawke's Booth in Moorefields about eleven at night, was attack'd by a single man; but he defended himself so well, that he got the better of his adversary, and knock'd him down; Whereupon two others came up, and asking him if he intended to rob their friend, he found it in vain to resist; by which time the fellow that was down got up; and what is most remarkably honourable in one of that stamp, finding his companions about to abuse the master, threatened to strip him and tie him to a tree, he interposed, declaring he was a brave fellow, and had given him fair play, and that it was enough to rob him; and after much opposition got off, with the lost only of his silver buckles, and about 24 s.

LONDON AUG. 9. The Lord Propriators of South Carolina having sign'd at the Treasury a deed of conveyance and surrender of their rights and title of that province, to the Crown for the sum of 20,000 £. was on Wednesday last issued out of the exchequer, being the purchase money agreed for; It is now expected a Governour and other officials will soon set out for that colony, which very much want them.

On last Wednesday in the evening, her Majesty, the Prince of Wales, his Royal Highness the Duke, the Princess Royal, and the Princesses Amelia and Carolina, were entertained with a new farce, which was performed in the Gardens at Richmond, by the comedians of the theatre Royal in Lincolns-Inn Fields.

A sloop bound from Jamaica with 180 Negroes, and a very valuable cargo, by firing a gun, took fire in the harbour and blew-up by which means the vessel, cargo, and crew (consisting of about 40 persons) were lost. But about 40 negroes were taken up alive, though in a miserable condition.

LONDON AUG. 9. Yesterday a stray'd ox going through King Street, Covent-Garden, went into an empty house, and having taken a survey of the shop and garden, walk'd into the dinning-room, where he stay'd a small time, then jumped out of the window thro' the sash upon the penthouse next door, which he broke all to pieces fell into the street & walk'd off.

Yesterday the Reverend Rowland, a clergyman, stood in the pillory at Chancery-Lane End, for the second and last time, pursuant to his sentence, for writing a letter to the Lord Chief Justice, highly reflecting on two worthy Justices of the Peace in Westminster. He was not pelted; but on the contrary, had wine and money gave him. A certain Brokade Knight, being up stairs in the coffee-house near the pillory, had a very eliquent learned charge deliver'd to him by the chairman of the mob, who was design'd to print the same.

LONDON AUG. 13. This morning Sarah Williams, in Lumber-Court by the Seven Dials, got out of her bed in her sleep, and throwing up the sash, sat down on the frame of the window in her shift only, which a woman that lay with her, observing, scream'd out, so that the said Williams was waked out of her sleep, and fell down into the court, by which she was so bruised that her life is in great danger. She was the same day carried to St. Bartholomew's Hospital.

LONDON AUG. 14. We hear from Coventry, That when the judges came there and opened their commission there were only three criminals to be tried, who all broke out of the goal during the time of the Assize Sermon, and escaped.

LONDON AUG. 16. They write from Mansier in Westmorland, that on the 2d instant, in the night time, Randolf Clarkson of that place, on his return from Whidington, was scorched to death by a flash of lightning.

They write from Aulchester in Worcestershire, that last Thursday se'nnight one Gile Hall, who travelled the country with a bear, to show for his livelyhood, was killed by the same, between that place and Preshore, and tore in a miserable manner.

Last Saturday a man in Spittlefields hanged himself, before being charged with committing a rape on the body of a girl between 14 and 15 years old.

On Monday John Harris, who sold glasses, unfortunately slipping as he pass'd along White-Chapel, pitched his head among his basket of glasses, which cut so dangerous a manner, that it is believed he cannot recover.

Some few days past, one of the King's sloops attack'd a smuggler off Harwich, and after an obstinante skirmish, which lasted a considerable time, and wherein one of the smugglers had his arm shot thro', and shatter'd almost to pieces, took her, and imprison'd the men, who are since discharged upon bail: He that was wounded is brought to town to be cur'd.

Henrietta Doyley, alias Smith, alias Edwards, alias Berry, who has, for many years, by her extraordinary grandeur and unparallell'd artifices, from time to time, obtain'd large credit from many honest tradesmen, was last week taken into custody, on a charge of defrauding a gentleman of 7 guineas, by forging a person of quality's hand, since which she has been charged with defrauding another gentleman of a sum of money by the same artifice, and was thereupon committed by Justice Lambert to Newprison.

LONDON AUG. 16. Yesterday two haystacks near Gravesend, took fire by the hay being stack'd too green, and were both entirely consum'd notwithstanding no help was wanting.

They write from Turnbridge-Wells, that several ladies have of late appear'd on the walks with shoulder-knots, a fashion led up by a certain Great Dutchess.

On Wednesday last a boy of six or seven year old went to wash himself in a little shallow pond by Hanover Square, and was drowned. Yesterday a victuallers son of six or seven years of age, fell down in Bishopgate-street as he was endeavouring to avoid a cart that was comming by, and the wheel running over him, he was kill'd on the spot.

LONDON AUG. 19. On Monday a boy of 10 or 12 unfortunately killed a child of 8 on George Key, by shooting him in the head with a fowling-piece which they were playing with.

On Thursday last one Thomas Manley, a scaffolder at Greenwich Hospital, fell off from one of the scaffolds there and was so much bruised, that he died the next day.

LONDON AUG. 19. On Sunday evening one of the Stratford stage coaches, which had been hir'd that day to go to Woodford, in its return to London the axel tree by the motion was set on fire and burnt through, so that the coach fell in White-Chappel, by which accident a gentlewoman was much bruised and wounded.

Yesterday one Thomas Tayler was killed in St. Clements Lane in the Strand, by a piece of timber falling upon him.

We have an account from Cara-Bay in Cornwall, this the beginning of last week a man well dress'd cast up by the tide, who appeared like a seafaring man, he had his watch, money, and a banknote in his pocket, in all to the value of between 200 and 300 £.

We hear from Walton in Leicestershire, that George Quadle a sawyer in Black-Fryers, who had been to see his friends in the country, was unfortunately drowned going over a wooden bridge near Hilton in Northamptonshire, on his return to London.

Yesterday about one o'clock at noon a middle aged woman, handsomely dress'd threw herself into the sluice that communicates Rosemond's Pond with the canal in St. James's Park, and was dead before she could be taken out.

LONDON AUG. 28. Yesterday about 3 o'clock in the morning, a fire broke out at the Queens Head Ale-House adjoining to the basin belonging to the York Building Water-Works in Marybone Fields, and in less than an hour's time entirely consumed the house. Mr. Lloyd the keeper and owner of the house (which was insured for 900 £.) had locked up his doors, and was gone with family to Smithfield where he keeps a booth, during the time of Bartholomew-Fair. Some persons broke into the lower part of the house, when the upper part was all in flames, in order to save some of the goods, but found the rooms stripped of all goods that could have been moved off with conveniency, from which it is generally believed that some villains had robbed the house, and afterwards set it on fire.

LONDON AUG. 30. On Wednesday evening a gentleman sent a porter from the New-England Coffee-House to Cross-Key-Inn in

Grace-Church-street for a portmanteau trunk; but the porter being in liquor, thro' mistake brought his horse, which the gentleman order'd him to take back, and let the trunk alone, thinking him incapable of carrying it, but the porter being officious would bring the trunk, and at the door of the house where he was to carry it, stood a person well dress'd, who pulling out his watch and looking on it, damn'd the porter for staying so long, and bid him to put it down, which he did, and the sharper march'd off with it, containing linen and other things of value.

Last week some workmen who were at work on the new bridge at Fulham, by accident let a large piece of timber fall into the river, which happening to light upon a boat that was passing thro' the lock at the same time, struck the head of the boat short off, and split it quite thro' the middle; but the lives of the six men that were in it were saved by two watermen, who seeing their distress, went immediately with their boats to assist them.

This week two young fellows, Taylors near Hungerford Market, which made love to the same damsel, (she not knowing which to chuse) resolved to decide the affair by single combat; accordingly they went into the fields, attended by a great crowd of spectators, and fought manfully, till at length one of them was beat, and it is supposed the other will be married; so that it is a dispute which gets the worst of it.

LONDON AUG. 30. Last Sunday was se'nnight, at the opening of Mr. Bragg's Meeting-House, which had been just beautify'd and repair'd, there was a numerous assembly, with some rogues mixing themselves, carry'd off several watches both gold and silver, notwithstanding the notice given them to take care of their watches and pockets; one lady in particular, laid hold of the chain of her gold watch, but lost her case.

LONDON SEPT. 4. Yesterday about 2 in the morning, the inhabitants of the lower Hay-market were greatly alarm'd, such vast quantities of earth having fallen into the sewer; which shock the houses as it was an earthquake had happened and the foundations were so greatly endanger'd that it was apprehended some of them would have fell. The York-Building Company's main water-pipe was again broke, which did considerable damage in several cellars which had stocks of wine, brandy, &c. and if a man had not been let down with a rope about his body and stopt the pipe, the whole neighbourhood must have been very great suffered.

A Negro named Pawpaw, belonging to Mrs. Littlepage in Virginia, having discovered a certain remedy for the venereal disease, by which he has wrought very speedy and surprizing cures, the Governour and Council have purchased him his freedom, and settled on him an annuity of twenty pounds per annum.

LONDON SEPT. 4. From Eglos in Wales, that one George Simpson, a dealer in salt, was accidentally run over with his loaded cart near Snoden Hill, and bruised in such a manner, that he died soon after.

NORTHAMPTON SEPT. 4. We have an account from Stanton near Lawry Ferry in Nottinghamshire, that some weeks since Mr. Pilkinton's man threw up with his plow a large piece of plate weighing seven pounds, four square, and a large cup in the middle of it; the inscription was Erauperius Episcopus Ecclrsia Ebojense dea'it.

BRISTOL SEPT. 6. Scull, the old man, condemn'd the last Assizes at Wells, for the murder of Sell the baliff & his followers at Wi-comb near Bath, which murder was committed 13 years ago, was brought last Wednesday to be executed at Bath and hang'd in chains on Odd Downs but the colliers rose in a body, and would not permit it: whereupon it was convey'd to Wells, and there executed the next morning in the most private manner, and the same day his body was convey'd to Odd Downs, where a gibbit was erect'd but pull'd down before they came, and being put up again, his body in chains was fixed thereupon; but the same night his body and chains were entirely carried off, and are not yet found.

LONDON SEPT. 6. On Tuesday last a cricket-match was play'd in Penshurst Park, the seat of the Earl of Leicester, between Kent headed by Edwyn Stede, Esq; and Sussex, Surrey, and Hampshire, by Sir William Gage, for 100 guineas, eleven on a side, and was won by the latter.

LONDON SEPT. 6. On Monday night between 11 and 12 o'clock a waterman's boy taking a gentleman into his boat at Stangate, in order to cross the water, three villains leapt into the boat, threw the boy overboard, and row'd into the middle of the river with the gentlemen, who crying out murder, two watermen with oars came up to his assistance, upon which a battle ensu'd, and in the fray one of the rogues fell overboard, but being immediately taken up they were all three secured.

Last Wednesday one Everet, of Fleet-lane sold his wife to one Griffin on Long-lane for a 3 s. bowl of punch; who, we hear hath since complain'd of having a bad bargain.

We hear on Friday last a melancholy misfortune happened at Faringdom in Berkshire, where one William Sokey, a soap-boiler, being disordered in his senses, went into the house of one Mrs. Sparks, who was then absent from home, and taking a young child out of the cradle, play'd with it for some time, saying it was an innocent lamb, and a pity to hurt it; but the child's brother of about five years old standing near the cradle, Sokey fell upon him with a truncheon, and beat him in so unmerciful a manner, that his brains came out, and the boy immediately died; another boy seeing this, ran out of the house, and called his mother, whom was at a neighbouring gentleman's at work: The poor woman no sooner entered her house, that Sokey knocked her down, and repeated his blows with such violence that she also expired; The place being alarmed, he was secured, and committed to Reading Goal; when he was examined before the justice, his reason for committing this horid fact was, that he thought that there were to many poor people in the country, and that had done some good service in ridding the town of them; the coroners jury have brought it in murder.

LONDON SEPT. 6. A letter from Bilton in Derbyshire, we have an account of farm house, with stabling, barns, &c. being consumed by fire which lately happen'd, wherein was all their new crops; and the house of a neighbouring farmer who came there to extinguish the same, in the interim of time broke out in flames, and was also consumed; by which it was conjectured they were set fire by some vile person. The damage is computed to be near 2,000 £.

BRISTOL SEPT. 6. On Monday and Tuesday, the weavers rose in a great body without Lawfords Gate, and broke open, and rufled many places where looms were, and carried 'em away, which chains and other effects, and burnt them in the open street. They got to such a head that several companies of the regiment in quarters here were sent to repel 'em; they had no orders to fire but only prevent them from entering the warehouses, and pulling down the houses, which they attempted. The reason they gave for it was, that the masters had combined to lower 6 d. in piece of their wages; but all is quiet now again.

The coroners inquest having sat on the bodies of Sarah Sparks and her son, a boy of 5 years, who were a few days ago kill'd by Wm. Sokey Sen. brought in their verdict, wilful murder.

LONDON SEPT. 7. On Friday last Mr. Cock and three other officers of the customs, belonging to the Port of Penzance, seized at a place called Goldzithney, nigh the Mount of Cornwell, six and twenty anchors of rum and brandy having got everything in readyness to carry off the same to the Kings warehouse in Penzance, some of the people from Goldzithney disguised themselves by blacking their faces, and put on women's apparel, fell on the officers, very much beat and wounded them, and forcibly carryed off the brandy and rum; the officers fought with great courage, but being outnumbered were forced to submit, glad to escape with their lives. The same night one Ely Davy, a Scottish fellow, one of the smuggling gang, who lived near Goldzithney, go into a barn where the brandy &c. taken from the officers was put, and drank so much of it, that he died on the spot, and was buried this day.

LONDON SEPT. 9. On Sunday in the afternoon an apprentice of Mr. Meadows, an anchor-smith in Rotherhithe, was drowned as he was washing himself in the Thames.

Last Saturday night two Scots sailors crossing a plank to go on board their ship at Hermitage Dock, the plank broke, and they fell between vessels and were drowned.

A servant maid of Mr. Grey of Glassdrumen in Ireland, was lately committed to prison on suspicion of poisoning her own mother, upward of 86 years of age, who she maintained for several years.

Last Thursday morning, a poor aged man, miserably ragged, was found dead in the foot path between Woolhampton and Reading in Berkshire; 'tis supposed he died of want.

LONDON SEPT. 11. Yesterday the sessions were held at Guildhall for the discharge of unsolvent debtors, above 30 were discharg'd from Woodstreet and Ludgate, one of the latter had been confin'd 24 years. Several likewise discharged who had been fugitives for debt, and were out of England on the 1st of February, and had since surrendered themselves pursuant to the Act.

Last Monday a youth of Spittlefields, who had been raking about town came to his mother for money, she refusing to give him any, he beat her with his cane till he split the same, and then robbed her of some linnen of a considerable value, and went off.

We have account from Ruck Bank in Herford-shire, that on the 25th of last month Thomas Herbert, servant to Mr. Cudbert of that place, accidently fell off a corn-mow upon the barn floor, and was killed on the spot.

BRISTOL SEPT. 12. On Wednesday night happen'd a terrible fire in the town of Whorton-Under-Edge; which consumed 16 tatch'd houses, but we don't hear as yet what the damages are in general.

LONDON SEPT. 12. On Wednesday last John Kitchen, a bricklayer's labourer, standing on a gutter of a house in Cousent-Lane near Lowgate Hill, fell off of the same and was kill'd on the spot.

LONDON SEPT. 16. Last Saturday evening, between 5 and 6 o'clock a carman going up the Gateway with his loaded cart into King's Arms Inn in Holborn Bridge, a child of the smith's in the yard, of between two and three years of age, ran between the wall and one of the wheels, and was crushed to death.

The French cook at the Tatch'd House Tavern in St. James's Street, went (seemingly in perfect health) into the Earl of Penbroke's House in James's Square, and died sudenly in the hall a few minutes after.

LONDON SEPT. 17. We hear that a marriage is negotiating between Prince William of Hosse Castle, youngest brother to the King of Sweden, & her Royal Highness the Princess Emilia, second daughter to his most Sacred Majesty King George.

Yesterday morning happened a storm of thunder and lightning, which was followed by such a prodigious shower of rain, for an hour successively, that the likes has not been known for many years past. It is observed that this storm began with a noise in the element, not much unlike the rumbling of a cart in the streets, till at length it increased to that degree, that one clap of thunder about half an hour past one o'clock, shook the houses in the city in a very surprizing manner which by some judg'd to be attended with the shock of an earthquake, and soon after ensued a storm of wind from at the S. W. which lasted till it was light.

Some days ago, Mr. Tilmer a Kentish gentleman drinking a glass of wine with some friends, after drinking the glass, said he had swallowed a warsp; whereupon he caugh'd it up; but the warsp had so stung him in the throat, that he died in less than a quarter of an hour.

About the beginning of October next all the convicts in Newgate and all the other county jails in England, will be shipp'd off for his Majesty's plantations in America.

CANTERBURY SEPT. 20. We have an account of the following affair which happened at Faversham the 12th instant: A poor man and his wife quartering at an ale-house there, were sick, and the wife in danger of death; which the landlord seeing removed the woman to the waterside in order to send her by the hoy to London where they formerly lived in good circumstances, and by trade the man was a distiller; though now reduced; but when she was brought to the waterside, the boatman perceived the woman was dying; and refused to take her on board, but sent his servant to acquaint the overseer that the woman was dying; and he being a man of more business, than Christianity, took no notice of it: So the poor creature was left with her sick husband on the key, and in the night died, the poor man lying by his dead wife till next morning, when being persuaded to go to the mayor, he was ordered to be taken care of in the work-house, and the dead corpse also to be carried thither. The miserable man however received but little of their charity; for on Sunday morning, he died also, and on Monday night they were both buried in one grave.

LONDON SEPT. 20. Last Saturday morning, two men, a woman, and a child, in a small boat, crossing the water between the Needles and Atherfield Rocks, over-set the same and were all drowned.

Yesterday John Viccari, a waterman at Fulham, having taken into his boat a young woman in order to bring her to London; he being in liquor, in their passage began to be rude with her, and she resisting, in a scuffle he fell overboard and was drown'd.

We are credibly informed from St. Edmonds-Bury That on Saturday last, a physician there, sent to a widow woman who kept a bakehouse, to ask if an earthen pan of such size would go into the oven and presently afterwards sent the said pan covered over with paste, to be bak'd: The woman desired to know what was therein, which required so large a pan, the servant who brought it, said it was a present of very fine pears sent to his master, and they must take a great care of it, and placed it to the middle of the oven, which was duly observed (the doctor being a good customer) but having left no vent in the paste, for the evaporation of the smoak, the pan burst and scattered liquid therein all over the oven; The smell was so excessively strong, that they could hardly remain in the bakehouse; whereupon they went and examined the pan, and found a child of about 3 years old in full proportion, the hand and arm of a grown person, and several other parts of human flesh and bones: The doctor was carried before two Justices of the Peace, but he refusing to answer their demands, how he came by the human body, &c. was obliged to find special security for his appearance.

LONDON SEPT. 23. They write from Sheffield in the County of York, that last week a snow fell upon the moors and other places adjacent, about a foot thick, which is looked upon as very remarkable, such a thing having never happened in these parts at this time of the year in the memory of the oldest men living.

Last week a very melancholy accident happened in or near Bakerstreet in Endfield: A poor woman which had taken a child to nurse from a certain family of good fashion in this city, going some little way from her house, gave the child to her daughter a girl of about 12 or 13 years old to take care of till she came back, which it seemed was in less than a quarter of an hour. The girl tending and playing with the child, according to the best of her skill, carry'd it to the side of the New-River, which ran just by the door, thinking that shewing the child the water would please and divert it, and at last dropt it in. The poor infant sunk immediately; and the girl cry'd out, and help came presently, it could not be found for some hours, the stream having carried it down some distance from the place, so that it was irrecoverably lost.

LONDON SEPT. 23. On Tuesday morning William James, going to Knight-Bridge, was run over by a gentleman's coach coming out of Hyde-Park into Picadilly, the first wheel beat him down, and the other running over his breast killed him on the spot.

BRISTOL SEPT. 29. Here has been a very great riot communicated by the weavers, who would force their masters to raise their wages. They were going to pull down Mr. Fetcham's house on Castle Ditch; but the soldiers were called to his assistance, in which fray one serjeant and six weavers were killed, and several more wounded, before the mob went off, without the gate, they took away the looms of the weavers, and all they could find, and burn them. The drums are now beating about to arm; God knows the consequence of it; the mob is now in Temple-street as past nine at night.

GUILFORD SEPT. 30. John Parkhurst, a basket-maker being poor, and his family seized with the small pox, sent his wife abroad for bread, and hanged himself in the meantime.

LONDON OCT. 4. Yesterday morning before it was light, a new born child was drop'd in an empty house in Sea-Coal-Lane; the windows where one pair of stairs were open, and had it not been timely discovered by its crying, it would of necessity have perished for want of necessary subsistence, the child was soon baptiz'd and sent to parish nurse.

LONDON OCT. 6. Last Saturday in the afternoon, one Joseph Spriggs, a bricklayer's apprentice, who was repairing the house of Lord Windsor, in Queens Street Westminster, fell from the top of the same and died immediately.

LONDON OCT. 9. We are informed from Andover in Hampshire, that last week there was an extraordinary marriage consummated between a boy of 15 years old, and apprentice to a barber, and a girl of nine years and a quarter. The latter whose father was a clothier, and left 2010 £. was under care of four guardians, three of which intended her for their own sons or relations, when she was marriageable; but one of them having a suspicion of the other's design, sent for her home from school on Monday was se'nnight, and married her to his son, the lad above mentioned.

LONDON OCT. 11. We hear from Sibley Hethingham in Essex, that one Edw. Finch, being disturb'd in his mind, shot himself in the body; the ball lodg'd in the wound, and probebly he might have surviv'd the hurt; but being desperately bent, threw himself into a river, but was immediately taken out by some people who saw him; His father was so afflicted with his son's misfortune, that he likewise died in a few days after.

LONDON OCT. 11. On Tuesday last, the Justices of the Peace, gentlemen, and principal inhabitants in Goodman's Fields, and places adjacent, had a general meeting at the Hoop and Bunch of Grapes in the Minories to concert measures to put a stop to the further progress of the New Theatre, intended to be erected in Aylisse-Street.

The latter end of last week, as workmen were taken down a house in Little-Queer-street near Lincoln's-Inn-Fields they found between 30 and 40 guineas, and Jubileed the day of the occasion.

Yesterday about two in the afternoon, the Don Carlos, Captain John Barnaby (formerly the King George, Captain John Houghton, in the East India Company's service, a ship of above 500 tons 30 guns, and 60 men bilged on an anchor at Black Wall and sunk, and it is thought has broke her back. She was bound to Cadiz, being designed for a galleon) for which place she was to have departed in a few days, and had on board a very great quantity of woolen goods, &c. but as proper measures were immediately taken, it is hoped the goods (tho' damaged) will be saved.

The same afternoon, about 4 o'clock, the post-boy of Chester Road, and another person, were committed to Bridewell by William Billers, the former for breaking open a letter he received on the road, and taking out 30 £. note, and the latter for being confederate, and demanding payment of the same.

Isabella Eaton, alias Gwynn, who keeps the Crown Tavern in Sherrard-Street near Golden-Square, was on Thursday last commited by Justice Cook to the Gate-House, on the oath of three constables, for threatening to shoot them thro' the head in execution of their office, and also for keeping a disorderly house.

And the same day her sister Mary Harvey, alias Philips, in Shugg-Lane, who keeps also an house of ill fame, was bound over to Westminster Sessions by Justice Ellis, for insulting and grossly abusing the said Justice Cook in the execution of his office.

LONDON OCT. 11. They write from Foulney in Lancashire, That on the 23d of last month, a vessel, loaded with iron ore, was lost in a sudden tempest, and two men drowned, between Wallasey and the point of Pile Fuder.

We hear the affair of Sir Thomas Coleby, deceas'd are become the subject of all conversation, and it is thought it may occasion some amendments or at least explanation to be made in the law of the land next Session of Parliament; for some persons that have rich relations, appear not a little alarmed from an apprehension, that if a rich man should die intestate, his relations will be obliged to prove his legitimacy after his death, which they think may be attended with great difficulties, and render private property very precarious for the few they are able to prove the marriage of their grandparents, fathers or uncles when they are all dead; and therefore it seems reasonable, that if a bastard, his legitimacy ought not be call'd in question after his death.

But happy is the land where there is no lawyers.

LONDON OCT. 12. Last Monday noon there was a Regimental Court Martial held at the horse guards, Whitehall, before which two private centinels belonging to the guards were try'd, the one a grenadier of the First Regiment for mutiny and desertion, and found guilty, and order'd to be shot; the other a hatman belonging to the Third Regiment, for speaking approbious words against his present Majesty, of which he was found guilty and order'd to be whipt, and afterwards drumm'd out of the regiment with a halter about his neck.

LONDON OCT. 14. From Bath we hear there was a great concourse of people at Capt. Goulding's celebration of the King's Coronation Day, and more people was seen drunk at one time then ever was before, by drinking the Royal family's health out of the many hogsheads of punch, the barbicu'd ox was fallen foul of by the populace before it was quite ready, and the silver bowl was won by the famous Dorsershire King.

Last Saturday in the afternoon great quantities of earth fell into the new sewer, against the corner of the St. James's Square in Pall-Mall, which did considerable damage to the works.

Last Friday night late, a French gentleman was robbed in the road between Islington Church and the Turnpike, by two footpads, of his money, watch and sword.

On Saturday last, Thomas Butler, and another running footman who lately lived with the Duke of Chandos, walked fifteen times round the upper Morefields, for a considerable wager; the former did it in 59 minutes and the latter in 61. The ground they walked is computed at seven miles and a half.

LONDON OCT. 18. The convicts who lay in our Castle for transportation knock'd down the turnkey, and 2 or 3 made their escape; so that yesterday only 9 man and a woman (who cut two of her children's heads) were sent from the Castle, and two men and a boy and a woman, from our city goal, were sent forward in a cover'd waggon for London.

On Tuesday last a man dress'd like a sailor, who had been taken with a bundle of stolen goods upon him, was carried by a constable before the justices then sitting at Hick's Hall, but as three of their Worships had him under examination in a room up stairs, and were going to sign his commitment the window being opened, the fellow clapp'd both his hands upon't, and crying, Hey over leap'd out clean into St. John's Street, tho' it was of great height and got off.

Thursday the last pile of the bridge between Fulham and Putney was drove, the first being drove the 5th of April last; The Thames where the bridge is built is about 800 feet wide, and about 600 of the bridge, is cover'd with plank already; the planks are oak of four inches thick, upon which is laid loam four inches deep, upon that chalk six inches, and on that, gravel 10 inches thick.

Tuesday a gunsmith in Ragg-Fair, near the Deans Church, putting an old barrel into the fire, it happen'd to be loaded with a ball, and burst when it took the heat, which killed him on the spot.

Friday se'nnight a mad bullock ran one of his horns into the neck of a woman in Longlane in Smithfield, by which she soon expired.

LONDON OCT. 18. On Monday night a woman going into the shop of Mr. Rawlings, a grocer near Church Court in the Strand, fell through the hole of a trap door in the shop, which unluckily stood open and was killed.

LONDON OCT. 23. Mrs. Clark, who was some days ago run thro' the side by a soldiers sword, dy'd on Tuesday night.

LONDON OCT. 23. Edward Gregory, a tobacconist in St. John's Street was try'd on an indictment for being confederate with Michael Moore, in breaking open to lodging of Mary Poule, and feloniously taking out of her box, 60 guineas, and wearing apparel to the value of 10 pounds (who is beyond the sea) except 10 guineas; but upon full hearing, it appere'd by the evidence for the defendant, had liv'd with the prosecutor for some time, as her husband, and that she had gone by the name of Moore, so that the jury acquitted the prisoner.

At the same time Edward Lloyd, who was charg'd with counterfeiting the current coin of the Kingdom, was discharg'd, no bill being found against him; but a bill of indictment was found against Elizebeth his wife; for the like offence, and she was order'd by the Court to be continued till next sessions.

LONDON OCT. 25. From Exeter That a fellow was lately committed to the county goal there, upon his own evidence for breaking open an house about 6 or 7 years ago, in conjunction with two others, whom he has impeached, but are since fled.

N. B. A young man was condemned & executed about the above time, for the said fact, upon the evidence of this villain, whose conscience has so sorely afflicted him ever since, that he went voluntarily to a Justice of the Peace, would not be denied, and made an open confession of the same.

LONDON OCT. 25. This morning a mare is to drag a load of hay from Chigwell to the Turnpike near White-Chapel, in 6 hours & a half, on a wager of 6 guineas. If she wins, the loser is to give 10 pounds for her.

On Thursday an infirm man watering a pair of horses at Knights Bridge, was taken with a convulsion fit, & fell from one of the banks into the pool: Two troopers coming by, judg'd him to be drunk, and neglected at first to raise him, till seeing him, continuing in the water without making any effort to help himself, they drew him out bearly in time to save him.

On Tuesday night, when the workmen in his Majesty's Dock Yard at Woolwich were going home from thence, the sail makers were stopt, and lock'd in the pay-office, while their lockers in the sail loft were opened, in which considerable quantities of sail cloth were found.

This day 7 nights in the evening the sessions ended on Middlesex Side at Old Baily; when Robert Oliver, for robbing his fellow servant of 47 guineas; and Esther Morgan for robbing the Lady Thorald her mistress; in money and goods to the value of 3000 £. (in conjunction with Margeret Lawrence now under condemnation) received sentence of death.

Before sentence was pass'd Mr. Buckham came into the Sessions House, and humbly moved the Court on the behalf of John Showlwood, his late servant, praying he might be recommended to his Majesty's clemency, as being decended of a very honest and reputable parents in Scotland, who might be greatly scandalized by his suffering ignominious death; and Mr. Serjeant Raby promised request should be taken notice of in a proper place.

LONDON OCT. 25. Tuesday last 5 ships in the East India Company's service fell down to Gravesend; A squall of wind took them in Gallions, which laid them gunnel to, at which time a man was wash'd overboard, and drowned from the Princess of Wales; a gun broke loose on board the London, and the Barrington lost her flying jib boom.

LONDON NOV. 6. There have been great rejoycing for these two days past, in the cities of London and Westminster, &c. in commemoration of the Glorious King William, who was both born and marry'd on the 4th of November, and on the 5th landed at Torbay to deliver the nations from Popery and slavery.

LONDON NOV. 15. They write from Greenwich, that a pensioner in the hospital there, who was much troubled with the stone, died some days ago, aged 53; a surgeons apprentice having afterwards, searched his bladder, found in it a stone of an uncommon size, weighing thirteen ounces.

DOVER NOV. 23. On Friday night some Englishmen being in company with two Dutchmen, and a quarrel arising, the Dutchmen drew their knives, and one of the Englishmen received three stabs in the body and a cut in the throat. The man now lies dangerously ill, and the Dutchmen are committed to our goal by the Mayor.

EXON NOV. 28. They write from Plymouth, that on the 18th, about four in the evening, the ferryboat for foot passengers between that place and Tarr-Point attempting to get to the point with 4 men, and two women, and a young child on board; the ferryman set sail, and before they had got one third of the passage, the sea fill'd and sunk the boat: His Majesty's ship the York, being nearest, sent her boat to their assistance, and fortunately took up the man of the passage-house and another; but getting hold of the third, they got him in also, he never spoke afterwards; and the other man 85 was drowned; as they were getting in the woman and child, the child drop'd and the woman just spoke and expir'd. The woman that was sav'd, is a foot post between Sir Wm. Carew's house and Plymouth.

LONDON NOV. 29. They write from Warrington in Lancashire, the 21st, that above 20 people returning home last Wednesday from the market there, on horseback, some single and others double, in passing the River Mercy, which parts Lancashire and Cheshire at Wilderpool, over a high causeway, had the misfortune either to miss it, or be carried off by the rapidity of the floods, occasioned by the late great rains, and were all of them, with their horses, drowned, and on Friday last the bodies, except two, were taken up: among whom were one Mr. Percival, an eminent cheese-factor in Cheshire; the rest were chiefly farmers, &c.

DEAL NOV. 29. The ship which on Thursday morning run on Goodwin Sands, proved to be the Endeavour, William Reynolds from Maryland, for London; She lost all her anchors in the storm off New Forland, when the wind was at N. W. and stood in a fair for the Downs under their foresail, mizens and mizen topsail; but the ship fell off to leeward; before they could get their mainsail (they being all jaded) she struck. They staved their long boat in getting out, upon which they all got into the yawl, (being 19 or 20 in number) and left the ship; but their boat soon filled with water, and a little distance from the ship one of the town boats took them in, as their boat was sinking, and brought them safe on shore about three in the afternoon.

LONDON NOV. 29. We have an account from Sherborn in Dorsetshire, that the keeper of that jail was murder'd by a prisoner on the 31st instant at night, as he was going to lock him up; the fellow made his escape, but about two hours after was retaken and then brought back.

LONDON DEC. 1. On Friday morning last, a cart loaded with lumber broke down in Aldergate Street turning into Barbican, and a piece falling on the carman, beat him to the ground, and bruised his breast and stomach so much, that he died the next day.

They write from Ailesbury, That last Wednesday 3 men broke out of the goal there. One of whom was John Gillet alias Shock, who was whipped the sessions before last from the King's Head at Harrow on the Hill to the church for stealing a game cock. After which he and one Robinson were removed to Ailesbury by Habeus Corpus, the first for horse stealing, the other for the highway. The third was taken in the country for the said fact. But they were retaken by the diligence of Mr. Woodcock the keeper, in the said town, after much opposition. They had off their irons when taken.

LONDON DEC. 3. Monday night last, between 10 and 11 a-clock, Dr. Mead the physician, was attacked in Holbourn, by one footpad who commanded the coachman to stop, and told the footman behind, if he offered to stir he would shoot him, and demanded of the doctor his money, watch and rings; but the footman crying out villain the villain fired a pistol at him and run off, but being persued by the footman, crying out stop thief, he was seized; and being immediately carried before Sir William Billers, proved to be the notorious street robber James Dalton, who about 12 months ago was admitted as evidence with Thomas Neives (since executed at Tyburn for shop-lifting) against 12 street roberies; whereupon he was committed to the compter, and being yesterday further examined he was committed to Newgate.

LONDON DEC. 6. Yesterday Thomas Bambridge Esq; was brought to the bar at the Old Baily, and tried for the felony whereof he stood indicted (for stealing the goods of one Elizabeth Berkley). It appeared by the evidence given on the part of the Crown, that the said Bambridge was, at the time the goods alleged got stolen, Deputy Warden of the fleet, and in vertue thereof he had made a seizure of said goods for nonpayment of rent; and it likewise appearing that such seizure was regularly and publickly made, the jury acquitted him.

LONDON DEC. 6. They write from Warwick, that in September last the tomb of the famous champion, Bold Beauchamp, who had been buried in St. Marys Church there 293 years, fallen in, his corpse was discovered entirely; and what is most remarkable his hair was very fresh and strong.

BRISTOL DEC. 6. We have the melancholy news of the True Love, Capt. Rogers of this port, southward bound from the Straights, with wines, castile soap, &c. being wreck'd in our channel, in Bude Bay, near Briddeford, last Thursday se'nnight: she was drove on a rock, and beat to pieces; there was a gentleman and a gentlewoman came passengers in her; the former was by sea carry'd overboard, and wonderfully left by it on shore, whilst the rest on board were left in the utmost distress, the gentlewoman and three men were drown'd, and those that had good fortune to save their lives, were stript and robbed by the country people; a boy they entirely left naked; it was probable, that after the storm had abated, a great part of the cargo might be saved, to the owners use, if the humanity of the people on the sea-coast, were so just as not to apply it to their own.

LONDON DEC. 13. On Wednesday last the tyde in the River Thames flowed so high, that several boats floated, in the New Palace Yard, Westminster, and the inhabitants were forced to be carried out of their houses in them. The water was five inches high in Westminster-Hall, in so much that the shop keepers were forced to quit their shops, and caused the gates to be all shut up; the cellars and lower rooms of several houses in Channel Row were filled with water, which hath done a considerable damage to most of the cellaring thereabout.

1730

LONDON JAN. 3. On Sunday night about 11 o'clock, a fire broke out in the dwelling house of Mr. Allen, a waterman, who kept an Ale-house known by the sign of the Two Brewers at Dick Shoar near Limehouse, which soon spreading in a short space consumed near 20 houses: Mr. Sherman Godfrey, an eminent distiller who lived next door to the ale-house had time to get his family out before his house was in flames: The Benjamin and Anne, Capt. Vavassor, which was in Mr. Graves's Dock, whose house was burnt down, was much damaged in her rigging, and with difficulty preserved. A boy at the ale-house, and a maid-servant in the neighbourhood, are missing and 'tis believed are burnt.

LONDON JAN. 7. Yesterday about 12 o'clock a fire happen'd at the house of Mr. Hobbs in Botolph-lane; And about 2 o'clock another fire happen'd in the house of Mr. Heather, pastry-cook the corner of Avy-Mary-Lane in Ludgate-street; but by timely assistance of firemen and porters, they were both extinguish'd without doing any other damage than the floors, in which part of the house that it happened.

LONDON JAN. 8. Tuesday last a woman well dress'd was observ'd by a centinel to throw herself into Rosamond's Pond in St. James's Park, but he could not come time enough to prevent her being drowned; It appears she was an eminent butcher's wife in St. James's Market.

Last Monday Mr. Arthur of Red Lyon Square, was robbed on his return to London from Uxbridge, by one highwayman, who took from him 6 guineas and 9 s. 6 d.

LONDON JAN. 10. A few days since, a woman near fourscore years of age, who had begg'd alms in Ironmongers-Lane, Cheapside and the adjacent neighbourhood for upwards of 15 years, was married to a barber 84 years of age in the same lane: and since her marriage she has carried her spouse to her own lodging, which was exceedingly well furnish'd; and she has since acknowledged herself worth 3,000 £.

LONDON JAN. 15. One night last week two young gentlemen concern'd in liquor, went to Edward's Chocolate House in Drury-Lane Play House Passage, and call'd for a bowl of punch, which they drank, and was going away without paying their reckoning: whereupon the gentle woman of the house telling them, that she hoped they would pay their reckoning, one of the gentlemen, in a very reprobate manner, swore she should die that minute: & forcing her to kneel down, he, with his drawn sword, push'd at her breast in order to run her through, but by good fortune miss'd her body, so that the sword went thro' her cloaths and stuck in the wainscot; upon which several persons enter'd the room and secur'd them, took their swords and their canes from them, and carried them to Covent-Garden Round-House, where one of them privately took a penknife out of his pocket, and without the least provocation, stabbed the waterman belonging to Covent-Garden in the breast with the said penknife, in such a desperate manner, that the wound was at first thought mortal, but we hear he is now likely to recover. The two young sparks were the same night committed to the Gatehouse, but has since been admitted to bail.

LONDON JAN. 17. 'Tis talk that a duty of five shillings will be laid on every pack of cards, and one guinea upon every pair of dice, which, if it be true, will be a great service to the many thousands of his Majesty's subjects, and in particular those of low rank, by preventing in a great measure the excessive gaming, which is so frequently practiced by such persons, whose families many times are miserable sufferers there by.

LONDON JAN. 21. On Sunday morning Mrs. Bendish coming to town from her house at Chich Ford, and seeing on Epping Forrest a person who she suspected to be a highwayman, she took off her rings and watch, which she concealed in the coach, with her gold; Soon after the fellow came up, ordered her to let down the glass, and then demanded her green purse, which by the same time she had prepared for him, having put 3 s. 6 d. and some half pence and tied it in a hard knot. He then asked her for her watch and rings but seeing she had neither, he told her she might go on and if she met two persons at the bottom of the hill, she need only say poor Robin, and they would not molest her.

LONDON JAN. 21. They write from Northampton, That one day last week a remarkable wedding was celebrated within a few miles of that place, between one William Chester of Ashby, leger, and a woman of Badby, whose age computed together do not much exceed 180 years; and what is observable that this is the second time the woman has been married since she was 80 years old.

We are credibly informed, That the Royal African Company intend to present a petition to Parliament very speedily, seeking forth the necessity of keeping forts and castles in Africa, for the preservation of that trade, and praying for such relief and assistance for enabling them to keep and maintain them, as the Parliament think fit; but they have no intention to apply for an exclusive trade, nor for any thing in prejudice of seperate traders to Africa.

CAMBRIDGE JAN. 26. On Monday, Tuesday and Wednesday last week the sophs were examined for their degrees, and on Friday one hundred and nine were admitted Batchelors of Art.

LONDON JAN. 27. Mr. Bambridge late Warden of the Fleet went out a shooting, in company with two or three other gentlemen, near Bromley in Kent, several of them shot at a bird flying that they sprung up in a wood thereabouts, and Mr. Bambridge brought him down; but one of the gentlemen gunners miss'd his mark so very much, that he lodg'd a great many small shots in Mr. Mosely's face of Bromley, and several in Mr. Bambridge's, and it was thought the latter gentleman would lose an eye by it: Mr. Coletheart, an able surgeon, hath them both under care.

LONDON JAN. 27. Yesterday James Dalton was brought to the Court in Old Bailey to be arraign'd, a woman, said to be one of his wives, took an opportunity to strike him over the head with a weapon that cut him in a very desperate manner, which put the crowd in such disorder and confusion, that three felons, viz. two men and one woman found means to make their escape.

We hear, that in lieu of the duties on soap and candles an inpost of 10 £. per ann. will be laid on all noblemens coaches and chariots. And 10 s. per ann. on persons wearing swords in Great Britain, the officers of the army, navy and train'd bands only excempted.

The Marquees of Carnavon lost a gold snuffbox of very great value as he was attending his Royal Highness the Prince of Wales last week at the Play-House.

The Lord Bruce's Lady lost a diamond earing of great value at the opera, which being found by one of the Dutchess of Buckingham servants, was very honestly restored to her Ladyship.

LONDON JAN. 29. We hear from Bath, that one day last week, a young highwayman was taken there, and committed to goal, for several robberies committed within a mile and a half of that city: He says, he is of a good family, and that his father possessed a good estate, but having been guilty of some extravagancies had incurr'd his ill-will; that he often wrote to his father for money, but he taking no notice of his petitions, it forc'd him to rob to keep him from starving; but that it was very much against his conscience to wrong any person, and those that he had robb'd were but three persons, from whom he took but trifling sum and that he would chose rather to be hanged than undergo such a miserable circumstance of poverty; His lodging was in a quarry at Odd-Down, where he had a bed, a bottle of wine, and some provisions.

LONDON JAN. 29. Monday evening, four highwaymen, mounted on horseback, and with pistols, attack'd four men coming to our fair, on Barrow Common, about three miles from this city, and robb'd 'em of 105 £. The rogues treated 'em very roughly, and because one of the men said some expressions at their parting from his money, not agreeable to the villains ears, had one of his eyes beat out by the but end of a whip, and was in miserable pain all Monday night.

Wednesday evening a porter belonging to a shop in the fair, was trick'd out of a piece of broad cloth by two sharpers; he was directed with it to a shop in Winestreet and asking where the person lived he was to deliver it to, one of the sharpers directed him to a wrong place by All-Saints Church, where another sharper was ready, and told the porter he was the man the cloth belonged, left it with him.

Several persons that came from Bradford the same day reports, that there were three footpads on the road, who had robb'd several persons, particularly from an old woman on horseback they took 13 s. 6d. and at the same time a young woman coming to this city happening to come by, one of 'em endeavour'd to take ho'd of her horses bridle, and threatn'd to shoot her if she did not stop; but she, regardless of what they said, kept on a swift tilts, and saved her money.

LONDON JAN. 29. On Friday se'nnight Mrs. Harding, a waterman's wife at Battersea in Surrey, was brought to bed of three daughters, and dy'd in labour of the fourth; and on Sunday last (being all very well) they were Christend, viz. Mary, Sarah, and Rebecca.

LONDON FEB. 7. On Saturday last a considerable body of dealers in Bone-Lace from the counties of Buck, Northampton and Bedford, waited on their Majesties (being introduced by the Lord Grantham to his Majesty) with a petition in behalf of their manufacture, and carried with them a parcel of lace, to shew the perfection they had brought it to; and their Majesties shew'd their Royal intentions to encourage the British manufacture, by receiving them very graciously, and bought a considerable quantity for the use of the Royal Family.

LONDON FEB. 14. Last Thursday as they were craining up a hogshead of sugar at Wiggens Key by custom house, the rope broke, and it fell down upon a porter, and kill'd him on the spot.

Last Saturday night, a maltman of Deptford was coming from Dartmouth in Kent, on Blackheart near the corner of Greenwich-Park Wall, his horse fell with him; by which accident his collarbone was broke; and seeing two men at some distance, he called out for help. They came to his assistance, got the horse off him, robbed him of his watch and money, to the value of about 15 £. and notwithstanding the misfortune of his collar-bone being broke, the rogues beat the maltman so cruelly that his life is in great danger.

LONDON FEB. 17. Yesterday morning her Majesty the eldest Princess, his Majesty the duke, and the Princess Loisia walk'd round St. James's Park.

Yesterday came the trial between the Lord Abegavenny and ____ Lyddalli Esq; before the Lord Chief Justice Eyre, at the Court of Common Pleas at Westminster, in relation to the latters having criminal conversation with the formers wife, when after a full hearing, which lasted from nine in the morning to three in the afternoon, the jury went out for about the space of half an hour, and brought in a verdict for the noble Lord of 10,000 £. damages.

On Sunday morning about 10 o'clock, one Briget Harris, who lived at Mr. Bensons near Cow-Cross, was taken ill, on a sudden, and sat down in a chair, and leaning her head on her arm, died immediately.

LONDON MARCH 13. We hear that a great number of Palatine families having lately proposed to the Lord of Trade to go settle in South Carolina, so that the province in a short time will, in all likely hood, be in flourishing condition, that delightful country assuming all necessaries of life, and wanting only people to cultivate it.

LONDON MARCH 25. Yesterday being Maunday-Thursday, according to a very ancient custom, there was distributed in the forenoon at Banqueting House, Whitehall, to 47 poor men and 47 poor women, (the Kings age 47) boil'd beef 7 shoulders of mutton in plenty, and small bowls of ale, which is called dinner; after that, large wooden platers of fish and leaves, viz. undress'd large old ling and one large dry'd cod; twelve red herrings & four half-quartern loaves, each person had one platter of this provision: in the afternoon at four, being prayertime, after the first and second lesson, Dr. Gilbert, Sub-Almoner to the Archbishop of York (who was girded about with a white cloth and his scarf-place supply'd with the same) distributed to the above objects shoes and stockings, linnen and woolen cloth, and leathern bags of silver, with one penny, two penny, three penny and four penny pieces of silver and shillings; after service was over, each object had about one gill of wine: The whole value to each is supposed to be worth about four pounds.

LONDON MARCH 28. Yesterday a Board of Admiralty was held at their office near Whitehall, at which was present the Lord Torrington; and upwards of 120 disabled seamen were minueted down to be admitted into Greenwich Hospital.

On Monday last, the Exeter Carrier was robb'd about 12 miles beyond Dorchester, by three highwaymen, who took off some of the packs from the horses, open'd them, and stole from thence to the value of 950 £. 13 s. in guineas and moidores.

GUILFORD APRIL 6. This day five malefactors condemned here at the late Assizes for this county, was executed on our new gallows erected on this occasion, viz. John James, for robbing Lambert Church; Patrick Carr, Wm. Carter, John Sike, and John Goodbury, for robbing on the highway; but William Jones and Wilby Fates, convicted of burglary and Robert Acherton, for horse-stealing, have received his Majesty's most gracious reprieve. Money was collected yesterday in our church for coffins to bury them in, and notwithstanding their bodies had been begg'd by surgeons, our bargemen brought them off, and saw them interred.

LONDON APRIL 7. On Sunday night Hugh Norten charged with robbing the Bristol mail, now a prisoner in Newgate, attempted to make his escape, by filling off his irons; but finding it impracticable, he took a quantity of poison, which began to operate before the keeper discovered it, when proper means being used to expel it, had the desired effect; and it is expected he will be tried tomorrow at the Old Bailey. This timely discovery is chiefly owing to the care and diligence of Mr. Langley, one of the turnkeys of the said prison.

Yesterday in the afternoon one Anne Deber, an ancient woman, living in Plough-Stable Yard near the new church in Bloomsbury, dropt down dead, as she was going to cross the same with a tub of water.

Yesterday a party of the Cripplegate Grenadiers; and another of Fusillers, met in at Bridgewater Square, whence they marched to Bloomsbury, where having joined the Grenadiers from St. Clement's Danes, they proceeded to Westminster, and performed a handsome exercise in Tothill Fields, and made a mock seige of a fortress at the Alms-House. There happened at the same time an unhappy accident to a soldier of Col. Chidleigh's Company in the Second Regiment of Foot Guards, who standing before one of the pieces of small artillery, a spark from a squib fell on the touch hole, and the piece went off, by which his leg was very much shatter'd: Also a woman lost her eye by the throwing of a squib.

LONDON APRIL 8. On Tuesday last Mr. John Cardwell, a Quaker, and an eminent clothworker on his return to his house in the Curtin near Holloway Lane, Shoreditch, was attack'd by some street-robbers about a quarter past seven o'clock under Moorgate Postern, who came behind him, and knocked him down, and took 100 £. out of his pocket, tied up in a bag, which he received at the bank that afternoon, besides 17 s. in silver, and a pocketbook, in which several promissory notes, to the value of 60 £. They endeavoured to take his watch but the chain broke in pulling it out; which he saved. The rogues stabb'd him in the right side with a penknife as it is supposed by the wounds; and bruised him in a violent manner, and then made off with their booty undiscovered. Soon after some gentlemen coming by, they carried him into Moorgate Coffee House, and sent for Mr. Wheeler, an eminent surgeon in Basinghall Street, who dressed his wounds, none of which appear to be mortal.

LONDON APRIL 11. On Thursday evening a new married couple of this city, returning with their friends in coaches from Edmonton, where they had kept their wedding-dinner, were attacked between Newington and Kingsland by two highwaymen who robbed them of watches, rings, jewels, and money, to a very considerable value.

Robert Halsey, late master of the Good Providence sloop, who was to have been discharged out of the fleet, upon the fugitive Act on Monday last at Guildhall, was on Saturday charged with piracy, and likewise with the murder of his cabin boy, by a warrant from the High Court of Admiralty, and thereupon he was removed from the fleet prison to the Marshalsea, there to be confined till a session of Admiralty to be held at the Old Baily. The sloop was bound on a voyage from Sicily to Lisbon with corn, when the crimes are supposed to have been committed, but she proceeded to Cagliari, and there the master and others on board her, sold and discharged it, and then changed her name, and proceeded to Plymoth, and there quitted her.

LONDON APRIL 13. They write from St. Albans, that a gentleman upwards of 70 years of age, who set out from London on the 4th instant, in order to go to Sheffield in Yorkshire, to settle there for the remainder of his days, was set upon by two footpads on Tuesday last who robbed him of a guinea and a half and some silver which had been given him, it seems by a nobleman in Piccadilly, to defray his journey. They knock'd him down twice, because he refused to deliver his money, and they bound him, and laid him in a ditch, where he must have perished, had he not been unbound by a man and his wife, that were passing by, they brought him with much difficulty, to St. Albans, and gave him half a crown, and left him in a dying miserable condition. The same rogues about two hours after, committed another robbery on a country woman: but one of them is since taken, and he offers to make a large discovery.

LONDON APRIL 13. Yesterday one Horsey was committed to Newgate, for marrying a second husband, her first being living.

LONDON APRIL 14. Yesterday several owners and masters of ships attended to the Navy Office, with proposals for letting their ships to the Government; but none were taken up, the Commissioners not thinking their terms low enough. The ships which they require must be square sterned, upward of 200 tons, having 5 feet height between decks. They propose to hire them for 4 months certain and to have power to discharge them in the Mediterranean.

LONDON APRIL 16. On Monday last a new born dead infant was left at a church warden's door in Bush-Lane by Cannon-Street, decently wrapt up in a shroud, and put into a coffin, upon which was fasten'd a paper with this inscription, Bury it for charity.

LONDON APRIL 17. Yesterday an attachment was granted by the Court of King's Bench against one Wm. Brine a baliff for not shewing or delivering to a prisoner he had arrested a clause in the Act of Parliament, entitled An Act for the Relief of Debtors, with Respect to the imprisonment of their persons. Before any victuals, drinks, &c. were called for in pursuance of the said Act, and likewise for extorting two guineas from him for civility money (as they call it) contrary to the said Act.

The same day a motion was made against a certain attorney at law, for a rule to oblige him to show cause why an attachment should not be granted against him for oppression and illeagle practices, and the same was granted by the Court.

On Tuesday morning a man well dressed, who had a suit of deep mourning, and scarlet great coat, was found gagged and tied a fields breath out of the foot road between Kingsland and Hackney, when the evening before was met and robbed by 3 foot pads of his money and watch.

LONDON APRIL 17. Yesterday a servant of Mr. Stubbs at the White Lyon in Shoe-Lane, by firing a gun which was fastened in a wooden carriage, the breech flew out, which shatter'd to the bone of his leg very much; He was immediately sent to St. Bartholomew's Hospital.

LONDON APRIL 18. Yesterday about four in the afternoon, two gentlemen met in Pig-Lane and fought a duel; One of them wounded the other three times in the sword arm, and a fourth through his left hand: The last thrust which was received, was one of the three, before mentioned in the arm, which bent his sword double: The other had so much honour (though so much wounded) that he gave him his life without asking for it; and both went to town in a coach together. The person who gave the other his life, was very ill, and bled extremely, and he that received it, had one slight scratch on his wrist.

We hear that the widow Lovejoy of Nettlebed in Oxfordshire, and several other farmers who dressed their land with Mr. Living's Compound Manure, have an appearance of the greatest crop of corn and grass that ever were seen in England: And several noblemen and gentlemen who have large estates in Ireland, having desired him to erect offices, and make the same there. His Majesty hath ordered letters patent for his sole making and vending the same in Ireland to pass the Great Seal of that Kingdom, in the same manner as the letters patent already granted him, for the sole making and vending the same in England.

LONDON APRIL 22. Yesterday the Duke of Devonshire and Richmond, the Earl Albimarle, Lord James Cavendish, and about 12 more, diverted themselves at cricket in Hyde-Park, & next week they are to play a match for 100 guineas.

His Majesty has been pleased to order one John Carter, under sentence of death in Newgate, who was reprieved this day to be transported; and yesterday the keeper of Newgate received a warrant for that purpose.

Yesterday some workmen were shoaring the front house turning into Air-Street from Hockley in the hole, part of the wall fell in, and bruised one of the carpenters in the rubbish; he was taken out alive, but died in about three hours after.

Last week one Meuse of Plymouth was committed to Exeter Goal, for burying goods, knowing to be stolen from his Majesty's stores.

The Queen has purchased several hundred acres of land, lying between Richmond and Kew Green off the Lady Molineux, which is to be laid to the Royal Gardens at Richmond, to enlarge and make them more commodious.

LONDON APRIL 25. Col. Chariteis, who was thought to be gone to Bath, hath hired lodging at Kensington Gravel Pits: And last Saturday night, as he was going in a hackney coach to Chelsea, the mob fell upon him and beat him in a barbarous manner, for no reason than that there were two women with him in the coach.

LONDON MAY 13. Hugh Norton, alias Horton, who was yesterday to have been executed at Tyburn, for robbing the British Mail, found means to hang himself in his cell, about 6 in the morning, by taking his belt that buckled his irons, and making it fast to the bars of the cell window, and to make it a convenient length, he tied his handkerchief to it, putting the same about his neck, without making a knot, kept hold of the end of it with his left hand, kneeling down till he was dead, in which posture he was found by the keeper, who had not been from him 8 minutes. The said person had been purposely hired to watch him, to prevent his laying violent hands on himself, he having declared, when the poison he had taken was expelled, that they should not hang him. His body is this day to be carried from Newgate to be hanged in chains on Hounslow Heath.

LONDON MAY 16. On Wednesday last the main topmast fell down on board the Diamond man of war at Wollwich, whereby one man was kill'd and two more wounded.

On Thursday last as some workmen were repairing some old houses at Deptford, one of the houses and two chimnies fell down and kill'd one labourer.

Yesterday the sessions ended at the Old Baily, when the three following malefactors received sentence of death, viz. John Doyle for robbery on the highway who pleaded guilty; John Young for robbing a person of three broad pieces of gold, and other things, near Uxbridge; he had kept him company all the way up from Bristol, and had lent him money to defray his charges on the road, and after he had robbed him shot him in the neck with a pistol; and Anne Bambrey for privately stealing from Roger Smith two gold rings and other things.

The said John Young's wife was also try'd for felony, in stealing a sum of money, and cast for transportation.

A man was try'd for having two wives, and a woman for having two husbands, both now living; but they were both acquited for want of sufficient evidence.

LONDON MAY 22. A vault is building in Hammersmith Church Yard for the family of Richard Robenson, Esq; of Blue Green near the said town, a daughter of whom is to be interred there this evening.

Several soldiers belonging to his Majesty's Foot-Guards, at Hanover, who were lately discharged there, upon account of their being under size, are come over hither, and petition'd his Majesty's on Sunday for the pension that is allow'd to disabled and supperannuated soldiers at Hanover; and his Majesty was graciously pleased to order them a sum of money to defray their expenses back to Hanover, and to give directions to Baron Bothmar to send word over, that they may be admitted into pension they petitioned his Majesty for.

LONDON JUNE 4. On Saturday evening happened the following melancholy accident: A cart going from Croydon Market to Godstone, in which Mrs. Moor the owner, the widow Rossey of Coulsdon, and Mr. Canston's daughter of Croydon, of about 12 or 13 years of age, was overturned on Rickles Down about 4 miles beyond Croydon; and being loaded with goods and tilted, they were all smother'd to death before they could get out.

LONDON JUNE 4. On Saturday last two persons in single chaises in the back road to Klington strove which could run faster, when the one running against the other overturned him into a ditch, whereby his arm was broke, and he was so bruised that he is likely to die.

LONDON JUNE 12. On Friday last came on a trial in the Court of Exchequers at Guildhall between the King plaintiff, and Mr. Dingley, a gold smith of this city, defendant, on an action brought against Mr. Dingley, for a considerable sum of money, for duty of 5,400 ounces of wroth plate exported beyond the sea; and after a full hearing, the jury found a verdict for the defendant.

LONDON JUNE 19. Yesterday the dwelling house of Mr. Jones in Henrietta-street by Covent-Garden, and that of Mr. Lloyd the woolen draper next door, fell down to the ground, to the great damage of the aforesaid persons. The houses cracked some moments before they fell, so that the inhabitants narrowly escap'd out at the back door. The same day a dwelling house fell down in Prince's-street by Leicester-fields, but no person received any hurt.

LONDON JUNE 20. We have received an account from Amsterdam, That it was observed by the populace there, that sixteen coffins were carried from their City-House, or Guildhall, which coffins were supposed to contain bodies that had been privately executed for sodomy, of the richer sort of people; and that morning about 29 persons, of mean extraction, were to have been publickly executed for the like crime; but the populace arising in arms, and demanding publick execution of the rich as well as the poor (there then being 300 of all ranks in prison in that city accused of that crime, and for some of them of great note and subsistance) the magistrates were obliged to send to the Hague for assistance. A list is published of those wretches that are now in custody.

LONDON JUNE 23. The latter end of last week or the beginning of next a great number of new fire arms, swords, bayonets, & other proper accoutrements, will be sent for his Majesty's Armory in the Tower, to the Lord Mark Kerr's Regiment, which will completely equip them for their intended expedition. The officers of said regiment having received pikes, colours, &c. some time ago on that occasion.

Most of the transport vessels lately hired are fallen down the river, to take on board part of the forces that are to assist in the intended expedition.

On Sunday last Peter Bluck, Gent. voluntarily came before Justice Burdus, and confess'd and sign'd his confession, that on or about the

19th of February gone two years, he strangled & murdered Anne Bluck his daughter, a child aged five years, and that ever since he had been troubled in his conscience for the said murder, whereupon the said gentleman was committed to Newgate.

LONDON JULY 10. The Birch galley, Capt. Joseph Turner, is arrived at Bristol from Jamaica; but her passage, on the 19th of May last, she was taken by a Spanish guard de coast, belonging to Havanna, which carried her to one of the Florida Keys, and there came to an anchor, kept the said Turner and his people 4 days on board the guard de coast, plundered the ship of all her stores, and part of her cargo, put the thumbs of all her company under the cock of a gun, to force them to say they had money or logwood on board; which they had not. They also stript them of their cloaths and bedding, and kept them prisoners 4 days. The truth of the aforegoing article they have sworn to before the Mayor of Bristol.

CHESTER JULY 17. This day the coroners inquest is to sit on the body of an Irishman lately killed on the other side of Brandywine in this county. It seems the deceased and one Bourk, his countryman, both lately out of servitude, were reaping together all the morning, and about noon Bourk stabb'd his companion in the breast with a knife of which wound he languished a few days and then died, charging the said Bourk with his death; who is now in irons in our County Goal. This affair makes a great noise in the country, the rather because some of the more ignorant sort, have been so indiscreet as to give out threatning words against authority, of what they would do in case any Irishman should be executed in this country; and two of them, for saying they would fetch the prisoner out of goal, with some other ill behavior of the like kind, have been sent to keep him company. There are various reports about the circumstances of the murder, so that we are impatient to hear the verdict of the inquest.

We have hired an unlucky She-Wrestler who has lately thrown a young weaver, and broke his leg, so that 'tis thought he will not be able to tread the treadles these two months. In the mean time however, he may employ himself in winding quills.

LONDON JULY 20. They write from Great Ness, and other adjacent villages in Shropshire, that, a violent sickness rages there, which seizes them in the bowels and head, attended with a shaking raunch like an aque, which carries them off in three or four days. Great number of them die daily; especially the poorer sort of people, there being scarce labouring men enough to get in the harvest; and those that are, will not work under twelve pence per day, and their victuals; which is reckoned an extraordinary price to that county, and has not been given these many years.

LONDON JULY 21. One Haslett, a water-carrier of Chapham, being on Saturday afternoon fetching stones from Vauxhall, his carriage broke down on the road, but a gardner lent him a cart to carry them to Clapham, on his promising it to him that night. The old man, when at Clapham, got his son and one Clare, a neighbour, to accompany him back with the cart, and being then past ten o'clock they took a pitch-fork with them, the better to defend themselves if attack'd: When they got to the White-Post, a lusty man attack'd young Haslett, (who drove the cart) and got him down, and a little man attack'd Clare, who sat in the cart's tail, and knock'd him off; then bid the old man, who was farther in the cart, get down and deliver his money. He accordingly got out, and by the help of the fork not only kept him off, but with it, as often as he could, struck the rogue that was on the ground grabbling with his son, who by that help soon got the uppermost: Clare in the mean while recovering, was getting up, which the little man seeing, knock'd him down again; and finding he could not assist his companion without demolishing old Haslett, he, after two or three times snapping, fired a pistol at him, which doing no execution, he endeauvour'd to get over the hedge into the field; his antagonist pursued him, pushing at his buttocks with the fork, but the prongs being unluckily doubled would not enter, therefore with the other end he beat him so that he made a loud outcry till he tumbled over the hedge, at which time the horse ran away, when Clare recover'd again and soon follow'd in order to stop them. The two Hasletts gaining a complete victory over the lusty rogue, carry'd him to the county goal, where on Sunday two persons saw him, who had been lately robb'd and swore to him before Justice Welch. When taken, two pistols were found upon him, which he was unable to pull out during the action, his opponent engaging to fighting so closely.

LONDON JULY 23. On Tuesday morning an unhappy accident happen'd between Kensington Gravel-Pits and this town, to a woman that was coming to St. James's Market with a cartload of pease, who meeting with another cart on the road, some dispute happen'd about giving the way, and in the scuffle the woman fell out of the cart, and beat out her brains, her husband, to whom she had been newly marry'd was gone to Clare-Market with another cart of pease.

On Tuesday last a person who is supported by being a zany to several persons of quality, was secured at Tunbridge for commiting a rape on the body of a girl eight years old.

LONDON JULY 23. We hear that on Friday last came on at the Quarter Sessions at Hick's Hall in St. John's Street, before a Justice of the Peace for the said County of Middlesex, the trial of one William Richards, formerly a servant to Sir John Williams of Llangibby-Castle in the County of Monmouth, Bart. for a villainous conspiracy, in endeavouring to charge Sir John Williams with the murder of one Capt. Charles Williams about two years ago; whereas it appear'd that Capt. Charles Williams was lost in a Bristol ship, between the Downs and Petersburg in Muscovy, above sixteen years ago, and neither ship, the captain, nor one soul on board her, were ever heard of since.

Note, William Richard was sent over about a year ago from Placentia in Newfoundland by Governour Philips, and hath lain in the Gate-House ever since.

It appears to be a vile and base accusation, no such man as Capt. Williams having been heard of these sixteen years and Sir John Williams, a gentleman not only of a large fortune, but of an excellent good character. William Cowper, Esq; the chairman, observ'd the danger which the most innocent gentleman might run, not only in his reputation, but also in his life and fortune; and he wondered what could induce the prisoner to be guilty of so base an action, and that he ought to be dealt with, with utmost rigour; but the Court considering the length of his imprisonment, and his extreme poverty, were pleased only to fine him one shilling, to suffer two months of imprisonment, and to stand in the pillory at Charing-Cross.

LONDON JULY 25. A certain young Baronet of a good estate having lately married a young woman of a small fortune, living near Clare-Market, and soon after was taken ill of the smallpox, and died about six weeks after his marriage, the next of kin to the deceased, petitioned the Court of Chancery this week for a Commission of Enquiry, in order to be satisfied whether she was with child, which we hear was not obtain'd; but thus far it was granted, that the petitioners may, if they please, appoint two women to attend her during the time of her pregnancy, whether real or pretended, to prevent any unfair practice.

On Thursday the chairman and committees of Justices of the peace, appointed at the last Westminster Sessions for the suppressing of the night-houses, and other disorderly houses in Covent-Garden,

Bridge Street, and other places contiguous to Drury-Lane, met for the second time at Covent-Garden Vestry, where there were present ten Justices of the Peace; and a considerable number of the substantial inhabitants in the near White-Hart Yard, made a complaint of several disorderly houses in that neighbourhood, whereby they were frequently disturbed by many dissolute and wicked persons harbour'd in those houses, the justices immediately issued out their warrant, and sent a High-Constable and a great many petty constibles, to apprehend the persons who keep these houses, several loose and idle persons and suspected thieves and pickpockets, taken last night at several of these houses, are committed to Tothill-Fields Bridewell to hard labour; and amongst others, a bailiff, forowner, who is a notorious bulley in the hundreds of Drury, as well as solicitor; and his doxy is also committed with him.

LONDON JULY 25. Late Thursday night three boys made up to a gentleman's coach in Kingstreet by Covent Garden, with an intent to rob, as is supposed; upon which the gentleman who had observ'd them follow the coach a considerable time, jumpt out upon them, the watch seized another, and the third made his escape.

The two prisoners, the oldest of which was not 13 years of age, were taken to the Roundhouse and search'd, but no arms were found upon them; And being asked what account they could give of themselves, one of them said he was lock'd out of his lodging, and the other that they were going to Windsor by four o'clock the next morning, and that they only followed the coach to hide themselves from being taken up by the watch.

Yesterday one Charles Stewart, a young lad, about fourteen years of age, was apprehended with three more, on suspicion of being concerned with Hugh Morris and Robert Johnson, who were taken last Sunday at Datchet; at which time Stewart was committed to New-Prison, when not knowing Morris and Johnson were taken, he Impeach'd them with about fourteen more, which the constables, &c. are now making diligent search after: This pernicious gang is reckon'd to consist of near forty in all, who used frequently to resort to Covent-Garden every night.

Some of these informants have given an account of the several robberies they have been guilty of, and particularly that of robbing a gentleman in Lincoln-Inn-Fields of his silver hilted sword, (which they said was their first attempt), and being persued by the gentleman and the watch, they threw the sword from them, and narrowly escaped.

The second robbery they committed was that of Captain Pitts in King-Street, Golden Square of his silver hilted sword, and some money and a gold headed cane.

MANCHESTER JULY 26. About an hour and a half after the publick-worship was concluded, in the afternoon, we had a very terrible storm of thunder and lightning, which broke at a place call'd Moses's Hill, about a mile from our Meeting-House: By which seven sheep near the top of the hill were kill'd; a tree in the decent was broken and shivered; a rock of considerable bigness was split both perpendicularly and horozontally, out of which latter rent there came some stones in the shape of large wedges, and on the back side of the rock, part of it was seperated, and turned, as it were round; about a rod or two from the rock it went into the earth and made a large furrow, out of which several larger rocks were thrown quite up. In spots (about the quantity of an acre) it touched the earth separating the soil.

OXFORD JULY 29. Yesterday Wm. Fuller was executed for the murder of his wife, by choking and strangling her with his hands, which, however, he denied to the last. After he was cut down the scholars insisted to have the body, but the proctors were present and order'd it to be deliver'd to his friends, who put it into a coffin; but the mob got the coffin from them and threw it into the water; the gownsmen then jump'd in like spaniels, drew the body out of the water, and carry'd it to Lincoln College; thither the proctors went, and took it from thence to a house in Bullocks Lane; But the gownsmen came soon after, broke open the door, and had carry'd it about half a mile, when the proctors came and got possession of it again, and secur'd it in the castle: Now the mob dispers'd, though a proclamation, which had been ready by the town clerk, was not regarded. About 11 o'clock at night the body was bro't out of the castle, in order to be carry'd and convey'd in a boat; but in the way of the water side they were surprized by a party of gownsmen, who lay in ambush, and seized the corpse, which is now disected in Christ Church College.

LONDON JULY 30. Information having been given to Sir John Gonson of a gang of pickpocket boys, to the number of thirty, who nightly infest the Plazzas in Covent Garden, the Strand, Temple Bar, and the other streets thereabouts, he issued out a warrant for the searching several night-houses and night-cellars, which harbour and entertain them; and several of this gang being apprehended by the constables, eight of the most notorious were on Tuesday committed to Tothill Fields Bridewell to hard labour: The oldest of the these boys is not above thirteen, and most of them curs'd and swore in a dreadful manner as they were carrying them to Bridewell.

LONDON AUG. 1. On Sunday morning an unhappy alarm happen'd in Parish Church of St. Gile's in the Fields, a pickpocket being taken up by the Beadles over night, whom they had secured in the Round-House, was attempting to break out in sermon time, but some people observing him came running to the church crying out Fryer! (that being the name of one of the beadles,) which surprized the audience, thay some thinking the church had been on fire, and others that it was falling down, by the cracking of the pews that was made by those that endeavoured to get out first; the pews being fast they were burst open; The minister jump'd out of the pulpit; several had their legs and arms broke, and others were very much frighted.

LONDON AUG. 6. On Tuesday last a Committee of Council held at the Cockpit, Whitehall, a petition of the late Mr. Wood and others concerned with him, for a charter to make iron with pit coal, came under their consideration; several facts shown; nails, an anchor, and many tools made of the said iron were produced to the said committee; certain affidavits were read, and witnesses examined, and amongst the rest an eminent iron master, who gave a plain and rational account of that method of making iron; several questions were ask'd him, to which he gave such answers as seem'd to be to their satisfaction; but we cannot say whether a charter will be granted or not.

On Saturday last the son of Mr. Capper an attorney in Chancery Lane, was passing thro' Little Jemair-street a rotted cornish of a small house fell down upon his head, so that his brains came out, and he died Monday last.

On the same day a young man of sixteen years of age, went to swim in the Thames near Chelsea, and was unfortunately drowned. He was design'd to be brought up a scholar, and that very evening his mother went to a boarding school at Chelsea, to treat about his boarding, and learning.

LONDON AUG. 6. Last night about 6 on the clock Mr. Theophilis Rogers, an eminent attorney of Northampton, was found dead upon his bed in his night-gown, at his chamber in Clifford Inn. He went to bed very well on Tuesday night; last night his landress not going to make his bed before 6 o'clock, was the reason that his death was not before discovered.

LONDON AUG. 10. They write from Weston Underwood near Oney in Buckinghamshire that a few days ago a carpenter having a little wheat near that place, went with his apprentice to reap it, the former struck the latter, for not doing his business according to his instructions, the other return'd the blow, both fighting with their sickles, in the combat the man struck the master with the point of the sickle, with such violence, that it ran in one side of his belly and out the other, tearing his entrails to pieces, specially as he was endeavouring to pull it out, so that he died on the spot.

LONDON AUG. 11. Friday last Nathaniel Gould of Hackney, Esq; one of the directors of the bank, received a letter, directed to him from some unknown persons who intimated there being gentlemen reduced by fast living, and going to visit our American Plantations, in hopes of retrieving their lost fortunes. Therein they required him under the penalty of imminent danger of life, to deposit the sum of 30 pieces, under 3 bricks, within 3 yards of the corner of the wall behind Buckingham-House, going towards Constitution-Hill, exactly at 10 that night; which money, they say was to help defray their expences thither: Some will have it that these reduced gentlemen, were so reasonable as to demand only 10 guineas. The bricks were afterwards situated according to directions: But Mr. Gould (not hastening to comply with so modest a request) next day he received another still more peremptory summons: doubtless from the same quarter, the writers swearing if the guineas were not sent that very evening they would have his blood; concluding with, Utrum, Horum Mavis Accipe i. e. take your choice. Sure these gentlemen are in haste to be on their voyage, and apprehensive of losing their passage.

LONDON AUG. 12. Thursday last ended the Assizes in Bridgewater, for the County of Sumerset, before Mr. Thompson and Mr. Justice Lee, when the three following malefactors received sentence of death, viz. Francis Taylor, and George Hipsley for burglary, who are both reprieved in order to 14 years transportation; and John White for the robbery and murder of Robert Sutton: which fact seem to be exceeding barbarous. The case was as follows: The said Sutton was going with a letter to a gentleman's house, and meeting with White, told him, if he would shew him the way he would treat him, thereupon he carried him to an alehouse by the roadside where he treated him accordingly; after Sutton had paid the reckoning, he pulled out a gild counter, which White took to be a half guinea; afterwards White, instead of shewing him the way he led him out of it into a by-place, and taking a stick from a hedge, he knocked him down, beat out one of his eyes, and run a stick in his mouth, and out the side of his neck, mangling him in a most cruel manner. He is to be hanged in chains, to-morrow, on the Cross-Road at Bratton in Sumersetshire, near the place where he committed this inhuman murder.

Yesterday morning at four, a horse belonging to Mr. Robert Underwood, innkeeper at Henly upon Thames, set out for Oxford, and was to go from S. Guiles's Pond and back again in twelve hours, for a wager of 100 guineas. He came in three minutes before nine, baited about 12 minutes at Mr. Worsley's Stag and Hound by S. Giles's Pond and then set out on his return.

The horse which was made to run last Monday from Oxford to S. Giles's Pond and back again to Oxford, performed his merciless task in 11 hours and a half, and so got his owner 100 guineas, winning the wager by half an hour, but died in 21 minutes after. This is riding a free horse to death, with a vengeance! A vile inhumane practice too much in vogue. A good natured gentleman said this morning in a coffee-house, that for his own satisfaction he would freely have lost ten guineas, if the horse had lost by half an hour.

LONDON AUG. 12. Yesterday morning the wife of one Rawlings, a journeyman turner in Jermyn-street, St. James's was safely delivered of four boys all living.

Tho. Barnes of Wiltshire, Esq; had made a bett of 100 guineas, that he rides 200 miles and walks 30 in one day: To be performed in October next at New-Market: Half forfeit.

A few nights ago a certain officer of the militia, and a mercer in Covent-Garden, being in company together at a parish entertainment, the mercer unbraided the captain with male-practices scandalous to his commission, in sending a fowl, wine, &c. home to his family at an entertainment of the like kind. This so enrag'd the captain, that he challenged the mercer out; but he desired to be excused till the next morning, when he promised to meet him sword in hand. The captain went at the time appointed, but not meeting with his adversary at the place, went to his house and enquired for him, but the mercer thinking himself safe in bed than in a combat with so brave an adversary, did not appear; which adding a fresh whet, both to the Captains courage and passion, he stabbed his sword in the door, saying, Damn you for a scoundrel! take that! then went home in triumph with the same valour and conduct as he came. Since which, as the bravest spirits are the most forgiving, he has suffered his indignation to cool, and laid up his trusty sword till the next campaign, in Tothill-Fields, gives him an opportunity to use it with more glory, and the quarrel has been amiable adjusted.

LONDON AUG. 12. Yesterday at about five o'clock in the morning three young fellows from London were seized in bed at the Widow Meredith's, a publick house in Prescot-Street, New Winsor, information having been given to John Owen, Esq; recorder of the corporation, that they had been guilty of several robberies on the highway, in the counties of Middlesex, Bucks, and Berks; upon the examination they impeach'd two of their accomplices, who were seized then in bed at an aleshouse in Dachett, with two loaded pistols under their pillows. They were all committed to Reading Goal. The eldest of them is not above twenty years old.

LONDON AUG. 12. On Friday night a gentleman was attack'd in Maggots-Court over against St. James's Church, by two street robbers, one of whom presented a pistol to his breast, and demanded his watch and money; but the gentleman calling for help, and running from them, the villains fired a pistol at him, which alarmed the watch, &c. notwithstanding which the rogues escaped.

The same night Mr. Walker a Counsellor of Lincoln-Inn accompanid by a painter, coming from Cambray House at Islington, was attack'd by two footpads on the causeway between Frog-Lane and the Pest-House; the painter being foremost was knock'd down into the ditch, and immediately recover'd and ran away; then the counsellor drew his sword, and push'd one of the villains who fell. When the other seiz'd him by the arm, wrested his sword from him, stabbed him several places with a knife, and threw him into the ditch, and then stabbed him in the back with his own sword, and very much bruised him with a stick; after which they robbed and stript him, leaving him nothing but his shoes and breeches: When the villains were gone, he made shift to get out of the ditch, and went to the Queens Head in Islington, where he now is, in a very dangerous condition, attended by Mr. Singleton the surgeon.

On Saturday night two sharpers went to the shop of Mrs. Coxon, a haberdasher of small wares, in King-Street, near Covent-Garden, and asked to look upon some garters, when one of them endeavoured to engage Mrs. Coxon in talk, while the other carry'd off a drawer, in which were 16 dozen of silk garters, value 9 £. but Mrs. Coxon perceiving the cheat, seized the man she was talking with, cry'd out for help, and held him till he dragg'd her into the channel, when getting loose he made his escape; but his accomplice who carry'd away the goods; was taken, and the goods found upon him; whereupon he was carry'd before a justice, who committed him to the Gatehouse.

On Friday night last the following persons were committed to the New Goal in Southwark, viz. John Perkins, William Morris, John Turry, and John Lawen, for breaking open a closed lighter in the river, and stealing thence goods to the value of 100 £. Joseph Ervice was also committed to the Poultry Compter, for being an accomplice; and 'tis said he is to be made evidence.

On Tuesday night near the Chain at Horsley-Downs Stairs, a loaded sloop, Capt. Isaac Friend, master, outward-bound, (for post as we hear) took fire by some accident, and was consumed; and two boys that were in her were burnt to death. She was cut off from her mooring as soon as possible, and fasten'd at a distance from several other ships that were near her, to prevent their catching fire.

On Sunday night at ten o'clock Mr. Charles Bishop, a noted butcher in Newgate-Market, in coming to town from Endfield was set upon between Kingsland, near the Turnpike, and Islington by three foot-pads arm'd with a blunderbuss and two clubs; they rush'd on upon him from behind a great elm tree as he was riding by. The fellow that had the blunderbuss bid him stop or he would shoot him; but he not stopping the barbarous villain discharg'd the blunderbuss at him, being about 10 yards distant. It is likely that the blunderbuss was loaded with ten or twelve balls, for five were taken out of the mare that he rode upon, three lodged in her shoulder, having narrow miss'd the riders side, one in her side, another in her leg; The mare though so much wounded carry'd him near half a mile farther but dropt down dead at Islington.

Yesterday one Macdonald was committed to Newgate by Justice Gifford, on the oath of Anne Davies, for frauduently getting from her into his possession two pair of stockings and a pair of gloves, under pretence of being a servant to the Right Hon. Lord Baltimore, from whose service he had been discharged two months before he had the said goods deliver'd to him; he is also charg'd on the same oath with cheating other tradesmen in the like manner.

On Saturday last about three in the morning a sudden and surprizing accident happen'd at St. Thomas's Hospital in Southwark, where three men being employ'd to empty a vault; when they had almost finish'd their work, one of 'em was observ'd to drop down dead suddenly from the ladder, a second going to help him had the like fate, and a third tying a rope round his waist, as he was letting down, called immediately for help, and being drawn up again, lay some time for dead, but is since recovered. One of the dead persons was Mr. Shermon, one of the beadles of the said hospital.

LONDON AUG. 24. They write from Oxford, that, last Sunday morning four Scots peddlers being there, one of them having drunk a little too much, was determined to go for Reading; the others, with a view of dissuading him from the design, offered to see him part of his way: and seeing a light at an alehouse in St. Thomas's Parish, knocked, but were refused entrance; on which one of them, named John Armstrong, took up some small stones &c. and flung at the window, Franklin the landlord opening the casement, presented a gun, shot him in the face, so that he lost both his eyes, and was elsewhere so much wounded that his life is in the utmost danger. The over-rash publican was instantly seized, and is now in city prison.

From Edinburgh we learn, that the law against wearing printed callicoes and Indian damasks were, the 26th past, begun to be strictly put in execution, and several women were apprehended in the streets, with gowns of the same, who are to be fined as the law therein directs. The penalty for wearing Damasks and chints is 200 £. sterling, and for wearing printed callicoes 5 £. sterling for each offence.

Last Tuesday a lad, of about 16, fell from a second story window, in Leading-Hall-Street, and broke his thigh bone. He was carried to the hospital.

Yesterday morning, a woman very well dressed was found dead, in a field beyond Islington, with several marks of violence about her; particularly her finger cruelly mangled and bruised, supposed to have been done by villains by whom she was robbed and murdered.

LONDON AUG. 24. On Tuesday last some gentlemen coming for London in the Colechester Coach, were informed at Witham, That Mr. Edward Munday, who keeps the Crown-Inn in Woodbridge in Soffolk, had been robb'd by one of his drawers of a considerable sum of money. Afterwards one of the gentlemen that was a passenger in the coach, sitting at a door at Harestreet near Rumford, saw a young fellow indifferently mounted without boots or whip, whom by the discription he supposed to be the person that had committed the robbery; and accordingly charged him with it, which he at first deny'd, but being carry'd before Justice Fanshaw at Rumford, confess'd the fact; and upon searching him, there was found in his pocket 56 £. 3 s. 3d. which he confess'd to be the money of the said Edward Munday, and that he took it out of his closet, which he said was left open.

LONDON SEPT. 1. They write from Plymouth, That on the 26th of last month put in there the Anna Constantia, of and for Amsterdam from Smyrna, where the captain came on shore, but was shortly ordered on board again to perform quarantine, and the custom-house officers, who were placed on board her, were soon afterwards order'd on shore, for fear of what might otherwise happen, and a strict guard is order'd to be kept on her, she has on board 30 men, six of whom are sick, but the captain reports only ill of the scurvy; He had a long passage upwards of three months, and the captain was obliged to put in there for fresh water and hands.

LONDON SEPT. 5. Signor Senision, the famous Italian eunuch and singer, was contracted to come over hither against the winter, to perform under Mr. Heydegger in the Italian Operas.

LONDON DEC. 5. Yesterday morning Mr. Woodyier who keeps the King's Arms Tavern on Ludgate-Hill, having had some differences with his wife, she rashly cut his throat: but she did it not effectually, there is hope of his recovery. He is now under the care of a very able surgeon.

Last night fire broke out in the house of Mr. Gorwall, a noted tobacconist, in Watling-Street; which, with those of Mr. Gostelow, a distiller, and Dr. Douglas (which lay backward of Bow-Lane) were soon utterly consumed; and some of the adjoining houses were greatly damaged. The lost is very considerable; but we do not hear of any lives lost, tho' the inhabitants narrowly escaped, particularly the doctor and his family, most of them little better than naked.

LONDON SEPT. 8. Yesterday was rid from Oxford a little horse of 13 hands high, to London, with a boy for his rider, for a wager of 10 guineas; The boy was to be back in 18 hours, but he performed it in 16 hours and a half, and came in very well. It is remarkable, that the boy and horse had but two eyes; so the boy at starting was heard to say to his master, there is nothing that can hurt us except the loss of an eye: The horse and the boy are very well.

LONDON SEPT. 11. It is wrote from Jamaica, July 5. That 100 white men being sent out against some runaway blacks, were all destroyed by those Negroes, & from March 26, 1729, to June 24, 1730, 11,421 hogsheads of sugar has been exported from that island, and 4,621 Negroes brought in there from the Coast of Africa.

BRISTOL SEPT. 12. Monday last, Mr. George Parker, on St. Augustine's Back, had a letter sent him by two persons unknown, threatening to murder him if he did not comply with their request of leaving 6 guineas under a particular stone, by the stocks, under St. Augustine Church Yard Wall: which so alarmed the said gentleman and the family, that a guard is kept in the nighttime, to prevent the authors of this letter from affectuating this villainy. Tuesday a letter was sent to the same gentleman much to the same purpose wherein the authors hint, that the occasion of the second notice was upon account that they suspected he had not received the first. Wednesday the said gentleman received a third letter, to let him know they were sensible of the guard they kept, &c. but notwithstanding, if he did not have the above sum under the particular stone by the New Draw-Bridge, if they waited two years after they would certainly murder him. They gave him to understand in one of the letters, that they were gentlemen who had spent their fortunes, which occasioned them to fall under necessities, &c. The Boys who carried the above letters were both taken up and examined at the Council-House; one proved to be innocent of the matter; the other, an Irish lad, equivocated much in his examination, but being closely put to it, said, he had the letter from a person who use to lie of lodge with his mother at a house in or near Marsh-Street, that his mother had sold him her head of hair for 6 s. since which she was taken up; and since that an Irish peruke-maker; but neither have confess'd anything to the purpose yet.

LONDON SEPT. 15. 'Tis wrote a certain Term in Court, that some officers having indurred their master's displeasure for not obeying his orders, which they took upon themselves to think too severe, has been castier'd, stripped of their regimental cloaths, and vested with coarse linnen frocks, sent to hard labour, and order'd to be kept on bread and water. Those letters add, that a person of distinction who has been for some time in confinement, has been denied the use of pen, ink and paper; and the valet de chambre, the only person who had the liberty to attend him, was forbidden to stay with him above two hours in four and twenty.

LONDON SEPT. 17. We have an account from Hereford of a very barbarous murder committed lately near Weoby by two highwaymen, who stopt one Mr. Moningrew on the road, and without giving him time to deliver his money, shot him dead upon the spot: The rogues are since apprehended and committed to Hereford Goal.

The following is a poscript of a letter, dated at James River, in Virginia, July 30, 1730.

We have at this instant an account of an insurrection of the Negroes about Williamsburg, occasioned by a report of Col. Spotswood's arrival, that he had direction from his Majesty to fire all baptized Negroes; many masters and mistresses having baptized their slaves, in order to instruct them in the Christian Faith: The people of distinction took notice of this, and the Negroes have improv'd it to a great height; 'Tis said some of the ring leaders are taken: Five counties are in arms persuing others, with orders to kill them if they do not submit.

LONDON SEPT. 19. The account in our last of the insurrection of the Negroes in Virginia, is confirm'd by other letters; and Capt. Wills of the Amity, as he was coming from thence, discover'd a Negro who had hid himself in his ship, and being examin'd how he came aboard, said, he was going ambassador from the Negroes to his Majesty King George, however, his ecellency was turn'd ashore and whipt, thro' every county to the place from whence he came.

LONDON SEPT. 21. Yesterday about 1 on the clock, a girl, about 14 years of age belonging to the Charity School in St. Martins in the Field, having absented her self from the school contrary to the order of the said school and for fear of being corrected, threw herself in the canal in S. James's Park.

A boy about 10 years of age seeing her, strip'd his cloaths off and went into the water, and took her up and saved her life. Several persons of distinction saw it, and gave the boy money for his courage, and gave a woman some to take care of the girl.

LONDON SEPT. 22. On Saturday about two o'clock, the son of Mrs. Jones at the Crown and Pearl in Cornhill, fell off of the house upon a back room in the King's Head Tavern, and fractur'd his skull, and expired about seven o'clock in the evening.

On Saturday last one Joseph Davis, servant to Mr. Heavyside, sugar-bake of Ratcliff Cross, was kill'd as he was craining up a barrel of sugar, one of the hinges of the pully breaking, it fell down upon him and dash'd his brains out.

LONDON SEPT. 29. One Mary Muffet, a woman of great note in the Hundreds of Drury, and lately committed to Tothil Fields Bridewell by the chairman and eight other Justices of the Peace of the committee apointed at the last Westminster Sessions, for surpressing the night houses and other disorderly houses, &c. brought his Majesty's Habeas Corpus, and was Wednesday carried before the Rt. Hon. the Lord Chief Justice Rayman, at his chambers in Serjeants Inn in Chancery-Lane, expecting to have been either bail'd or discharged; but the commitment appearing to be legal and just, and drawn up with great care, his Lordship thought fit to remand her back again to Bridewell, where to her no small mortification she is still beating hemp, and bestows many hearty curses upon her lawyers, as well as the civil part of the neighbourhood, who complained of her to the justice.

Last Saturday the Reading coach was robbed near Twiford Turnpike by one highwayman well mounted, who made off. Two farmers happening to come by, pursued him towards Oakingham, and were within 100 yards of him at the turnpike there. They cry'd stop the highwayman, and he cry'd that the highwaymen were pursuing him; so he got through by that means, but in such confusion, that he left his great coat, and made off towards London.

The Greenwich, Capt. Brokie, which arrived in the river from East-India, has been seized by an exchecker, Capt. Writ, obtained by some custom-house officers, on account of her not performing according to the Act of Navagation. It seems so many of her men either died or deserted in India, and necessitated them to hire a number of Indians to bring her home, which exceeded one 4th part of her company, which is the foundation of this seazure, by which means the ship is kept at an expence, and the company prevented from getting their goods, which they want for the sale, which begins next week.

BRISTOL OCT. 5. I have a melancholy account to relate to you of what happened in this city, and perhaps history does not afford a parallel of such villainy. About a month ago one George Parker a merchant of this city, received an anonymous letter, directing him to put 6 guineas under a certain stone, at a time prefixed, and in case of non compliance, his life was threatened: However Mr. Parker did not comply with it, but set a guard to watch the place in order to discover the person, but without success; whereupon he had another letter sent him, proposing another place, enlarging the sum; but still Mr. Parker did not comply, but kept a guard always in his house, and went abroad; and in about 10 days time I believe he received half a dozen letters in very insolent terms, threatning not only the distruction of him, but all his family and that they would burn his house, whereupon a reward of 50 £. was offered, and diligent search was made to find out the author, but to no purpose, and yesterday morning about one o'clock the rogues actually set fire to his house, which was entirely consumed, but Mr. Parker and his family escaped the flames tho' with great hazard. It was a great mercy the wind happened to be easterly for the house standing St. Augustine's Back opposite to the key, the ships lying there would have been in great danger. Last night Mr. Parker received another letter letting him know they had with a great deal of pleasure seen his house in flames, and hoped to have seen him in them; but tho' he had escaped, yet they were resolved to have his life. Three of four letters have been dropt about the city, threatening others in the like manner, so that where this villainy will end is uncertain.

P. S. Just now I hear 5 or 6 Irish fellows are taken up; they are now before the magistrate, &c. 'Tis reported they have confessed the fact, discovered near 20 concerned with them, were to have put the whole city in fear.

LONDON OCT. 8. Tuesday morning about 2 o'clock, the night men being at work, emptying the bog-houses in the palace that while they were gone to refresh themselves at a publick house hard by, a woman well dress'd fell into one of the offices that was open up to her arm pits, and must certainly have been smothered, had not a centinel that was near, heard her cry out; who came to her assistance, and got her out, and that she liv'd in Westminster, and had lost her way.

We hear from Cirencester, that last week three children having by mistake drank some aqua forris instead of small beer, two of them died immediately, and the life of the third is very much endangered.

On Saturday last early in the morning, the house of the widow Moore, in Shoemakers-Row, was broke open by a villain, who as soon as he got in found out the old woman, and endeavour'd to cut her throat, but being in the dark, cut her along the jaw, which making a large wound awaked her, and she endeavouring by her hands to defend herself, had her fingers cut in a sad manner; upon her crying out thieves and murder, he stabbed her in the belly very deep, and made off leaving his knife and chisel behind.

LONDON OCT. 22. Yesterday the Right Hon. Earl Ferrers, who had been several years a lunatick, appeared in person before the Right Hon. High Chancellor of Great Britain at his house in Lincoln-Inn-Fields, where after a short hearing, the Commission of Lunacy formerly granted was order'd to be suspended, the said Earl being perfectly restored to a sound mind, to the great joy and satisfaction of the truly Honourable and Noble family.

Yesterday a person walked from Hyde-Park Corner to Windsor, which is 20 miles thither, and back again, for 20 guineas, and had 12 hours allow'd to perform it in, but he did it in ten hours and a half.

LONDON OCT. 24. Yesterday the man who is suppos'd to have robb'd the Bristol mail on the 30th of August last, was taken near Reading in Burks, with sundry bank bills and notes about him, which we know to have been taken out of the said mail, and is committed to Reading jail.

Yesterday morning, as his Royal Highness the Prince of Wales, and the Princess Royal, were taking the air in an open chaise; they were overturn'd between Richmond and Kew-Green, but received no hurt.

LONDON OCT. 24. Yesterday Thomas Flower, who was to have stood in the pillory at the end of Russel-Street Covent-Garden, pursuant to his sentence at the Old-Bailey, for putting off bad money, was brought there accordingly at twelve o'clock; but being very ill of the prison disease, the sheriff indulged him so far as to let him sit, in a chair, on the stage of the pillory; after which he was remanded back in a coach to Newgate.

READING NOV. 2. We gave you account three years ago, of a great quantity of money being found by a cooper in this town, that was digging a place in his shop in order to set a choping block; and since that, another of the same trade is come into the same house, and by digging found some more money, but digging deeper than ordinary he found the scull and thigh bones of a man, with his coat buttons, a sword and spurs, and the heel of one shoe, which gives room to judge, that some person was murder'd and buried there.

LONDON NOV. 5. Last Sunday an unhappy accident happened at a house in Tyburn Road, where two men, being in liquor, viz. one Bolton and one Case and quarelling, Bolton struck Case on the head with a poker, and fractured his scull; whereupon Case stabbed Bolton in the right breast with a penknife: Case's wound proving mortal he linger'd till yesterday when he died.

LONDON NOV. 7. We hear from East-Redford in Nottinghamshire, that a fine spaw was lately discovered there no way inferior to the German spaw; and that several eminent physicians have given their approbation thereof, which hath encouraged the corporation to begin a subscription to making the place very commodious, and it hath met with success among gentlemen of the neighbourhood, &c. that it is thought it will be a great advantage to the publick, many remarkable cures having been perform'd already by the use of it.

DEAL NOV. 9. Two several nights the last week, Admiral Morris's seat at Great Berrarshanger, about four miles from Deal, was beset, as also the farm house near it; on which we are told, the Admiral's Lady fired a pistol out of the window, and one of the servants a musket from the top of the house, on which the rogues made off.

LONDON NOV. 11. We hear an anonymous letter demanding money and fill'd with menaces in case of refusal, has been sent to a noble Lord in Surrey.

On Thursday last Thomas Best of Chatham Esq; had a letter thrown into his court yard, signifying that unless 200 guineas were out in a bush in a neighbouring wood where he used to walk, upon which they had left a white rag for a signal, his house should be burnt.

COVENTRY NOV. 11. Sir, Inclosed is a copy of the letters put under the master-weavers door. It had alarmed the city; but we think we have the man in goal, that wrote the letters; but he will not confess it, but all the magistrates making him to transcribe the letters it seems to all it is his handwritting; so believe the villainy is stop'd here, though our magistrates are very dilligent, and our watch doubled, and one sits every night, the inhabitants being very willing to sit up and watch in their persons. I am, &c.

Friend Towers.

By these lines we let you understand, that we are a body that consider'd the distress of the poor weavers, and are fully bound by oath, upon pains of death, to have the burden of these poor sufferers eased, by raising the price of all sorts of work twelve pence per piece: But upon the refusal of the request, your house shall be laid to ashes at the time when your bodies shall have much ado to escape; for you are the sort of men who delight to grind the face of the poor. It will be justice to extort the greatest judgement upon you, and not only you but also all the master weavers in general. I cannot but be loyal to the government.   God save the King.

LONDON NOV. 12. Yesterday morning about two o'clock a sad accident happened at Angel Inn behind St. Clements Dane in the Strand, where Mr. Olden and Mr. Sifler, two attorneys at law, who were lately come to town from Devonshire, in order to be sworn before one of the Lord Chief Justices, persuant to a late act of parliament, being in liquor, and quarreling, Mr. Olden received a thrust with a dagger thro' the left shoulder and breast, which went thro' his heart, and kill'd him on the spot.

Mr. Olden was possessed of an estate at Tiverton in Devonshire of between 3 and 400 £. a year, and was just about the point of marriage with a young lady of Tiverton.

The same day one Anne Kirkill, an elderly woman, was found dead in her bed, at her brothers house in Dogwell-Court, Whitehall, having strangled her self with her garter.

LONDON NOV. 12. On Monday night about five o'clock a fire happen'd in the stillhouse of Justice Rolse in Barnaby-street, Southwark, by the head of the still flying off, which very much alarm'd the neighbourhood; but by the coolness of good temper of the justice in the midst of the hurry, in immediately sending for the firemen and giving them proper directions, the same was soon extinguished and no great damage done.

Last Monday night about nine o'clock, Mr. Longman who keeps a publick house in Oxford Road was robbed in Lincoln-Inn-Field by three foot pads, all very young who after they had taken his watch, silver buckles and money tied his hands and legs with his garters, then made off.

Last Thursday Mr. Serjeant Ruby made a report to his Majesty in council of the seven convicts who receiv'd sentence of death at the last sessions held in Old Baily, and we hear his Majesty was pleased to order the four following for execution, viz. Hath Morris, Robert Johnson & James O'Bryon, for the robberies on the highway, and Thomas Rivers, convicted of burglary, and stealing out of the dwelling-house of Nicolis Fendwich the value of 50 £. and upwards. Last night the dead warrant came down to Newgate ordering their execution to be on Monday next.

His Majesty has been graciously pleased to extend his Royal mercy to James Rogers, Humphry Belmossett and George Beavis, and to order them to be transported.

LONDON NOV. 12. The pavement a few steps N. N. W. of the statue in the Royal Exchange having sunk for the breath of a yard lower then the rest of the pavement, on Monday morning paviours were employ'd to mend it, but finding the ground not firm, they having on Tuesday dug about twelve or thirteen feet deep, found themselves on a level with an arched vault built with chalk, which went about five yards to the southward, being about 5 feet broad and near six feet high, and in it a human scull and some bones and decay'd wood, and in digging they found a stone, which by the form and workmanship is supposed to have been part of a pillar.

'Tis written from Flintshire, That the villains who wrote letters to Mr. Jackson of that town, and he not complying with their demands, broke into his shop, with a design to murder him and his family, but having a good guard, they were repulsed and got off, but next day Mr. Jackson seeing them at a fair three miles distant, he had them seized, and being carried before a justice, they were all committed to Flint-Castle and laid in irons.

LONDON NOV. 14. On Thursday last, his Majesty in Council was pleased to order a proclamation to be issued out, for the apprehending and taking of the incendiaries for sending threatning letters to several persons, demanding money to be left them in the places specified in their letters.

And we hear that a reward of one thousand pounds, as a future encouragement for the apprehending and taking of such person or persons, as shall be brought to justice, will be immideately paid by order of his Majesty out of the treasury, upon their conviction, besides his Majesty's free pardon to such as shall discover any of his or their accomplices.

LONDON NOV. 14. A few days since 9 barges and lighters were sunk under one of the locks of London-Bridge, occasion'd by a barge of Deals sticking against the sterlings, which sunk down, and stopt up the lock.

LONDON NOV. 17. Last Thursday two men, companions, went out a fowling in the Parish Pangborn, near Reading, and in the County of Berks, viz. Francis Dell and Thomas Dean, Having had some sport, they charged their pieces again, and pursuing their game, cocked both their pieces: The latters foot slipt and in falling, his piece went off, and shot the former through the body; that he died instantly.

LONDON NOV. 19. Last Monday morning there were found under Mrs. Jackson's door in Exeter, a letter, signed Leagion, requiring her to put 5 guineas in a post by the Pryers Gate, adjoining to her house, or in case of noncomplience, she might expect Mr. Parker's fate.

Yesterday Mr. Clement a baker at Milford-Lane in the strand, received an anonymous letter, demanding 15 guineas to be left at a certain place therein mentioned. The following is a copy of the said letter.

Mr. Clement, This is to warn you to put 15 guineas this night between 9 and 10 o'clock under the post at your bakehouse door, and if you do not, expect that your wife and you shall not live an hour after, and your house shall be consumed by fire. Likewise inform your brother Mr. Smith, that he is warned also to put 7 guineas, his watch, and a ring that he wears, at the same time, under the spout that carries the water from off his your house, or between the window and the said spout; and upon his not doing so, he and his wife likewise must expect to suffer immediate death, with you and yours.

The same afternoon the above mentioned Mr. Smith received a letter directed to him, at his house in Hanover-Street to the following purport: That he and his brother were resolved upon not complying with their former demands, and that they intended to set a watch at night, but that it would be more advisable for them to leave the money, watch, and ring, as required; for that if all the parish were to watch, they and their wives should certainly be murder'd and their houses consumed by fire.

LONDON NOV. 28. On Saturday their Majesties, accompanied with several persons of distinction, took the air at Richmond, and dined there; but on their return in the evening, it being very dark, and blowing so hard that they could not keep their flambeux lighted, the King's coach was unhappily overturn'd near Peterborough-House by a great hill of gravel that lay for mending the road. The coachman finding he was going, stopt his horses: by which means the coach fell easily, and their Majesties, and two ladies of the bed-chamber that were in, the coach, received no hurt. Two of his Majesty's foot men that were behind, were flung some yards distance, and much bruised. The guard immediately dismounted, and the King and Queen got out of the coach; which being lifted up again, about nine o'clock their Majesties was very pleased to order the guard 30 guineas.

LONDON DEC. 7. From Dublin they tell a merry story of a dreaming woman in George-Lane in that city. That woman lives in good repute in her neighbourhood, and being in bed, dream'd her husband was unkind to her; she in revenge gets out of bed (in her sleep) going down stairs, and opening the street door lay herself down on her shift before it; She was so found by the watch, who suppos'd her to be dead, but in a while after she awak'd and coming to herself was much surpriz'd at what she had done; as are most of her neighbours, at the strength of her imagination.

LONDON DEC. 12. We hear that the following melancholy accident lately happen'd in Yorkshire; A servant to a gentleman of considerable rank and figure, having refus'd to obey his masters command, the gentleman reprimanded him for his sauciness; where upon the servant had the impudence to draw a poker out of the fire, and made a thrust at his master with it; the gentleman avoided it, and the servant repeating his attempt, the master drew his sword and kill'd him on the spot. The coroners inquest have sat on the body, & bro't in their verdict defendo.

LONDON DEC. 23. One Margaret Cox of the Parish of St. Saviours, Southwark, died lately, aged 104. She was 21 years old when King Charles the 1st was beheaded, and was a servant then at Whitehall; she saw the executioner hold up the head after he had cut it off, and remembered the dismal groans of the spectators when the fatal blow was given. She lived on a milk diet for 20 years past, not eating any flesh all that time.

BRISTOL DEC. 24. On Tuesday last we have an account given us by two sailors, lately belonging to the Expedition gally of London, Capt. Leopard, that about the beginning of November last, the said gally struck upon a ridge of rocks; call'd St. Patrick, off of Barmouth in the County of Merioneth, in Wales, 18 miles from land, and the men had but just time to get into their boat before she sunk down all of whom got safe on shore. She had been out on a trading voyage almost three years and came last from Leghorn, bound for Hillsborough, laden with oranges, lemons, cotton and cocheneal.

LONDON DEC. From Dublin Dec. 12. Some accounts of Mr. Johnston and Porter of that place of execution, who were lately tried and condemned here for murder.

All application to the Lord Justices for respite having prov'd in vain, this day Mr. Rich. Johnston, son to the late _____ Johnston, Esq; and brother to Counsellor Gab. Johnston of this city; and Mr. John Porter, eldest son of Mr. Alderman Porter, late Lord Mayor, were executed according to their sentence at St. Stephen's Green, being hang'd and quarter'd on account of the murthers of Pat Murphy, a salter, who was kill'd the 21st of October last (as is generally believ'd by a knife he had thrust hastily into his side pocket, which catching in the lining of his breeches hung so as run up in his thigh, on his hastily sitting down in a low chair at the Union on Temple-Bar, at the time he was pursu'd by these unhappy young gentlemen.) They were all allow'd the favor of a mourning coach by the high sheriff Mr. Dobson, and were attended to the gallows by an eminent & learned Divine, and the common ordinary as his assistant; and after some time spent in prayer and speaking to the people, wherein Mr. Johnston solemnly declared, as he was a dying person, he was not guilty of the fact he was condemned for, which was stabbing, and murder of the said Murphy; for that, on the salters drawing a knife, he had drawn his sword and persu'd and struck the said Murphy: Yet hoped that this his unhappy end would be a warning to all young gentlemen to shun all irregularities, the too frequent practicing of which had lost him his character & therewith his life; he forgave the jury, and begg'd pardon of all that he offended, and dy'd with the greatest penitence and resolution, tho' he appear'd very sad when first he was ty'd up, yet he continued smilling a long time after he had disburthend his mind, and declar'd his innocence, and seem'd pleas'd with the hopes that God would accept his life as a sacrifice for the sinful follies he might be guilty of for which he prayed forgiveness.

Mr. Porter also declared he even dy'd with pleasure, when he thought how little he was guilty of the fact, on having any design of murdering the deceased person, who he confessed to have persued down Essex Street, yet said he was not near him when he got his deat's wound: He earnestly hoped no one would impute his untimely end to his unhappy parents, or cast reflection on his relations on his account, since it pleased God that he should be cut off; that however undutiful he had been, they had all done their parts by him; after which, earnestly recommending his soul to God, they were turned off, but had scarce the breath out of their bodies, when a person arrived with a reprieve for 40 days, from his Grace the Duke of Dorset, Lord

Lieut. of this Kingdom, to the inexpressible grief of all the beholders, who greatly lamented, their misfortune.

After the hang man had cut down the body of Mr. Porter, he mangled it in so inhumane manner (whether thro' fear or haste) that he enraged the mob and they began to pelt him so with dirt, &c. that he could hardly get leave to cut off Mr. Johnston's head which however he did with much addo, and then was convey'd away by a strong guard of constables.

INDEX

ABDIN, Thomas 82
ABEGAVENNY, Lord 241
ACHERTON, Robert 242
ACTON, William 214
AEYNHAM, Lord 60
AIRS, Mr 204
ALBEMARLE, Earl of 139
ALBIMARLE, Lord 246
ALBRIDGE, Acton 192
ALLAN, Mr 71
ALLEN, Mr 195 237
AMELIA, Princess of ? 195 199 218
ANDERSON, 87
ANDREW, Mary 19
ANGEAU, Claudius 110
ANGIRE, Humphrey 65
ANNE, Lady 121 122
ANNE, Princess of ? 92
ANSLO, Thomas 73
ANTIF, John 152
ARCHER, Elizabeth 164
ARHURTNOT, Dr 144
ARISTOW, Anne 54
ARMSTRONG, John 259
ARNOLD, Edward 82 Moll 146 Quilt 146
ARTHUR, Mr 237
ASHBURN, Michael 8
ASHE, Benjamin 57 Mr 57
ASHLEY, 190 John 170 189
ASTALL, 1 Mr 3
ATHBOTHNOT, Dr 32
ATTERBURRY, Mr 46
ATTERBURY, Dr 156
ATWOOD, Mr 66
AUDIBER, Capt 145
AYERS, Mrs 71
B, A 120
BACON, Edmund 185
BAKER, 93 Earnest 65
BALDWYN, Acton 107 Mr 107
BALL, Mrs 71
BALLY, David 73
BALTIMORE, Lord 258
BAMBREY, Anne 247
BAMBRIDGE, Mr 239 Thomas 234
BAMPSTON, Mr 137
BARBIER, Mrs 10
BARKER, Abraham 159 Mr 111
BARNABY, John 228 Mr 55
BARNES, Mr 112 Tho 256
BARNS, Capt 175
BARRYMAN, Rev Dr 113
BARTON, 54
BATCHELLOR, Mr 48
BATTYMAN, Rev Mr 36
BEACH, Isaac 24
BEALE, Margaret 121

BEAUCHAMP, Bold 235
BEAUCLERE, Vere 209
BEAUFORT, Duke of 119
BEAVIS, George 268
BEDFORD, Duke of 119
BELL, Capt 51
BELMOSSETT, Humphry 268
BENDISH, Mrs 238
BENEDITTE, 8
BENSON, Jane 132 Mother 132
BENSONS, Mr 241
BERKLEY, Elizabeth 234
BERRY, Henrietta 219 Thomas 140
BERRYMAN, Capt 42
BERYMAN, Mr 60
BEST, Henry 123 Thomas 266
BEVAN, Joseph 83
BICKERTON, John 24
BICKNELL, Mr 1
BIGLOE, Capt 20
BILLERS, William 229 234
BING, Admiral 3
BIRD, 37 68 Mr 98
BISHOP, 124 Charles 258 Creel 195 Mr 119
BISHOP, Lord 36
BLACKERBY, Justice 140 Nathaniel 44
BLAKE, Joseph 97
BLEWER, William 140
BLEWIT, 149 Moll 146 William 146
BLEWSKIN, 97
BLUCK, Anne 249 Peter 248
BLUNT, Charles 8 John 8 14
BOLTON, 265
BOOTLE, Mr 180
BOTHMAR, Baron 247
BOURBON, Duke of 129

BOURK, 249
BOWEN, Mr 48
BOWER, Messieur 56
BOWLER, Capt 114
BOYTE, 46
BRADFORD, Earl of 122
BRADFORD, Mr 98
BRADSHAW, James 21 23
BRAGG, Mr 221
BRAKES, John 146
BRETTON, John 216
BREWERS, Capt 129
BRIGGS, Laird 186
BRIGHAM, Mr 121 Orlando 121
BRINE, Wm 245
BRISDEN, Matthias 46 48
BRISKFORD, John 93
BROKIE, Capt 263
BROOKE, Edward 185
BROOKMAN, Henry 155
BROUGH, Mr 183
BROWN, George 21 J 124 Justice 119 Mr 67 68 Thomas 146
BRUCE, Lord 240 Mr 172
BUCKHAM, Mr 232
BUCKINGHAM, Dutchess of 240
BUCKINGHAM, Joseph 54
BUCKINHAM, Duke of 181 182
BUGGS, Charles 153
BULL, Capt 125
BURDUS, Justice 248
BURK, William 58
BURNET, Gov 210
BUSHEL, Capt 116 117
BUTHURST, Lord 41
BUTLER, James 64 Mr 46 199 Thomas 230
BYER, Justice 45

CAILOUS, Marquis of 11
CALMADY, Sheldon 5
CAMERON, Margaret 77
CAMPBELL, Daniel 116 Mrs 98
CANE, Mr 178
CANSTON, Mr 247
CAPPER, Mr 254
CARD, Richard 114
CARDIGAN, Earl of 108
CARDWELL, John 243
CAREW, Wm 233
CAREY, Capt 121
CARMICHAEL, Lord 55
CARNAVON, Marquis of 239
CAROLINA, Princess of ? 218
CAROLINE, Princess of ? 92
CARR, Mr 103 123 Patrick 242 Robert 123
CARROL, 62 Daniel 61
CARTER, 107 John 246 Wm 242
CARTER, Baron 189
CARTERET, Lord 6 7 24
CARTWOOD, William 124
CARY, Samuel 194
CASE, 265 266
CASEY, John 46 William 30
CASTER, John 123
CASTILL, Mr 200
CASTLEMAIN, Lord 22 119
CATER, Mathias 127
CAVENDISH, Charles 95 James 246
CHADWICH, Samuel 185
CHALK, Justice 140
CHAMBERLAIN, Capt 28 Dr 92
CHAMBERS, John 101 Mr 182
CHANDLER, Mr 93
CHANDOS, Duke of 230
CHANDOS, Dutchess of 119
CHAPMAN, Joseph 61
CHARITEIS, Col 246
CHARLES I, King of England 270
CHARLES, Lord 95
CHARLESWORTH, 37
CHARMOCK, Capt 194
CHARTRES, Col 57
CHESTER, Mr 15 William 239
CHIDLEIGH, Col 243
CHOJA, Coffan D 193
CIRRICK, 61
CIVE, Verney 150
CLAP, Margaret 146
CLARE, 250
CLARGER, Thomas 164
CLARK, Christ 21 Dorothy 39 Grace 39 Mathew 19 Mrs 231
CLARKE, Mr 133
CLARKSON, Mrs 21 Randolf 218
CLAXTON, John 146
CLEMENT, Mr 269
CLERK, Mr 14
COCK, Mr 224
COCKRELL, Mr 128
COFF, Mary 155
COFFORT, Messieur 56
COLE, Abigail 128 George 145 Mr 28 William 160
COLEAR, William 191
COLEBY, Thomas 229
COLETHEART, Mr 239
COLLAHEART, Mr 62
COLLINS, Mr 214 Mrs 89
COLLIS, Anthony 195
COLTHEART, Mr 57
COMBES, Capt 28
COMYNS, Mr Serjeant 180

CONNINGHAM, Mr 55
COOK, John 96 Justice 229
COOKE, Capt 177 George 162 Mr 107
COPE, Anthony 24
COPPARD, Mr 88
CORNET, Capt 21
CORNWALLIS, Mr 141
COTTER, James 4
COTTON, Thimothy 207
COWLER, Lord 9
COWPER, William 251
COX, 87 Margaret 270
COXON, Mrs 257 258
CREW, Mr 164
CRISPE, 36 Edward 35
CROSS, Daniel 96 John 62
CUDBERT, Mr 225
CUMBY, Capt 140
CUNE, Isaac 96
CUNNINGHAM, Mr 182
CUTLER, Joseph 146
CZAR OF MUSCOVY, 62 63
CZARINA OF RUSSIA, 154
D----, Lord 2
D----l, Mrs 33
DALKEITH, Earl of 4
DALTON, James 234 239
DAMEL, Mr Serjeant 180
DAMPSEY, Mary 9
DANZEL, Michael 189
DARBY, 67 John 214 Mr 160 161 162 166
DAVENPORT, Marmaduke 59
DAVEY, Robert 96
DAVIDSON, Mr 169
DAVIES, Anne 258 Capt 114
DAVIS, Joseph 262
DAVY, Ely 224
DAY, Alexander 59 Nathanial 40

DEAN, Thomas 118 268
DEBER, Anne 243
DECHICOYNECAW, Messieur 11
DECOSTA, Medez 144
DEFRIE, Marquess 69
DEGANNON, William 89
DEGOLTZ, Mr 15
DELAFAYE, Mr 49
DELASTORRES, Count 156
DELATORRE, Count 38
DELGARNOE, Capt 199
DELL, Francis 268
DELLAGAL, Capt 119
DENT, George 178
DEPUTRON, William 215
DERFLEY, 137
DESAGULLIERES, Dr 26
DETORRIS, Marquis 163
DEVAL, Capt 192
DEVONSHIRE, Duke of 58 95 246
DEWING, George 195
DIBLY, 21
DICKENSON, Emanuel 140
DINGLEY, Mr 248
DOBBINING, Mr 97
DOBINS, Justice 19
DOBSON, Mr 271
DODDINGTON, George 214
DOLZEL, Michael 189
DORMER, Stewart 167
DORSET, Duke of 271
DOUGLAS, Capt 174 186 Dr 260
DOUGLAS, Duke of 4 55
DOUGLASS, Jane 2
DOYLE, John 247
DOYLEY, Henrietta 219
DRIVER, John 157

DUCE, William 64
DUFFUS, Lord 63
DUFORD, Ambrose 158
DUNNING, Capt 63 Mr 171
EATEN, James 32
EATON, Isabella 229
EDGAR, Mr 147
EDMONDSON, James 63
EDWARDS, Francis 73
    Henrietta 219 Lt 209 Richard
    160
ELIZABETH, Queen of England
    115
ELLIS, John 193 Justice 31 87
    229
ELVES, John 91
ELY, Mr 1
EMERY, Mr 152
EMILIA, Princess of ? 225
EMPEROR OF MOROCCO, 36
ENGLAND, Capt 4 Nathaniel 90
ENGLISH, Mr 40
ERVICE, Joseph 258
ETHERIDGE, Mr 5
EVAN, Morgan 148
EVANS, Mary 148
EVERET, 223
EVERETT, 37
EVERSFIELD, Charles 139
EVERSHED, Mr 192
EYLES, John 21 Mr 98
EYRE, Lord Chief Justice 241 Rt
    Hon Lord Chief Justice 137
F----, 84
FAICHILD, Mr 91
FAIHOUT, Stephen 147
FAIRFAX, Bryan 210
FANSHAW, Justice 260
FATES, Wilby 242
FAUSTUS, Dr 100

FELLOWS, John 14
FELTON, John 114
FENDWICH, Nicolis 267
FERDINAND, Duke 154
FERGUSON, Mr 141
FERRERS, Earl 265
FETCHAM, Mr 227
FIELD, William 97
FIGG, Mr 122
FILEWOOD, 13
FILMORE, Mr 180
FINCH, Edw 228 Lord 162
FINHAVEN, Laird 186
FISHER, 167 H 161 Henry 166
    Mr 26 161 162 171 Mrs 171
    172
FITBAL, 168
FITCH, 59
FITWELL, 21
FITZSIMONDS, Mr 94
FLANDERS, Moll 36
FLETCHER, Ann 22
FLOWER, Thomas 265
FLOWERS, William 146
FONSECA, Mr 93
FORBES, Francis 128
FORD, Mr 138
FORSYTE, Mr 156
FORWARD, Mr 16
FOSTER, Mr 37
FOX, George 193 Tho 205
FREDERICK, Prince of ? 158
FRIAR, John 88
FRIEND, Dr 53 Isaac 258
FRISKY, Molly 99
FRY, Capt 164
FRYER, 254 John 55
FULLER, Wm 253
GAGE, William 222
GALE, Capt 169

277

GALLASPY, Thomas 162
GALLWAY, Lord 180
GANDRY, Henry 205
GATTS, William 123
GAUBERT, Mary 83
GAYLEY, George 205
GEORGE II, King of England 165 194
GEORGE II, King of Great Britain France and Ireland 165
GEORGE, King of England 50 164 165 225 262
GEORGE, King of Great Britain 135
GEORGE, King of Great Britain France and Ireland 164
GEORGE, Prince of Wales 164 165
GEORGE, Sir 209
GERRARD, Mr 197 198
GIBBON, Mr 15
GIBBONS, Samuel 65
GIBBS, Mr 72
GIBBY, James 122
GIBSON, Alexander 181
GIFFORD, Justice 258
GILBERT, Mr 242
GILLET, John 234
GLADWIN, Thomas 6 24
GLANDVILLE, Mrs 21
GLASS, 206
GODDARD, Mr 119
GODFREY, Mr 192 Sherman 237
GODMAN, William 157
GODOLPHIN, Earl of 56
GOLDERSTONE, Sarah 19
GOLDSTONE, Mary 24
GONSON, John 253
GOODBURY, John 242

GORBERT, Ann 24
GORDON, Duke of 143
GORE, Justice 62
GORING, Lord 157
GORWALL, Mr 260
GOSLING, William 24
GOSTELOW, Mr 260
GOUGH, Capt 207
GOULD, Mr 255 Nathaniel 255
GOULDING, Capt 230
GOW, 109
GRAFTON, Duke of 119
GRAHAM, Hannah 24
GRAND MUSTI, 63
GRAND SEIGNOR, 39 63
GRAND VIZIER, 63
GRANTHAM, Lord 241
GRAVES, Mr 237
GRAVESANDE, Sieur S 26
GRAY, Mrs 198
GREEN, Capt 21 James 96
GREENBERG, J 13
GREGORY, Capt 94 95 Edward 231
GRETTON, John 177
GREY, Lord 49 Mr 224
GRIGBY, John 14
GRIMES, Hannah 24 Mr 47
GROVE, William 97
GROWER, Mr 138
GUERIN, Mr 115
GUNE, Solomon 96
GUY, Mr 207
GWIN, Alexander 62
GWYNN, Isabella 229
HADDON, Mary 160
HALEWELL, William 54
HALL, Gile 219 Mr 136 Powell 6 William 160
HALLADAY, Capt 203

HALSEY, Robert 244
HALTON, Lord 157
HAMILTON, Capt 74 David 22
HAMILTON, Duke of 172
HAMMERTON, Capt 111
HANCOCK, Mr 40
HANDCOCK, Justice 40
HANDEL, Mr 92
HARDING, Mary 241 Mrs 240 Rebecca 241 Sarah 241
HARE, Mr 65 Reverend Dr 92
HARLEY, Lady 6 24
HARLEY, Lord 68
HARRIS, Briget 241 John 219
HART, Mr 212
HARVEY, 182 Mary 229 Mr 215
HARVEY, Lady 199
HARWOOD, John 151 Mary 151 Mrs 151
HASLETT, 250
HATTORF, Baron 110
HAVLEY, Edward 146
HAWKINS, 53 Mr 46 60 62
HAWKSWORTH, William 61
HAWS, Mr 15
HAYES, Mr 208
HAYNES, Thomas 159
HEARNE, 149
HEATH, John 180
HEATHCORE, Mr 22 Samuel 22
HEATHCOTE, Michael 199
HEATHER, Mr 237
HEAVYSIDE, Mr 262
HEFORT, Earl of 137
HEIDIGGER, Mr 66
HENRY VI, King of England 79
HENRY VII, King of England 4
HENRY VIII, King of England 171

HERBERT, Thomas 225
HEYDEGGER, Mr 260
HILBOROUGH, Earl of 138
HILL, Capt 174 Mr 44
HIND, Philip 89
HINTON, Richard 145
HIPSLEY, George 255
HIPWORTH, Mrs 186
HIYERS, John 142
HOBBS, Mr 237
HOLBY, Maj 138
HOLDITCH, Mr 15
HOLE, Rev Dr 189
HOLWORTHY, Justice 22
HOPKINS, Mr 71
HOPSON, Admiral 186
HOPTON, Admiral 156
HORSEY, 244
HORSFALL, Luke 205
HORTON, Hugh 246
HOSIER, Admiral 16
HOSKINS, Richard 88
HOUGHTON, John 228
HOUSTARE, Lewis 83
HOWARD, Charles 139 Mr 139
HUBBARDS, Mother 150
HUDSON, Thomas 46
HUGE, Mr 69
HUGES, James 172 Mr 69
HUGHES, Mr 95 Rev Dr 181 Rev Mr 181
HUGHS, Arthur 46 Capt 2
HUMPHREY, John 148
HUNT, Capt 101 John 6
HUNTER, Robert 24
HUNTINGFORD, Mr 111
HURLOCK, Benjamin 65
HUTCHINGS, William 83
HUTCHINSON, Samuel 160
HYDE, Thomas 152

INMAN, Mary 24
ISLA, Earl of 130
JACK, 107
JACK THE WALER, 93
JACKSON, 110 205 Mr 268 Mrs 269 Roger 8
JAMES, John 242 Thomas 123 William 227
JAMES, Lord 95
JAMES, Lord of Rochester 44
JAMES III, King of England 89
JAMSON, John 8
JANSSEN, Theodore 14 15
JEANE, Capt 141
JENKINS, Thomas 210
JENNINGS, John 143 Thomas 46
JENNY, Mr 55
JEPSON, John 90
JERVASE, Mr 199
JOBSON, Mr 112
JOHN, Mary 148
JOHNSON, 46 Jane 132 Jenny 133 Madam 111 Major 7 Robert 252 267 Roger 111 167
JOHNSTON, ---- 271 Gab 271 Mr 270 271 272 Rich 271
JONES, Elizabeth 44 Jezrrel 194 Mr 189 248 Mrs 189 262 Rice 159 William 242
JUBEENVILLE, 120
KEFER, 64
KELF, George 145
KENDAL, Dutchess of 82
KENNEDY, 46 Walter 21 23
KERR, George 93 Mark 248
KEYTE, Mrs 199
KILLAGREW, Lady 125
KING, John 41 193 Mr 44

KING OF HERENHAUSEN, 144
KING OF PRUSSIA, 186
KING OF SPAIN, 131
KING OF SWEDEN, 225
KIRKHAM, 204 Mr 139 Thomas 203
KIRKILL, Anne 267
KITCHEN, John 225
KITE, 106 Francis 109
KNEEBONE, William 97
KNIGHT, Mr 14 15 Robert 14 43 51
KNIPE, John 61
L'AQUA, Stopa 105
LADE, Justice 69
LAMB, Mr 138
LAMBERT, 91 John 14 Justice 219
LANE, Capt 52 Mr 52 Richard 144
LANGLEY, Mr 243
LANGLEY, Nathaniel 160
LANGWORTH, Mrs 30
LAWEN, John 258
LAWRENCE, Capt 62 John 188 Margeret 232 Robert 175 Thomas 153
LAYER, Christopher 60
LEE, Justice 255 Mary 132 Simon 121
LEEDS, Duke of 108
LEICESTER, Earl of 222
LEOPARD, Capt 270
LETIRANGE, Mrs 196
LILLY, Mr 23
LITTLEOR, Mr 148
LITTLEPAGE, Mrs 222
LIVING, Mr 245
LLOYD, Edward 231 Elizabeth

LLOYD (cont.)
   231 Mr 220 248
LOBBS, Capt 128
LODELL, Baron 80
LOISIA, Princess of ? 241
LONG, Capt 167 Will 131
LONGMAN, Mr 267
LOVEJOY, 245
LOWTHER, Christopher 24
LOXLEY, 213
LOYD, 137 Samuel 55
LUCAS, Thomas 65
LUN, Mr 100
LUTTRELL, Capt 108
LYDDALLI, ---- 241
LYNN, Wm 216
MACCLESFIELD, Earl of 111
MACCRA, Capt 18
MACCUINNIS, Constantine 79
MACDONALD, 258 Alexander 209
MACHIN, Justice 92
MACKDONNELL, 193
MACKINTOSH, Benjamin 146 Brigadier 1 John 1
MACKNEIL, Capt 47
MADDOX, Aaron 123
MAITLAND, Dr 37
MAJOR, 185
MALLONS, 61
MALTA, Great Master of 39
MALTA, Viceroy of 39
MANLEY, Thomas 220
MANN, Robert 185
MANSELL, Lord 92
MAPLE, Will 207
MARCHBANE, Mary 83
MARCHBANK, Ann 24
MARGASTROIDE, Capt 48

MARLBOROUGH, Dutchess of 94
MARTIN, George 74 Mr 72
MASON, Hampton 56 Joseph 180
MASSEY, Mr 45
MATTHEWS, Mr 186
MATTOCKS, John 136
MAWLEY, Mr 217
MAYNARD, Mr 217
MEAD, Dr 32 Mr 234
MEADOWS, Mr 224
MEALE, Mr 182
MEREDITH, Widow 257
MERICK, William 158
MERITT, Ann 24
MEUSE, 246
MEXICO, Viceroy of 52
MICOUR, John 207
MIDDLETON, Joseph 65 Lord 119 Mr 94
MILES, William 148
MILKSOP, 46
MILLS, Mary 148 Mr 37
MILTON, Mrs 216 Robert 216
MIST, Mr 86
MITCHEL, Anne 115 Col 123 John 193
MITCHELL, Capt 16
MOIER, Mr 61
MOLINEUX, Lady 246
MOLLAND, William 160
MONEMAR, Count 179
MONINGREW, Mr 262
MONTIGUE, Duke 43
MOOR, John 40 136 Mrs 247
MOORE, Michael 231 Rev Mr 53
MORGAN, Esther 232 William 108
MORRICE, Mrs 46 William 156

MORRIS, Admiral 266 Ann 46
  Hath 267 Hugh 252 John 115
  Mr 84 William 258
MORRON, Col 49
MORTIMER, Capt 85
MOSELY, Mr 239
MUFFET, Mary 263
MUNDAY, Edward 259 260
MURPHY, Pat 271
MURRAY, Col 40 Mr 91
MUSCHETT, Nicol 13
NAPLES, Viceroy of 39
NEGRO, Martinique 170
  Pawpaw 222
NEIVES, Thomas 234
NELLY, Dan 138
NEWELS, Capt 128
NEWLAND, Moses 145
NEWSHAM, Mr 63
NEWTON, Isaac 26 158 Justice
  79
NICHOLS, Justice 196 Mr 40
NICHOLSON, Gen 15
NICKOL, Mary 148
NICKS, 98
NORFOLK, Duke of 50
NORRIS, Henry 119 John 16 157
NORTEN, Hugh 242
NORTH, Lord 49
NORTON, 197 Hugh 246 Mr 66
NOST, Mr 157
O'BRYON, James 267
OAFENAN, Moses 97
OGLANDER, Mr 110
OLDEN, Mr 267
OLDFIELD, Mrs 199
OLIVER, Robert 232
ONSLOW, Lord 82
ORELEN, Lt 158
ORRERY, Earl of 49

OSBORN, 150
OUGHTON, Col 57
OWEN, John 257
OXEY, Richard 46
OXLEY, Richard 46
PAGE, Ambrose 10
PALMER, Daniel 160
PARADISE, William 152
PARKER, George 261 263 Mr
  263 264 269
PARKHURST, John 228
PARSON, John 3 Mrs 196
PARSONS, William 61
PAYNE, Mr 86
PECKETMAN, Mr 8
PELHAM, Col 113
PENBROKE, Earl of 225
PENNICK, Mr 56
PENRICE, Henry 189
PENROSE, Mr 56
PEPPER, Gen 23 119
PERCIVAL, Mr 233
PERKINS, John 258
PERTRAIN, Col 61
PETERS, Henry 156
PHILIP, Col 119
PHILIPS, Capt 85 Gov 251 John
  96 Mary 229
PIERCE, 132 Jane 132 John 88
  Mr 132 Mrs 132
PIERCY, Peter 145
PIERPOINT, Mr 21
PILCHER, Elizabeth 205
PILKINTON, Mr 222
PITT, Capt 187 Elijah 89
PITTS, 57 Capt 253 Gov 139 Mr
  194
POCOCK, Thomas 49
POLE, William 131
PORTER, Alderman 271 John

PORTER (cont.)
    271 Mr 270-272
PORTMORE, Lord 163 179
POST, George 24
POTTER, Mr 186
POULE, Mary 231
POWIS, Lord 10
PRATT, Lord Chief Justice 6 22 62
PRENTICE, Henry 23
PRICE, 8 Jane 132
PRIE, 190 John 170 189
PRINCE OF WALES, 36 37 164 218 239 265
PRINCESS OF COURTLAND, 154
PRINCESS OF WALES, 36 37 108 164
PROBYN, Justice 189
PRUETT, George 137
PULTENEY, Mrs 199
PURDY, Mr 60
PURVIS, Capt 156
PUTLAND, Mr 192
QUADLE, George 220
QUARMAN, Benjamin 96 Jacob 96
RABY, Serjeant 232
RAGLESFIELD, Capt 177
RAILTON, Justice 122
RAMBOUILET, Mr 166
RAMOND, Lord Chief Justice 182
RANSON, John 61
RAVEN, John 217
RAWLINGS, Mr 99 231 256
RAYMAN, Lord Chief Justice 263
RAYMOND, Lord Chief Justice 132 178
RAYNE, Mr 217
RAYNOLDS, Capt 179

RED, Mr 172
REE, John 203
REED, Capt 204
REES, Thomas 148
REYNOLDS, Edward 145 William 233
RHOCHE, 50
RICHARDS, Lawrence 205 William 251
RICHARDSON, Gr 124 William 157
RICHMOND, Duke of 246
RIGG, Mr 2
RIGGS, George 209
RIVERS, Thomas 267
ROBENSON, Richard 247
ROBERTS, Mary 24 Richard 56 96
ROBINSON, Hugh 64 William 64
ROCHESTER, Bishop of 56 58 59 62 69 83 84 156 Lord Bishop of 45 46 48 53 60
ROGERS, Capt 235 James 268 Theophilis 254
ROGIER, Mr 78
ROLSE, Justice 267
ROPER, Henry 60
ROSSEY, 247
ROWLAND, Rev 218
ROWLER, 127
RUBY, John 95 Serjeant 267
RUSSEL, Capt 31
RUTLAND, Dutchess Dowager of 111
RYLEY, Mr 169
SACHEVERAL, Dr 45
SAINTHILL, Mr 183
SALISBURY, Sally 54
SALT, John 48 Sarah 48 Silver

SALT (cont.)
   Sarah 48
SANDY, James 57
SAWBRIDGE, Jacob 14 Mr 15
SCAWEN, Thomas 149
SCOT, Capt 53 Col 73
SCOTSMIR, Mr 106
SCULL, 222
SEAFORTH, Earl of 47
SEARRIOT, Miss 199
SELDON, Thomas 147
SELL, 222
SELLS, Samuel 136
SENISION, Signor 260
SERGEANT, Capt 45
SEWEL, Adam 193
SHAMMY, Tom 161
SHELBY, Mr 149
SHELLY, John 149
SHEPARD, Mr 93
SHEPERD, 90
SHEPHARD, Martha 121
SHEPPARD, John 94 97 98 99 100
SHERMON, Mr 259
SHIPPEN, Mr 49
SHOCK, John 234
SHORT, Col 177 Mr 110
SHOWLWOOD, John 232
SICILY, Viceroy of 39
SIFLER, Mr 267
SIKE, John 242
SIMPSON, 53 George 222 James 55
SIRMON, Robert 14
SLOAN, Hans 32
SLOANE, Han 209
SLOENE, Mane 147
SMITH, 87 109 184 Capt 109 Constant 96 George 54

SMITH (cont.)
   Henrietta 219 John 29 80 143 154 Matthew 176 203 Mr 46 113 152 269 Roger 247 Thomas 109 145 178
SNAPE, Rev Dr 72
SOKEY, William 223 Wm 224
SOLGARD, Peter 109
SOULIER, Messieur 11
SPARKMAN, Capt 193
SPARKS, Mrs 223 Sarah 224
SPARROW, William 205
SPENCE, Miss 188
SPENCER, Miss 188
SPILMAN, Capt 199
SPOTSWOOD, Col 262
SPRIGGS, Joseph 228
SQUIB, Mary 4
STACKPOLE, Capt 131
STALKS, Capt 28
STANFORD, Mary 146
STAPLETON, Mr 107
STATERWAIT, Miles 8
STEDE, Edwyn 222
STEEL, Hurford 96 Sarah 96
STEVENS, 22
STEWART, Charles 252 Col 181
STOAKS, Mr 96
STOKER, Mr 172
STOKES, Mr 122
STRAFFORD, Earl 169
STRAFOLDI, Count 38
STRATMORE, Earl of 186
STUBBS, Mr 245
SUFFEX, Earl of 60
SUFFOLK, Earl of 107 127
SUMMERFIELD, William 54
SUNDERLAND, Earl of 39
SURMAND, Mr 15
SUTTON, Edward 172 Mr 122

SUTTON (cont.)
   172 Robert 255
SYKEY, 101
SYLVESTER, Mrs 115
TALBOT, Mrs 199
TALES, Charlotte 182
TAULOR, Capt 140
TAVENEY, 87
TAYLER, Thomas 220
TAYLOR, 27 Francis 255 John 65 Mr 172 Thomas 61
TEMPEST, Capt 47
TENENT, John 61
THOMAS, Elyzabeth 148 John 24 William 38
THOMPSON, John 7 Mr 255 William 161
THORALD, Lady 232
THORISBY, Thomas 24
THORNBILLS, James 68
TILMER, Mr 225
TINSEY, William 157
TIPLING, William 160
TOMKINSON, Margaret 56
TORRINGTON, Lord 242
TOWERS, 266 Capt 104 Charles 104
TOWNSHEND, Lord 40
TOWNSHEND, William 171
TOWSEND, William 158
TRANTER, Robert 108
TRIG, Mr 97
TRUNKETT, Mr 171
TUBERVILLE, Mrs 21
TURNER, Col 126 Joseph 249
TURRY, John 258
TYLER, Samuel 96 William 96
TYRELL, John 61
UNDERDOWN, Mr 118
UNDERWOOD, Robert 256

VALENTIA, Mother 114
VANDERY, Serjeant Maj 83
VARWICK, Jan 142
VAUGHAM, Joseph 193 Justice 55 192
VAVASSOR, Capt 237
VERNEY, Capt 55
VERNI, Messieur 11
VHOICK, John 80
VICCARI, John 226
VIVIUN, Capt 149
W----r, Mr 20
WADE, Capt 28 Maj Gen 116
WADHAM, Capt 78
WAGER, Admiral 157 Charles 6 209
WAKINS, George 67
WALDEN, Ann 24
WALKER, Mr 257
WALLER, Capt 17 Mr 137 Thomas 8
WALLIS, Richard 65
WALPOLE, Mr 16 152 Robert 164 197
WALTERS, John 150
WARD, Mr 71
WARNER, Edward 191 Mr 73 191
WARREN, Mr 71 127
WATERLAND, Dr 2
WATSON, Capt 134
WEBB, George 160
WELCH, Justice 250
WELD, Jonathan 105
WEST, Thomas 146
WESTBROOKE, Mr 216 217
WETACRE, John 105
WHARTON, Duke of 208
WHEELER, Mr 128 187 243
WHITAKER, 177

WHITE, 256 John 204 255
WHITWORTH, Lord 33
WILCOX, Henry 182
WILD, Jonathan 90 112
WILDE, Jonathan 93 97 113 146 Mr 97
WILKINSON, Capt 31
WILKS, John 73
WILL, Adjutant Gen 148
WILLIAM, King of England 101 232
WILLIAM, Prince of Hosse Castle 225
WILLIAMS, Capt 251 Charles 251 Edward 158 Francis 79 James 96 114 John 251 Sarah 218
WILLIAMSON, James 215
WILLIS, 185
WILLOUGHBY, Mr 162
WILLS, Capt 262
WILLSON, Mr 186 187
WILSON, Martha 75 Mr 209
WINCHIP, John 24
WINN, Mark 24
WINTER, Mr 69 Nehemiah 74
WITCHEL, Capt 36
WOOD, Mr 254 Thomas 142
WOODBURN, Benjamin 8
WOODCOCK, Mr 234
WOODYIER, Mr 260
WOOLANON, John 78
WORSLEY, Mr 256
WRIGGLESDEN, William 10
WRIT, Capt 263
WYNNE, Richard 65
YORK, Archbishop of 242
YORK, Duke of 165
YORKSHIRE, 185 Tom 180
YOUNG, John 247 Mr 98
YOUNGE, Mr 61

Other Heritage Books by Armand Francis Lucier:

1767 Chronicle

Boston, the Red Coats, and the Homespun Patriots, 1766–1775

*Central Colonies Chronicle: The Freeman, the
Servants, and the Government, 1722–1732*

*French and Indian War Notices Abstracted from Colonial Newspapers
Volume 2: 1756–1757
Volume 3: January 1, 1758 to September 17, 1759
Volume 4: September 17, 1759 to December 30, 1760
Volume 5: January 1, 1761 to January 17, 1793*

Jolly Old England

*Journal of Occurrences: Patriot Propaganda on the
British Occupation of Boston, 1768–1769*

*Newspaper Datelines of the American Revolution
Volume 1: April 18, 1775 to November 1, 1775
Volume 2: November 1, 1775 to April 30, 1776
Volume 3: May 1, 1776 to November 1, 1776
Volume 4: November 1, 1776 to January 30, 1777*

*Pontiac's Conspiracy and Other Indian Affairs: Notices
Abstracted from Colonial Newspapers, 1763–1765*

www.ingramcontent.com/pod-product-compliance
Lightning Source LLC
Chambersburg PA
CBHW070725160426
43192CB00009B/1316